Post-Qualifying Mental Health Social Work Practice

Post-Qualifying Mental Health Social Work Practice

Jim Campbell
and Gavin Davidson

Los Angeles | London | New Delhi
Singapore | Washington DC

First published 2012

SAGE Publications Ltd
1 Oliver's Yard
55 City Road
London EC1Y 1SP

SAGE Publications Inc.
2455 Teller Road
Thousand Oaks, California 91320

SAGE Publications India Pvt Ltd
B 1/I 1 Mohan Cooperative Industrial Area
Mathura Road
New Delhi 110 044

SAGE Publications Asia-Pacific Pte Ltd
3 Church Street
#10-04 Samsung Hub
Singapore 049483

Library of Congress Control Number: 2011937239

British Library Cataloguing in Publication data

A catalogue record for this book is available from the British Library

ISBN 978-1-84860-994-5
ISBN 978-1-84860-995-2 (pbk)

Typeset by C&M Digitals (P) Ltd, Chennai, India
Printed and bound by CPI Group (UK) Ltd, Croydon, CR0 4YY
Printed on paper from sustainable resources

Contents

About the Authors

Jim Campbell qualified as a social worker in 1986 and practised as a mental health social worker for five years before joining Queens University Belfast as a lecturer, then senior lecturer. He has a range of teaching and research interests including mental health social work and law and the impact of political violence on social work practice. He has recently been appointed as Professor of Social Work at Goldmiths, University of London. He is currently co-editor of the *British Journal of Social Work* with his colleague, Professor John Pinkerton, Queens University Belfast.

Gavin Davidson qualified as a social worker in 1995 then worked for 12 years in mental health services, in the Northern Health and Social Care Trust, as a Community Mental Team social worker, out of hours Approved Social Worker, project manager and team leader in assertive outreach and rehabilitation. He moved to Queen's University Belfast to be a social work lecturer in 2008 and his research interests are in all aspects of mental health social work, especially the deinstitutionalisation process, the effectiveness of mental health services, trauma and coercion, the recovery approach and mental health legislation. He lives in Belfast with his wife, Katherine, and two sons, Leo and Patrick. Patrick was born between Chapters 4 and 5.

Preface

This is a specialist text for post-qualified social workers, and other mental health professionals, who are interested in exploring the complexities of practice using a broad range of explanatory theories and evidence-based approaches. In writing this book we were mindful of the debates about the current mental health social work role (Ramon, 2009; Campbell, 2010) and how it might be changing because of the advent of the generic Approved Mental Health Professional (AMHP) in England and Wales, as well as the potential dilution of professional identity caused by the integration of social work practitioners in multidisciplinary teams.

As will become apparent, however, the book presents a forceful argument for a strong, recognizable identity for mental social workers built upon a solid knowledge base and broad-based application of skills that complement the work of other professionals in this field. We argue that, in the midst of the inevitable changes to role and function created by shifts in law, policy and organization, a discernible position can be identified and maintained for social workers in mental services. For these reasons we believe the text will be of particular interest to mental health social workers practising and studying mental health social work at various levels within systems of post-qualifying education and training across the UK.

The text begins with summaries of four 'core knowledge' areas which inform the rest of the book – an Introduction to the various forms of post-qualifying education and training in the UK followed by three chapters on Policy and Agency Contexts, Legal Contexts and Models of Mental Health and Illness. These provide essential, background contextual knowledge that then underpins the other chapters in the book. The following chapters, which focus on the application of theory to practice, are each preceded by references to National Occupational Standards, learning outcomes and case study material. Throughout the book you are encouraged to reflect upon your learning using selected questions, exercises and further reading. We hope you will find it particularly interesting in its use of diverse case material illustrating the many types of mental health problems that individuals, families and groups experience, and how these experiences are shaped by issues of age, class, gender, ethnicity and religion.

The Introduction presents an overarching discussion on the educational and training contexts that inform mental health social work practice in each of the four jurisdictions of the UK. It also explains the history of the specialism and contemporary arguments about the need for critical, reflexive learning approaches that can help us understand the complexity of the mental health social work role.

Mental health social workers are employed in a variety of quite diverse organizational settings across the UK, and their practices are informed by important policy drivers. Chapter 1 will help you to explore these factors. It highlights the way that policies and organizations have been shaped, in particular, by the process of deinstitutionalization in each of the jurisdictions of the UK. This has led to more community-based approaches to service delivery which will be familiar to readers. As with other chapters, we hope that you will be able to critically analyse the processes that inform practice in these organizations.

The next core knowledge chapter describes and discusses how mental health laws are used by mental health social workers. Thus in Chapter 2 we review the history of mental health laws in the UK and the mandates used by mental health social workers to compel service users to accept hospital- or community-based care and treatment. In deciding to coerce citizens in this way, mental health social workers face many practice dilemmas which you may be able to recognize.

The final core knowledge chapter, Chapter 3, focuses on models of mental health and illness. Mental health social workers are required to understand key paradigms and discourses about mental health and illness. In this chapter a number of key debates in this area are discussed and analysed. We argue that you should be mindful of the importance of the predominant discourses around the medical model but that mental health social workers also need to engage in alternative, critical views on how mental ill-health occurs, and therefore which interventions can be used to address service user needs.

The remaining chapters then use selected case study material to apply a range of theories to practice. The first of these, Chapter 4, discusses the way in which mental health service users experience many forms of discrimination; we argue that it is crucial that mental health social workers are aware of these issues and engage in strategies that can challenge them. We believe that such approaches complement the holistic nature of the mental health social work role that we recommend throughout the book.

In the last decade, partly because of movements from the ground up, but also as a result of government policies, mental health social workers have been required to listen to the voices of services users. In Chapter 5 we trace the history of service user movements and contemporary debates about how you can empower service users and we illustrate this with selected case material. We hope that these ideas will make sense in terms of your work with service users.

Chapter 6 complements the previous chapter and focuses on the needs of carers of people with mental health problems. We argue that there is a tendency on the part of mental health social workers and other professionals to ignore or neglect these needs. The second part of the chapter uses case material to explore how you can apply theory to practice in this important area.

The next three chapters explore how mental health social workers can work effectively with individuals, families and communities. Chapter 7, on addressing the needs of individuals, reviews the types and range of psychosocial theories and interventions associated with mental health social work with individuals. We believe that, as an experienced practitioner, you should be familiar with the 'toolkit' approach to interventions with clients.

Chapter 8 then discusses the importance of 'the family' in the lives of people with mental health problems. The family can be a crucial form of support for service users, but also an area of stress and strain. In this chapter you will learn about debates on the part that families can play in preventing mental ill-health. The chapter highlights a number of interventions that can be used by mental health social workers for therapeutic benefit or the prevention of relapses.

We complete these three inter-related chapters by using Chapter 9 to discuss and analyse the way mental health social workers can engage with communities. This chapter uses two ways of viewing the social work interpretation of the case material, the first by using a conventional community mental health team approach, the second a community work approach. We hope that, in your everyday practice, these ideas will resonate with you.

Multi-disciplinary working is a common feature of mental health social work practice. Chapter 10 reviews the literature on this subject and highlights the rise of specialist community-based teams across the UK. Some of the problems and opportunities faced by mental health social workers, which we think you will recognize, are identified and explained through the use of case material.

The final chapter focuses on the recent advent of the Approved Mental Health Professional (AMHP) in England and Wales. Many mental health social workers are employed in these jurisdictions, so it is important for you to critically analyse this role and consider the implications for your practice.

We conclude the book with a brief preview of where we think the role of the mental health social worker is heading as it faces the challenges of new forms of legislation and policy and pressures to deliver efficient and effective forms of service delivery. We will point to international experiences to help us speculate on how the role will change and develop over the next decade. This critical awareness of change is a constant reminder of the shifting roles that mental health social workers have adjusted to in the past and will have to adapt to into the future.

Acknowledgements

We are grateful to a number of people who made the writing of this book possible. Both of us have practised as mental health social workers in Northern Ireland and we are indebted to the service users, carers and multi-disciplinary professionals who have worked with us over the years, and to all the social workers involved in the Approved Social Work Programme in Northern Ireland. We want this book to be relevant to the everyday worlds of practitioners, by making connections between theory, evidence and interventions. And a mention should go to our colleagues at Queen's University Belfast who sometimes have had to suffer our interest in mental health social work, but, as they are repeatedly reminded, it is a central aspect of all areas of social work practice.

The idea about writing the book was first suggested to us by Professor Steven Shardlow, we thank him for pointing us the way to Sage, our publishers. At Sage we wish to thank Zoe Elliott-Fawcett Senior Commissioning Editor; Emma Milman, Assistant Editor; Sarah Gibson, Editor; Katie Forsythe, Production Editor; and Tamara Navaratnam, Books Marketing Manager. They have been consistently positive and encouraging as well as very tolerant with us in adjusting their work to suit our sometimes haphazard timescales. We would also like to thank Dr Martin Webber and Mike Maas-Lowit for their very helpful and informed comments during the drafting of Chapter 2 on mental health law in the UK. We are also indebted to our colleagues Dr Lisa Brophy and Bill Healy from Victoria, Australia and Anne-Marie O'Brien from Ontario, Canada for their long standing interest in helping us understand the complexities of community based compulsory mental health laws.

Last, but not least, we wish to thank our extremely supportive partners Anona and Katherine and our children, who carried on with their daily lives and missed some of our company whilst we were fixated on computer screens.

Introduction: Mental Health Social Work in the UK – Locating Policy, Practice and Post-Qualifying Education

Learning outcomes

1. To understand the origins and development of the mental health social work role
2. To locate your learning and practice in the context of the different types of PQ social work education and training in the UK
3. To develop an awareness of the need for reflective practice in PQ education and training

Introduction

There seems little doubt that mental health social workers in the UK will have to deal with increasingly complex issues when making professional judgements in a world that appears fragmented and less certain than ever before. Decision-making processes in this field therefore require holistic, reflective approaches that pay attention to a range of factors, including aspects of personal biography, levels of skills, organizational and policy dimensions and the requirements of legal mandates. Interventions should also be guided and underpinned by due attention to relevant, contemporary research across a wide range of academic disciplines from the social, psychological and medical sciences. This book is designed to help experienced mental health social workers make sense of these challenges in the course of their PQ studies and we believe its content is also relevant to other professionals studying in this field. In reading the book we hope that your interventions will be further informed by theory as well as reflexive and meaningful for clients. This Introduction begins by briefly tracing the history of mental health social work before highlighting policy, service and practice contexts that continue to shape the role. The impact of policy on practice is developed further in the next chapter and others in this book. The second part of this Introduction describes important features of PQ social work education and training in the UK, including an up-to-date account of current structures. It concludes with a discussion about the tensions that arise as a result of the need for mental health social workers to adhere to National Occupational Standards (NOSs) and National Occupational Mental Health Standards (NOMHSs), whilst protecting a necessary commitment to reflective practice.

Continuity and change in the mental health social work role

Changes to policy and law across the UK are key to understanding the historical development of the mental health social work role, a point we further develop in Chapter 1. It is tempting to view the modern origins of the profession as the product of the shift to generic training and education that occurred in the early 1970s. Certainly most of what we know about contemporary mental health social work is drawn from the growing body of literature which has emerged, particularly in the last two decades. A very good summary of research that is relevant to mental health social work (Ray et al., 2008) is provided by the Social Care Institute of Excellence at www.scie.org.uk/publications/briefings/briefing26. In the course of the book we will be drawing upon this and other such literature to explore the mental health social work role.

But first it is important to acknowledge, briefly, the period before the introduction of generic training and practice that followed the deliberations of the Seebohm Committee (1968). Although ongoing debates continue about the factors that shaped the development of mental health social work (Rapaport, 2005; Webber, 2008), there is some agreement about how the profession developed in the second half of the nineteenth and the first half of the twentieth century. A liberal perspective on this period suggests that a constellation of processes led to a drive for 'lunacy reform' in which charitable organizations, politicians and pressure groups slowly humanized the asylum (Busfield, 1986). The nascent professional groups of psychiatry, psychiatric nursing and, eventually, social work, it can be argued, played various roles in this project. A more critical perspective was that such changes only represented shifts in the power of the state and the profession, and that patients remained subject to different forms of coercion; we take this issue further in our discussion of contemporary practice, particularly in Chapters 1, 2, 3 and 4.

By the mid twentieth century, prior to the changes introduced by Seebohm which established generic functions for all social workers, the profession had gone through a range of guises, from its early manifestations in Duly Authorised Officers, to Psychiatric Social Workers (PSWs) and Mental Welfare Officers (MWOs). In particular PSWs had gained a distinct professional identity and respected system of qualifying and post-qualifying training, underpinned by regulatory requirements. MWOs tended not to be professionally qualified but performed limited functions in mental health law when nearest relatives were not available. Rapaport (2005) draws other contrasts about the characteristics of these mental health social workers. PSWs were mostly women working in child guidance clinics whilst MWOs were generally employed in the adult services field, either in hospital or community settings. It appears that PSWs were often viewed by other professionals as competent and knowledgeable, in part because of their perceived expertise in case work approaches, often underpinned by psychodynamic theories. At the time of Seebohm concerns were expressed that generic training would erode this foundation of learning and experience; to some extent these fears were realized as educational approaches arguably became more focused on functional and structural ideas at the expense of the therapeutic role for mental health social workers.

Despite evidence of a substantial growth in numbers of social workers during the 1970s and 1980s, a specific role for mental health social workers was slow to emerge, either during the fleeting moment of radical social work in the late 1970s or following the recommendations of the Barclay Report in 1982. The retrenchment of health and social care expenditure during the Thatcher governments of the 1980s, underpinned by an ideological critique of the post-war UK state, tended to challenge traditional assumptions about the efficacy and purpose of the social work role. A series of child care, and later mental health care inquiries, sometimes confirmed this scepticism and doubt about the knowledge base that social workers were using in assessing and managing risk (we discuss the issue of risk in a number of chapters in the book). Although mental health social workers were not immune to such criticisms, it can be argued that their positioning within the wider mental health and social care system was in some way protective, in terms of role and function. Before the widespread deinstitutionalization that gained momentum towards the end of the 1980s, most mental health social workers practised in psychiatric hospitals, or alongside other mental health professionals, despite the fact that they were usually subcontracted from local authorities. The institution may have bonded various professionals together, but practices were inevitably informed by traditional discourses about care and treatment and there was little awareness of ways of empowering clients and their carers (see Chapters 5 and 6).

Mental health policy and practice

Mental health social workers in the UK have constantly had to adjust to new sets of circumstances which have emerged as a result of complex policy drivers; the challenges are made more complicated because of local, regional and national contexts. For example, systems of mental health care and treatment vary across the countries of the UK. In England, Wales and Scotland there are well documented organizational problems caused by the split between local and health authorities whereas the integrated system in Northern Ireland has enabled health and social care professionals to work together more closely (Campbell and McLaughlin, 2000; Reilly et al., 2007). Government concerns about the lack of uniformity across systems of mental health in England and Wales partly explain a number of key policy initiatives, notably the Care

Programme Approach (CPA), the National Service Framework (NSF), the development of National Occupational Standards (NOSs) for Mental Health and the Ten Essential Shared Capabilities (Hope, 2004). The other countries within the UK have tended to adapt these approaches to address perceived organizational deficits within their own systems.

Although there continues to be great variation in the delivery of mental health services, mental health social workers are generally placed in multi-disciplinary teams which use a number of standardized approaches in their work with clients and carers. Statutory social workers can be found in community mental health, early intervention, assertive outreach, forensic and crisis teams (see Chapters 9 and 10). In addition they may be employed in a variety of specialist settings, for example, working with people with dementia, addictions and eating disorders, and children and adolescents who have mental health difficulties. Interventions may take place in hospital, prison, residential, day care and other community settings. The way in which such services are configured will depend on local circumstances which will include funding arrangements, decisions made by individual organizations and relationships with voluntary and community sectors.

It was, however, the introduction of new mental health laws across the jurisdictions of the UK in the 1980s that revitalized the mental health social work role, although for some critics this was at some cost to the development of more therapeutic and empowering practices which tended to be marginalized thereafter (Ramon, 2009). Mental health social workers acquired substantially enhanced mandatory powers to detain clients in psychiatric hospitals and engage in guardianship procedures. More recently they have become involved in using new powers of compulsion in the community; details of these functions will be described and analysed in Chapters 2 and 11. These changes to the law often mirror, sometimes belatedly, shifts in policy and service delivery (Bartlett and Sandland, 2003). For example, over half of all psychiatric beds have been closed since the Mental Health Act 1983 was introduced. Similar trends have occurred in Scotland and Northern Ireland (Audit Scotland, 2009; Department of Health, Social Services and Public Safety (DHSSPS), 2009a; Kelly, 1998). At the same time policy makers have attempted, often unsuccessfully, to strengthen community-based resources and services. These failures are often pointed out when homicides and suicides occur (Reith, 1998).

Mental health social work today

It is interesting to note that mental health social work in the UK has, in some respects, returned to a form of specialism that was not predicted during the period of genericism in the 1970s and 1980s. This can partly be explained by the enhanced legal functions that were embedded in mental health laws in the mid 1980s. However these legal dimensions to the role comprise only a small part of the day-to-day activity of mental health social workers. Most of their work takes place alongside other professionals in the types of services described above. Because of the variation in the delivery of these services and the mix of professionals within teams, it is difficult to ascertain, definitively, the non-legal roles that mental health social workers play in the UK. Nonetheless some themes are discernible. In her review of the contributions of mental health social workers to mental service delivery in the UK, Ramon (2009), drawing upon existing literature, highlights both strengths and weaknesses in the role. She argues that, at least in the past, the profession has shown signs of being innovative and progressive in the way it has worked with clients, but is concerned that this more radical tradition has been eroded by changing patterns of organizational delivery. A common complaint is that the social work discourses are often marginalized in a mental health system that is largely informed by medical and biological paradigms. This is not helped by problems with local and health authority organizational arrangements in Britain. Even when health and social care systems are integrated there is little evidence that the social model is any more influential in the planning and delivery of mental health services (Campbell, 1999). Although the profession of social work should be well positioned to use holistic approaches to gain an understanding of clients' needs (Department of Health, 2007a), Ramon suggests that they have not fully embraced new, empowering approaches with service users.

A number of other observations about the mental health social work role have reflected upon opportunities as well as challenges. For example, in one of the few critical reviews of the evidence base for mental health social work (Marsh et al., 2005), it is suggested that the profession might be well positioned to take advantage of modernizing agendas in mental health services in the UK, and a Social Services Inspectorate (SSI) Report highlights the positive value base that social workers can use in working with people with mental health problems (SSI, 2004). On the other hand, mental health social workers, like other professionals in this field, can both contribute to, and sometimes challenge, the forms of discrimination that clients with mental health problems regularly face (Social Exclusion Unit, 2004); we discuss these possibilities in Chapter 4.

We hope that, through the application of theory to practice in the second part of this book, you will be able to identify ways in which mental health social workers can apply holistic approaches that will empower the lives of service users and carers. But first consider the following exercise.

Exercise 1

1. At what period in the development of mental health social work did you begin your career?
2. How has mental health policy and law changed since you began as a mental health social worker?
3. What current policy and practice issues do you face?

We asked you to consider this exercise because we cannot think of mental health social work practice without reflecting upon the period in which we entered the profession and how subsequent changes to policy and law have affected the way we now view roles and function (we will be returning to these ideas in Chapter 1). More experienced readers might be able to think about a time when mental health social work services were 'institutionalized' within psychiatric hospitals, while for younger social workers community-based practice is more normative. The preceding sections on history and current aspects of policy and practice should be able to help you locate and understand your professional and autobiographical journey as a mental health social worker.

The development of systems of PQ education and training in the UK

After the move to generic qualifying training following the Seebohm Report (1968) a range of PQ programmes was developed by numerous providers, usually overseen by the Central Council for Social Work Education and Training (CCETSW). At times these programmes developed on an ad hoc basis, dependent on the initiatives taken by individuals, agencies and institutions of further and higher education. For the many social workers who have passed through countless PQ programmes, such stories reflect the long, but somewhat patchy history of education and training often defined by a complexity of local and national policy needs and drivers. Relatively few evaluations of post-qualifying programmes have taken place over these years, so it is unclear whether they have delivered assumed or desired outcomes for social workers and their agencies (Cooper and Rixon, 2001; Postle et al., 2002; Brown and Keen, 2004; Brown et al., 2008). One survey of a number of English consortia, carried out just before the introduction of the current PQ system (Doel et al., 2008), found positive levels of satisfaction amongst candidates, but respondents felt that quality was sometimes determined by external factors such as the availability of good mentors and work easement. These are common structural problems across many PQ programmes that you may have already experienced in the course of your studies. The need for more collaboration between partners to develop new, more imaginative programmes and modules is also a common feature of the systems across the UK. At the same time there has been considerable debate about the pedagogical underpinnings of PQ education, mirroring similar debates at qualifying level, around the issues of competence-based practice (O'Hagan, 2007) and reflective learning (Jordan and Parkinson, 2001).

Despite these limitations, we believe current systems of PQ education and training, introduced across all jurisdictions in the UK in the last few years, offer new possibilities in helping mental health social workers to develop their knowledge, values and skills. In every jurisdiction of the UK programmes are more firmly embedded in institutions of higher and further education than was the case with previous arrangements, although employing agencies continue to play important roles in processes of design, delivery and assessment. It is the case that there are inevitable nuances in the structure of post-qualifying systems across these jurisdictions, for example in terms of policy and legal contexts and the structure and delivery of programmes. However, all must consider National Occupational Standards (NOSs), Codes of Practice and other relevant documents to guide and underpin judgements about the competence of candidates. Each programme will operate within the specific requirements of the national accrediting regulatory body. There remain some concerns that arrangements for PQ education and training in the UK are often driven by a governmental preoccupation with the regulation of the workforce at the possible expense of the value base that social work should aspire to (Galpin, 2009). In the course of reading this book, we want to encourage you to think critically about such debates, and understand the tensions that will always arise between the demands of policy makers, agencies' needs and the duty of practitioners to adhere to professional standards.

Current structures of PQ education and training in the UK

The devolution of power to regional assemblies in the UK has led to a rethink about the PQ education and training of social workers, not least because such activity is now regulated and quality assured by four Social Care Councils. A common feature of the four country structures is an assumption that candidates can move between different levels, usually differentiated by notions of complexity of practice and analytical skills (Higham, 2009). It has been argued however that there is some vagueness in the description and comparison between these levels (Adams, 2007). In using this book you should bear in mind that your post-qualifying education and learning experience will be specifically determined by the requirements laid down by the social care council within your jurisdiction. We now briefly describe the current state of PQ education and training in each of the jurisdictions of the UK.

England

The English system currently offers three levels of awards. The Specialist award is designed to consolidate, extend and deepen professional competence in a specialist context (usually delivered at honours level). The Higher Specialist award should offer the skills and knowledge necessary to make complex judgements, discharge high levels of responsibility, and manage risk (usually delivered at postgraduate diploma level). Finally the Advanced Award focuses on the knowledge and skills required for professional leadership and the improvement of services (delivered at Master's level). The GSCC recognizes five specialisms: mental health; adult social care; practice education; leadership and management; and children and young people. Programme providers are expected to focus on, develop and deliver modules and programmess across these areas.

Northern Ireland

Three types of PQ awards are available to social workers in Northern Ireland – Specific, Specialist and Strategy and Leadership – with opportunities for both academic and professional awards. Unlike other parts of the UK all PQ awards in Northern Ireland are delivered at postgraduate level.

Scotland

The system in Scotland uses a broad framework to encompass education and training across the whole social work and social care workforce, with Specialist Training available from SCQF 7 – SCQF 11 (Master's level).

Wales

The post-qualifying system in Wales uses a modular structure leading to qualifications at undergraduate certificate, undergraduate diploma, postgraduate certificate, postgraduate diploma and Master's levels.

Each PQ system in the UK is designed to address the particular circumstances of policy and practice in their respective countries. This is because there is considerable divergence in programme aims, curriculum content and professional and academic requirements, depending on where you work in the UK. You should also be mindful that, at the time of writing, the social care councils across the UK are engaged in consultations about a review of existing regulations and requirements (Jerrom, 2011). You should now complete the following exercise on PQ requirements in your jurisdiction.

Exercise 2

Go to your social care council website and check the requirements for the programme you wish to apply for, or are currently a candidate for.

Find out what changes are being proposed to your programme as a result of the review of PQ education and training in your country

In addition to the requirements laid down by respective Social Care Councils, programme providers need to take into account relevant NOSs (and in the case of Scotland, the Scottish Standards in Social Work Education (SiSWE)). For example, all PQ candidates have to identify the six key roles and units described in the NOSs (and their equivalent in Scotland) and reflect upon how these are incorporated into learning and practice (see Appendix 1). In addition mental health social workers, and other professionals employed in the mental health field, are also required to use the National Occupational Standards for Mental Health (NOSMH) (see Appendix 2) to inform their practice. In each of the chapters that follow we will be asking you to consider how you can integrate selected NOS and NOSMH with the practice material that we want you to discuss and analyse. However, just a word of caution: the concept of NOSs is not without its critics. At one level many of the descriptors can seem straightforward, and the intentions of such government policies are on the face of it rational and incontestable. Take for example this statement about NOSMH:

> The key purpose of mental health services has been defined as work with individuals, families, groups, communities and agencies to provide equitable and non-discriminatory services, across all age groups and settings which promote mental health, address mental health needs, manage risk, and provide appropriate support to people with mental health needs and their carers. (NOSMH website).

We would expect that you and all mental health social workers would embrace the principles that underpin this statement, in terms engaging with holistic, thoughtful practice that is mindful of all stakeholders who access mental health services. But it is, at the same time, important to be mindful of the contexts in which NOSs were introduced in the UK. As Rogers (2009) points out, NOSs can be viewed, more critically, in terms of a preoccupation by successive governments with regulating and monitoring professional activity and setting targets and performance-related outcomes. The everyday practice of mental health social workers, like that of other professionals, is informed or stymied (depending on how you view these contexts) by such systems of governance. We take the view that practitioners should be critically aware of how and why such standards have become so important in the delivery of health and social care. For example we feel that, however helpful standards are in identifying key principles for practice, they are only meaningful when considered in the context of available resources and systems of support and supervision. In any case they cannot provide a blueprint when competing demands occur, for example between clients, carers, agencies, practitioners and the general public.

In addition there is a potential logistical problem in applying quite descriptive sets of NOSs. The NOSs comprise six key roles and 21 sub-units; in the case of NOSMH it becomes even more detailed, involving 11 sections containing 111 units of competence in total. Many of these are relevant to mental health social work practice and, if met, entail an occupational competence to: operate within an ethical framework; work with and support individuals, carers and families; and influence and support communities, organizations, agencies and services. The temptation (and this is one of the problems with competence-based approaches to learning) is to engage in a mapping process which can often become rather mechanical and which does not correspond to the realities of everyday practice.

Being reflective and reflexive: how to get the best out of the book

In this book we also want to encourage you to look beyond the simplistic use of NOSs and engage with the material in a more reflective way that will help you explore the complex nuances of practice. The notion of the reflective practitioner has become quite mainstream in social work education and training, and is just as important for busy practitioners as it is for qualifying social work students. Although much has been said about this subject in the last decade, reflection in social work is, like the other issues discussed in this Introduction, a concept that can be interpreted in many different ways. Paradoxically the application of the idea to practice can seem superficial and unthoughtful, so we want you to avoid this tendency when you consider the chapters in this book.

A common starting point in the literature is to consider the different reflective and reflexive (which suggests a more critical perspective) processes that are involved in the social work process (Schön, 1987; Fook, 2002). Sometimes these are characterized by the terms 'reflection in practice' at the time of the interaction with clients, and 'reflection on practice' when post hoc opportunities occur to consider the intervention. To these processes can be added an earlier event as practitioners, while 'tuning in' to the intervention, reflect upon a wide range of factors that may inform practice. Sometimes we can only roughly describe these complex and changing relationships, not just in terms of the here and now of an interaction between the mental health social worker and the client, but also in terms of the many layered constructions of knowledge and discourses that inform and shape practice. It can be very difficult to understand how these overlap and interrelate when important decisions are being made. To illustrate this point consider the following exercise.

Exercise 3

Choose a situation when you intervened to help someone who had a mental health problem. What knowledge and theories did you consider and why?

The more you consider the question about 'what knowledge and theories were considered and why' the deeper you can go into the reflective process and you might be able to understand how complicated such interactions, however simple on the face of it, can be. There could be a plethora of competing ideas that will confront you in these circumstances: legal and policy contexts; agency regulations; ideas drawn from psychiatry, psychology and sociology; ethical principles and professional codes of practice. Yet even an awareness of an exhaustive list of possible theories does not fully capture these notions of reflection and reflexivity. We also have to be mindful of how these ideas are formulated in the context of our life histories and how we relate to 'the other' (as we discussed in Exercise 1). Positive outcomes for social work interventions can depend on this notion of self-understanding as much as a functional, cognitive appreciation of 'objective' knowledge and theory. Even where practitioners are making decisions that are the product of a critical, reflective position they may be undermined by agency procedures and a lack of support and supervision in dealing with the inevitable dilemmas that characterize mental health social work (Archambeault, 2009a; 2009b).

Conclusion

In this Introduction we have provided a brief overview of the history of mental health social work and the location of the professional in contemporary mental health policy and service delivery. The chapters that follow will provide more detail of these contexts, using case material to illustrate relevant knowledge values and skills, alongside selected NOSs and NOSMH. The most important message that you should take from this chapter, and one that will be followed up throughout the book, is the need to develop your ability to reflect upon your practice and be open to the struggle in dealing with dilemmas that are a recurrent feature of interventions in the mental health field. That way we believe you will deliver a more thoughtful and progressive service to your clients.

Recommended reading

A good overview of the state of play in PQ education and training in the UK is provided by two edited texts, with individual chapters on mental health social work:

Higham, P. (ed.) (2009) *Post-Qualifying Social Work Practice.* London: Sage.
Tovey, W. (ed.) The *Post-Qualifying Handbook for Social Workers.* London: Jessica Kingsley.

The following is a specialised text that helps the reader in understanding reflective practice with a range of client groups in the mental field.

Archambeault, J. (2009a) *Reflective Reader: Social Work and Mental Health.* Exeter: Learning Matters

Recommended websites

The websites for the four UK social care councils contain a lot of constantly updated information about post-qualifying training and education:

Care Council for Wales: www.ccwales.org.uk
General Social Care Council (England): www.gscc.org.uk
Northern Ireland Social Care Council: www.niscc.info
Scottish Social Care Council: www.sssc.uk.com

1

Policy and Agency Contexts

National occupational standards

This chapter will help you meet the following National Occupational Standards for Social Work:

Key Role 5: Manage and be accountable, with supervision and support, for your own social work practice within your organization. Unit 15: Contribute to the management of resources and services.

Key Role 6: Demonstrate professional competence in social work practice. Unit 19: Work within agreed standards of social work practice and ensure personal professional development.

It will also help meet the following National Occupational Standards for Mental Health:

- Identify trends and changes in the mental health and mental health needs of a population and the effectiveness of different means of meeting their needs (SFHMH 50).
- Negotiate and agree with stakeholders the opportunities they are willing to offer to people with mental health needs (SFHMH 72).
- Assess the need for, and plan awareness raising of mental health issues (SFHMH 87).
- Work with service providers to support people with mental health needs in ways which promote their rights (SFHMH 3).

Learning outcomes

1 To increase your knowledge of mental health policy, mental health providers and organizational change.
2 To develop your skills relating to the management of change – both self and others.
3 To develop your practice working in agencies.

Introduction

All too often social workers will become immersed in practice without fully understanding the crucial policy and agency contexts which will inform and shape judgements made with and about clients and their families. In this early chapter we want you to take a step back from your busy workload and consider how policy making is determined, and then delivered, by the agencies you work in. The chapter begins with a brief overview of key debates about how UK social and health policies are understood and constructed. The sections which follow then focus on particular aspects of mental health policy, beginning with an account of the competing explanations for the rise of the Victorian asylum and the impact these institutions had on patients and professionals and wider society and then noting some of this period's enduring legacy for contemporary policy and practice. The chapter then describes and analyses the key policy themes which are now identified with the period of 'de-' or trans-institutionalization that has occurred in the UK in the last two decades. It then provides a broad overview of key policy themes that re-emerge in the chapters on practice later in the book. These include community-based mental health care, risk management, prevention, empowerment and recovery. We describe and analyse the way in which these policy drivers determine the types of organizations in which mental health social workers are employed and the services that are provided to people with mental health problems. The chapter concludes by arguing that competent, reflective practice is underpinned by a critical awareness of the links between policy drivers, organizational form and social work practice.

Social work and social policy in the UK

For mental health social workers, who have their every working day filled with case load pressures, it can be difficult to understand how and why health and social care policies shape practice. We argue that a core understanding of ideological positions taken about policy-making processes is crucial to the profession.

> Disagreements as to what constitutes good policy or social work practice are rooted in differing values, ideas, and problem definitions. Attempts to penetrate dominant ideas are important in that they force social policy analysts and social work practitioners to ask fundamental questions about possible future developments. (Denny, 1998: 27)

Although it is tempting to view policy making in terms of logical, linear processes, invariably it is the product of competing pressures and contested perspectives in which powerful discourses and constituencies are at play (Lister, 2010). For example, Clarke (2004) explains how the welfare bureaucracies that were constructed during the post-war settlement in the UK were critiqued and redesigned by successive Conservative governments to fit with discourses about new types of welfare delivery with a greater involvement by the market. This new mixed economy of welfare was further refined by subsequent Labour administrations.

Whilst acknowledging that these policy processes are indeed complex, this should not prevent attempts to explore how they function and the way they relate to everyday social work practice. Weiss et al. (2006) have developed a pedagogical model to consider how such questions can be answered when encountered by social work students. They argue that students should have a good knowledge of fields related to social structure and social policy and they should also acquire analytical skills exploring the dimensions of the links between social policy and the goals and values of social work. In addition students should be capable of undertaking a critical examination of social policy and its impact on social work practice. There are many aspects to this interface between social work and social policy; here are a few questions specifically about health and social care policies and the various implications these may have for your clients:

1 *Family policy* – how do such policies differentially affect men and women?
2 *Welfare rights policy* – why is there an increasing use of means tested benefits?
3 *Housing policy* – can you explain the reduced levels of social housing?
4 *Community care policy* – how well does policy and law deal with the burden of care?
5 *Criminal justice policy* – why has there been a shift towards restorative justice practices?

Change and continuity: the origins of mental health policy in the UK

As with generic health and social care policies there is also a need to critically analyse mental health policy. We can understand how mental health policy has developed by examining the many political, social and economic factors that have converged and coalesced at different periods in the history of the UK state. Given the complexity of these events and processes it is not surprising that there are a number of competing histories that seek to explain how and why mental health policies developed in the way that they did (Rogers and Pilgrim, 2009). A particularly influential set of discourses that supported the rise of the Victorian asylum was informed by liberal, Enlightenment ideas that viewed these institutions in terms of a necessary reform of pre-capitalist forms of care and treatment for 'the insane' (Jones, 1960). This positive view of the asylum emerges in historical and contemporary arguments in support of the benefits that psychiatric institutions could deliver both then and now. For example, Borthwick et al. (2001) compare the principles which underlay 'moral treatment' by Tuke in the early nineteenth century with those that underpin contemporary mental health policy two centuries later. Other, less favourable commentaries position the rise of the asylum alongside the political economy of capitalism (Scull, 1977) and with it the need to control and manage deviant behaviours (Foucault, 1975). At its most coercive, the state had sought to incarcerate and thus used a range of physical, psychological, and latterly medical forms of care and treatment that appear harsh and unforgiving in the light of history. Aspects of this history remain with us today, whether in the physical imagery of surviving Victorian hospitals or in the way the state uses mental health laws to deprive service users of their liberty (a discussion that we will have in the next chapter).

We want to encourage you to think about this notion of the enduring historical legacy of mental health policies and consider how, sometimes surprisingly, this past still has a resonance for contemporary practice. So, consider the following two questions:

Exercise 1.1

1. Is there a Victorian psychiatric hospital in your district? If so, can you trace its history and whether any of your social work colleagues worked there?
2. Have you spoken to older clients, who were patients before the 1980s? If so, what were their experiences of the hospital?

In completing this exercise you may think, as we do, that there are a mixture of possible responses, positive as well as negative. Hundreds of Victorian asylums were built in Britain and Ireland in the nineteenth century. Those that remain continue to be a brooding presence in many towns and cities, instilling fear amongst those citizens who are old enough to remember the hospitals when they were fully functional. For some patients, especially those who were incarcerated for long periods, the institution and its members (including professionals) may have been viewed, on balance, in terms of a collective 'good', offering protection, care and safety from the outside world. Each member of the institution knew and recognized the expected roles and relationships (see our discussion of the work of Goffman in Chapter 3). For others, the asylum was essentially oppressive, where rights and dignity were stripped away, professional power could not be challenged and there was little prospect of returning to the community outside the asylum. Institutionalization describes the largely negative impact of long-term institutional care in which people were rarely asked to make decisions, had little responsibility and spent most of their time relatively under-stimulated and inactive. Other histories also suggest that life outside the asylum could be just as coercive (Bartlett and Wright, 1999).

It is not easy to establish those moments when mental health policy significantly shifted in ways that dramatically affected the lives of service users, carers and professionals (Carpenter, 2009). Often these processes could be slow burning, erratic and hard to determine, but the history of mental health services in the UK can be roughly divided into three main phases: before 1845 when there was little formal system of care; between 1845 and 1961 when the asylum dominated; and from 1961 until the present with the development of contemporary practices of community care. Before the relatively progressive thinking that was embodied in the 1845 Lunatics Act, which compelled county authorities to establish asylums, people with mental health problems had mainly been subjected to arbitrary, haphazard and often brutal treatment in workhouses, prisons and private madhouses (Pilgrim and Rogers, 1993). Leading up to this legislation there was growing political and public awareness of the lack of mental health services and a number of innovative approaches had attempted to provide more humane care (Jones, 1998). Urbanization, industrialization and professional forces contributed to these changes but in the direction of segregation (Scull, 1977). Following the 1845 Act, the large Victorian asylums totally dominated mental health care until the first official discussions about moving towards community care began following the aftermath of the First World War. A Royal Commission (1924–1926) considered reform and recommended a community service based on treatment in people's homes. Its recommendations were included in the Mental Treatment Act of 1930. Over the next 30 years some progress was made through open door policies, a greater focus on acute care, outpatient clinics, increased public awareness and the development of therapeutic community ideas. However, it was not until the 1950s that the role of institutions as the base for care was first really challenged. Jones (1998) has described this time as involving three revolutions – legal, social and pharmacological. Another factor was the spiralling costs of maintaining the mental hospitals.

The legal revolution began in the early 1950s with a growing concern about the loss of liberty involved in institutional care. This concern led to the creation of another Royal Commission in 1954 whose work was to form the basis of the 1959 Mental Health Act. This legislation confirmed the need to re-orientate mental health services away from institutions towards care in the community. The social revolution was heralded by the publication of a World Health Organisation report in 1953 that offered a new model for the development of community mental health services. In the late 1950s and early 1960s a rush of literature that confirmed the detrimental effects of institutionalization reinforced the need to move towards community-focused services.

The World Health Organisation report was closely followed by the pharmacological revolution that introduced new drugs which alleviated some of the symptoms of mental health problems. Although there was initial optimism about these drugs, their role in deinstitutionalization has perhaps been overplayed. By 1961 Professor Morris Carstairs noted that 'few would claim that our current wonder drugs exercise anything more than a palliative influence on psychiatric disorders. The big change has been rather one of public opinion' (Jones, 1998: 150). The in-patient population in England and Wales had peaked in 1955 at 155,000 and due to the legal, social and pharmacological developments began to decline slowly, with some community services introduced in rather piecemeal ways across the UK. However, in 1961, Enoch Powell, the new Minister for Health, driven by a political desire to reduce public spending (rather than any more therapeutic motive) declared in his famous Water Tower Speech the intention to attempt to cut the number of psychiatric beds by half in 15 years. This announcement established the pattern that has caused many of our current difficulties – the reduction of hospital beds without the establishment of sufficient community services to support people. Subsequent policy approaches highlighted this concern. Warnings about pursuing dehospitalization without reprovision were identified in 'Better Services for the Mentally Ill' (DHSS, 1975) and by the Social Services Committee of the House of Commons (1985) who stated,

> A decent community-based service for mentally ill or mentally handicapped people cannot be provided at the same overall cost as present services. The proposition that community care should be cost neutral is untenable ... Any fool can close a long-stay hospital: it takes more time and trouble to do it properly and compassionately. (cited in Mind, 2010: 1)

A key theme that has influenced policy in this area throughout the developed world has therefore been the stated intention by governments to move patients from psychiatric hospitals and into the community (even though these concepts in themselves can be hard to define). There are disparate views on which factors can best explain the origins and delivery of these policy agendas, with Scull, in particular, questioning the conventional wisdom that the introduction of new psychotropic drugs in the mid to late 1950s enabled the trend towards rehabilitation in the community to take place. Yet it was not until the 1980s that such a policy began to be only partially recognized. Debates continue about the merits of hospital- and community-based forms of care, confirmed in Thornicroft and Tansella's (2004) review of the evidence. A key factor in assessing mental health systems is the resources available to governments. Where there are limited resources, the literature suggests that investment should take place at the level of primary care. When more resources are available then policy makers are more likely to move away from asylum-based care. This usually happens when governments release funds by engaging in a process of deinstitutionalization. When welfare regimes can afford a stepped care model then important planning and training processes are necessary for successful outcomes. The authors conclude by arguing that a false dichotomy which poses institutional versus community care is not borne out in the evidence and that a pragmatic, integrated approach is necessary in any modern system of mental health care.

Deinstitutionalization and community care

Service users, carers and mental health social workers have to deal with the consequences of this policy, however ill defined it remains. Although there has been a substantial reduction in hospital bed numbers, rates of detention remain high, as illustrated by the graph below taken from McKeown et al.'s (2011) paper on trends in hospital use in England from 1998–2008:

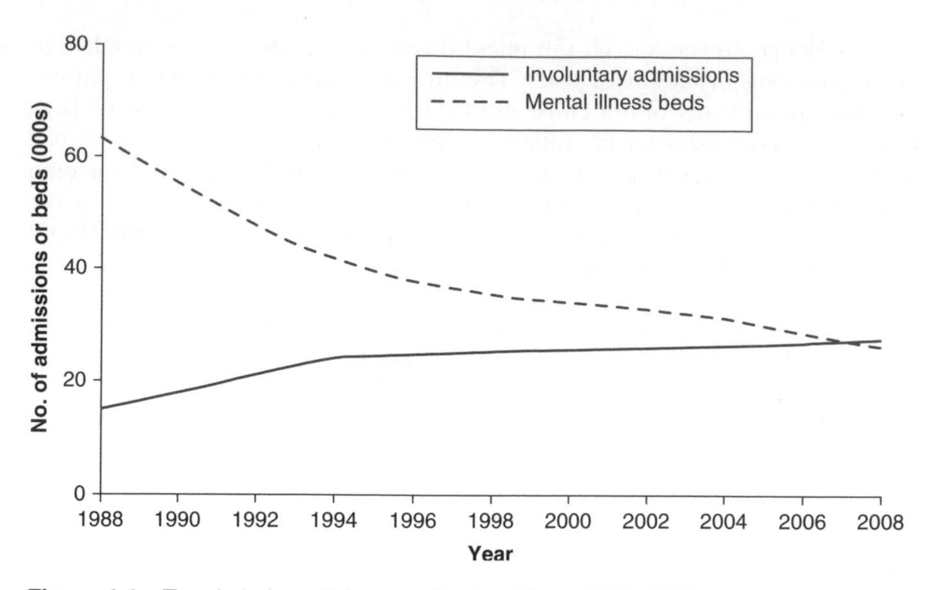

Figure 1.1 Trends in hospital use in England from 1998–2008

Similar trends occurred in Scotland and Northern Ireland, although services are inevitably configured in nuanced ways, depending on the patterns of deinstitutionalization and support for community-based care. As McKeown et al.'s (2011) figure implies, just because bed numbers had been reduced this does not mean that admissions also fell. What emerged during this period was the phenomenon of the 'revolving door syndrome'. This can briefly be explained as follows. As psychiatric bed numbers fell, time spent in hospital was reduced and quicker discharges occurred. In some cases service users were discharged too quickly, or community-based supports were inadequate, so a quicker than usual readmission to hospital occurred (Thompson et al., 2004). Increasing numbers of people were also detained – one assumes because of the lack of support and resource in the community to prevent admission and readmission.

Concerns about this 'revolving door' phenomenon had been recognized by the 1990s and a range of policy initiatives was designed to deal with these transitions. For example, a model of care management that described a process of assessment, planning, intervening and review was to be used with all adult services groups. This model of care planning continues to inform much social work practice in mental health and other services (Payne, 1995). Partly because of concerns about the haphazard nature of community-based care for, and risks to, people with mental health problems, the Care Programme Approach (CPA) was introduced. The idea was that clients judged to be vulnerable should be entitled to an assessment, and, where necessary, a care plan would then be delivered by a named professional, often a social worker. Two decades later, probably as a consequence of limited resources and the problems of organization, only the most vulnerable and those at immediate risk will receive these services (Golightly, 2008). Another feature of the CPA has been an attempt to record and track decision-making processes within and between the complex network of services that comprise the mental health system. A more recent, but related, policy process directly targeted at the improvement of mental health services is the National Service Framework for Mental Health (NSFMH) (DH, 1999b). Webber (2008) has argued that the standards set by the government in England and Wales (mental health promotion; primary care; access to services for people with severe mental health problems; effective services; caring for carers; preventing suicide) were rational in their intent, but not always underpinned by the evidence provided by government sponsored research projects.

Risk and protection

We mentioned at the start of this chapter that, however enlightened the policy process is in terms of government and civic aspirations towards more efficient, humane and inclusive services for people with mental health problems, concerns about risk and protection remain. These concerns have been intensified as broader principles of care management have been replaced with a more targeted, case management approach in dealing with service users deemed to be most at risk (Kemshall, 2002). In later chapters we will be using case material to illustrate how risk can be assessed and dealt with by mental health social workers, but first we must express a note of caution. In many ways risk can be viewed as a socially constructed concept that has been defined and redefined by policy makers over the years (Cree and Wallace, 2009). For example, many people in the past were admitted to psychiatric hospitals for social and not psychiatric reasons; often these practices adversely affected particular sections of society (Prior, 1999). The more recent policy initiatives (DH, 1999) that focused on one group of people with mental health problems, those described as having dangerously severe personality disorders, fuelled the debates that led to the eventual reform of mental health laws in the UK. This is an especially problematic issue for mental health practitioners because of difficulties with the assessment, diagnosis, care and treatment of people with personality disorders. There is little evidence that compulsory hospitalization leads to good outcomes in these circumstances, and the worry must be that civil legal processes might be used to incarcerate those who are viewed to be dangerous but not obviously subject to the criminal legal process.

Notwithstanding this assumption of some degree of social construction in the way that risk is perceived by policy makers and the wider society, attempts have been made to assess and empirically measure these relationships. Rogers and Pilgrim (2009) summarized the findings from a range of studies and, unsurprisingly, concluded that definitive trends and causal factors were difficult to establish. Findings will tend to vary according to the period studied, with contrasting claims of more or less risk in some populations of people with mental health problems. For example, there are strong claims that people with substance misuse behaviours and personality disorders are more likely to be dangerous than the normal population. These findings are interesting but not particularly helpful to practitioners and policy makers who would seek concrete answers to how risk can be judged in this field. Gaps in knowledge are also magnified when public inquiries examine homicides caused by people with mental health problems (Stanley and Manthorpe, 2001). What will emerge from these inquiries are appeals for more joined-up communication between health and social care professionals, particularly during the discharge process, and the development of skills and resources in carrying out multi-disciplinary assessments.

It seems ironic, and somehow reflective of public attitudes towards the problems faced by people with mental health problems, that the risk to service users from themselves and others is likely to be much greater than the risk they present to the general public. Mental distress, social isolation and stigma can contribute to feelings of worthlessness and lead to self-harm and suicide. As with the discussion on risk to others, it is nonetheless difficult to disaggregate the causes of these behaviours, not least in the case of suicide when coroners' courts do not always have the evidence of intention available to them to make a decision. Pritchard (2006) uses international figures to highlight the variations in suicide rates across the world and argues for multi-factorial explanations for these rates, including the significance of social and cultural norms and the sudden economic changes that adversely affect societies. For example, there has been an intense debate in Northern Ireland about the effects of the political conflict upon suicide rates (Tomlinson, 2007) and it is reasonable to conclude that, as before, suicides will increase during periods of economic recession. In the UK men are much more likely than women, and younger rather than older people, to be over-represented in statistics on suicide. Those who are depressed, use drugs and alcohol, and experience social isolation are also at risk. Recent figures indicate a general decline in suicides in the UK between 1991 and 2007, with an increase for the last year of combined records, 2008 (www.statistics.gov.uk). Governments across the countries of the UK have recognized the high costs of suicide and developed policies to help prevent suicide (DH, 2002b; Scottish Government, 2002; DHSSPS, 2006; Welsh Assembly, 2008). These policies share common aims in targeting groups at risk, responding to crises and developing preventative services, promoting well-being and recovery, engaging with how the media deals with suicide, and evaluating best practice in the field.

Social inclusion and recovery

There is convincing evidence that people with mental health problems often encounter disadvantages caused by social exclusion (Gomm, 2009). These disadvantages take different forms; for example exclusion from the labour market, which many service users face, is directly associated with the social consequences of being poor. Finding a job is made that much more difficult if you have had or have a mental health problem. In addition the pervasive forms of stigma and stereotyping to be found in the media and everyday discourses create barriers to social inclusion. During the last decade UK governments have attempted to challenge these forms of discrimination through a series of policy-based initiatives. For example, Standard One of the NSF highlights the requirement for service providers to address mental health promotion and the discrimination and social exclusion faced by mental health service users. The organization and delivery of mental health services should also be shaped by the key policy documents, *Modernising Mental Health Services* (DH, 1998) and the *Mental Health and Social Exclusion* report (SEU, 2004). Despite the fact that this policy agenda has been in existence for over a decade, concerns remain about its success.

Whereas government policies designed to reduce social exclusion seem somewhat remote and disconnected from the lives of people with mental health problems, recent interest in using the concept of recovery has generated a greater sense of hope for change in the mental health system (DH, 2001). Ramon et al. (2007) trace the history of the concept to its central presence in the UK mental health system (NIMHE, 2005). This concept is founded upon a critique of traditional, professional discourses about the care and treatment of people with mental health problems. This pessimism is challenged by ideas on recovery. Increasingly service users are demanding changes to the way services are managed and delivered. Embedded in the concept of recovery is the espousal of a strengths perspective where service users have a say in the services they receive and these services take more optimistic views about past, present and future experiences (Sayce, 2000). We further develop this discussion in Chapters 4 and 5.

Organizational contexts

In the second part of the chapter we now examine the ways in which organizations have developed to account for these policy drivers. We thought we would introduce this section by locating our own professional careers in the policy environments and organizational contexts that existed when we practised. One of us worked as a mental health social worker just at the crossover from hospital to community mental health teams in the late 1980s. This was the beginning of a large-scale process of deinstitutionalization, coinciding with changes to mental health law. The other author practised at a time when community care policy was much more developed and new services were designed to prevent hospitalization. The time was the late 1990s and the organizational unit was a Community Mental Health Team and then an assertive outreach team. In the decade between these two experiences much had happened in terms of the delivery of mental health services; these can be partly explained by factors that were discussed in the first part of this chapter. For example, there was a large reduction in psychiatric bed numbers, and a gradual increase in new forms of community-based care and multi-disciplinary working, growing worries about the management of risk and a greater recognition of the voices of carers and service users. At this point think about your career in the same way by completing the following exercise.

Exercise 1.2

1 Describe how mental health policies have affected the way your organization functioned during your career as a mental health social worker.
2 How have these policies affected the way that you practise?

We would imagine that there are many interesting stories about how your career has progressed in the context of these policy environments when these questions have been answered. Although there are, inevitably, large variations in organizational and practice styles, often determined by the policy contexts in each of the jurisdictions of the UK, it is possible to describe the types of services that have evolved to meet these policy imperatives. We now summarize the key features of these services.

Multi-disciplinary working and community-based care

One of the consequences of large-scale policy initiatives, such as the CPA, has been the pressure on organizations to deliver mental health services using models of multi-disciplinary working (see Chapter 10). This has been a difficult aspiration to achieve, particularly because of the diverse structures of health and social care in the UK. The problematic impact upon the delivery of mental health services caused by the split between health and social care authorities has been well documented (Onyett, 2003) while attempts to bridge organizational and financial arrangements to create a seamless, holistic service have often failed. It is also difficult to bring together professionals (social workers, nurses, psychiatrists, occupational therapists, clinical psychologists) who do not share common educational and practice paradigms. And even when an integrated service exists, it is not clear whether this necessarily delivers good outcomes for service users and carers (Reilly et al., 2007).

As a consequence of the NSFMH in England and Wales, and parallel policy processes elsewhere in the UK, a range of multi-disciplinary teams was established to deliver the promises of community-based care for people with mental health problems and their carers (De Chenu, 2007). Existing Community Mental Health Teams (CMHTs) were subject to various changes to meet new policy requirements. Thus some were situated in primary health care settings as part of a more preventative approach to mental health care and treatment. Other mental health social workers were located in teams that were designed to support service users with more chronic and enduring disorders and, hopefully, prevent their admission and readmission to psychiatric hospital. Assertive Outreach Teams (AOTs) provide intense, round the clock services for service users who have difficulty in functioning and managing everyday living. Crisis Intervention Teams (CITs) provide less planned services, rather their function is to respond to immediate crises, often dealing with situations of high risk and vulnerability. Early Intervention Teams (EITs) focus on younger people who are at risk of serious mental illness. Freeman and Peck (2006) used a stakeholder approach to evaluate the work of a number of such teams in England, revealing the strengths as well as the problems faced by such services. A significant problem was boundary disputes between generic and specialist teams about how service user needs would 'fit' with the teams' referral criteria. There were also some interprofessional conflicts within teams. On the other hand, these changes offered new opportunities to develop innovative services and therapeutic approaches and holistic assessments were made more possible through these organizational structures. Notably service users and carers were generally positive in their experiences of reconfigured specialist teams. While most mental health social workers will be employed in community teams, a smaller proportion will work in more specialized settings. For example, they may intervene at the interface between the criminal justice and mental health systems as part of a forensic team, deal with the needs of younger people in a Children and Adolescent Mental Health Service (CAMHS) team, or contribute to teams of professionals working with people who have addiction problems. We will use case material in the following chapters to help you explore these interfaces.

Conclusions: implications for mental health social work practice

We began this chapter by arguing that mental health social workers needed to be aware of the policy-making processes that would lead to changes in organizational delivery and professional practice. In particular the last decade has seen quite profound shifts in the way that governments view mental health provision in terms of rolling out community care policies, managing perceived risk and engaging more openly with service users and carers. We will return to these and other themes when we apply theory to social work practice in later chapters of this book. In the meantime, however, it is worth reflecting on the issues that mental health social workers face as a result of these ever-changing policy contexts. We believe that a critical understanding of policy processes can better equip mental health social workers to deliver practice that is mindful of service user and carer need. Bowl (2009) makes a number of important points in this respect. There seems little doubt that, as governments increasingly favour generic, shared mental health professional roles, some social workers will feel that their identity is threatened. Bowl cites the introduction in England and Wales of Support Time and Recovery (STR) Workers and the Approved Mental Health Professional (AMHP) to make this point (see Chapter 11). This concern about the diminution of a distinctive social work role in mental health services is the subject of continuing debate at the levels of both policy and practice, following the reconfiguration of services (NIMHE, 2005). The need for continuous education and training to enable mental health social workers to establish their credentials can be viewed as a positive response to such challenges. There is also a need to emphasize and re-emphasize the sociological, holistic perspectives that social workers can bring to the processes of assessment and intervention in mental health services (Gould, 2006). It may also be reasonable to assume that mental health social workers are better equipped to understand the impact of policy processes than other professional colleagues. Rapaport (2005), in her account of the development of the mental health social work role in England and Wales, traces a series of setbacks and some successes in the way that the role was constructed and re-worked in the post-war period. Her argument is that some of the erosion of the social work role occurred with the advent of multi-disciplinary teams and AMHPs in England and Wales. Although there are similar concerns elsewhere in the UK, the preservation of the sole legal function for social workers in Scotland and Northern Ireland at least partly assuages these concerns. The message, however, remains the same: social workers have to be more politically aware and prepared to advocate for their position at the level of policy making. We hope that now you have read this chapter this relationship between the professional activity of mental health social workers and wider policy agendas is clearer and its importance has been highlighted.

Recommended reading

For a comprehensive description and analysis of the historical development of mental health policy and services see the following Mind website:
www.mind.org.uk/help/research_and_policy/notes_on_the_history_of_mental_health_care

Pilgrim and Ramon provide a thorough, critical review of how mental health policy in the UK developed over the period of recent Labour governments:
Pilgrim and Ramon (2009) 'English mental health policy under New Labour', *Policy and Politics*, 37 (2): 273–88.

2

The Legal Context

National occupational standards

This chapter will help you meet the following National Occupational Standards for Social Work.

Key Role 5: Manage and be accountable, with supervision and support, for your own social work practice within your organization. Unit 14: Manage and be accountable for your own work.

Key Role 6: Demonstrate professional competence in social work practice. Unit 20: Manage complex ethical issues, dilemmas and conflicts.

It will also help meet the following National Occupational Standards for Mental Health.

- Respond to crisis situations (SMFMH 21).
- Assess the need for intervention and present assessments of individuals' needs and related risks (SMFMH 17).
- Respond to potential crisis and relapse for an individual in the community (FMH 18).
- Manage hostility and risks with non-cooperative individuals, families and carers (FHM 12).

Learning outcomes

1. To understand the key roles played by mental health social workers in mental health and related laws across UK jurisdictions.
2. To describe and analyse decision-making processes in assessing risk and capacity when using these laws.
3. To understand practice and ethical dilemmas in terms of client autonomy, paternalism, coercion, risk assessment and capacity.

Introduction

One of the most important decisions that a mental health social worker will have to make in their professional career is to deprive clients of their liberty by compulsorily admitting them to a psychiatric hospital and managing their compulsory care and treatment in the community. The statutory powers that mental health social workers and other professionals use in this field are substantive, and potentially coercive. What also makes this area of work challenging are the ethical dilemmas that arise because these powers are being applied in the context of civil rather than criminal law (Bartlett and Sandland, 2003). The chapter summarizes key features of mental health, capacity and human rights laws in the UK that underpin the statutory functions that are carried out by approved and accredited mental health social workers. Attention is also paid to research studies that critically analyse the role of mental health social workers in using these laws. The practice dilemmas faced by mental health social workers in fulfilling these functions will be discussed in the context of the case material used in the following chapters of the book.

The evolution of a statutory role for the mental health social worker

In considering how legal interventions might be used with your clients it is important to be mindful of how and why mental health social workers were given these powers. In the Introduction we provided a brief historical overview of the development of the mental health social work role from its origins in nineteenth-century philanthropic activity. Following the reform of mental health laws in the 1980s an assumption was made that mental health social workers could bring unique knowledge, skills and values to the multi-disciplinary assessment process. This would contribute to a more holistic assessment of risk and need, in which the clients' individual, familial and social circumstances would be fully considered before compulsory hospitalization would take place (Gostin, 1975; Olsen, 1984). The three new mental health laws that were introduced in the UK (The Mental Health (England and Wales) Act 1983; The Mental Health (Scotland) Act 1984; The Mental Health (Northern Ireland) Order 1986) reserved broadly similar roles and functions for mental health social workers. In the following two decades Approved Social Workers (ASWs) in England, Wales and Northern Ireland, and Mental Health Officers (MHOs) in Scotland, alongside other professionals, used substantial powers to compulsorily admit clients to hospital, apply for and administer guardianship proceedings, and play an important role in mental health review tribunal processes.

Although the acquisition of these new powers brought with it increased professional independence and esteem, consequent practice dilemmas have been associated with the use of these powers. It has been argued for example, that decisions made by mental health social workers to use mental health laws are characterized by a difficult, risky balancing act (Campbell and Davidson, 2009). Social workers have to take into account the often competing demands of a range of stakeholders, including clients, their families, the general public and policy makers. Although statutes and respective Codes of Practice are essential in guiding mental health social work practice, it is also important, when working with clients in this area, to consider what the research literature says about these competing demands. For example in carrying out your statutory functions it can be difficult to strike a balance between a duty of care and the possible legal requirement for paternalistic control (Beckett and Maynard, 2005). Such tensions were recognized in an early analysis of the ASW role. Prior (1992) argued that, however well meaning the view that ASWs could be advocates for their clients when using compulsory mental health laws, this position was compromised by legal function. The ASW had a responsibility to the state and wider society to restrict the liberty of mentally disordered clients who were presenting a risk to themselves and/or others; for this reason is was improbable that they could, simultaneously, seek to be their advocate. In some ways this argument has been recognized in current mental health laws where clients have access to professional and peer advocates at different stages of the process. In the years that have passed since the introduction of the ASW there is also greater acknowledgement of the potentially coercive nature of the use of mental health laws by mental health social workers and other professionals. There is now quite compelling evidence that, although it is the case that some service users are satisfied with professionals' use of coercion (Gibbs et al., 2005), many others have expressed dissatisfaction with these processes (Bradley et al., 1995; Canvin, 2002; Rose et al., 2005; Wilson and Daly, 2007; Hughes et al., 2009). Carers have also expressed concerns about their experience of professional interventions in this field (Rapaport and Manthorpe, 2008).

Unfortunately the positive use of mental health laws by social workers is often undermined by problems of organization and resource. Despite evidence of social workers aspiring to a positive, enabling role (Huxley et al., 2005; Quirk et al., 2003), these other factors conspire to make decision making problematic. A consistent finding from a number of studies has been the unevenness of ASW service delivery across the UK and a lack of adequate community-based resources (Barnes et al., 1990; Smith, 1991; Huxley and Kerfoot, 1994; Manktelow et al., 2002; Quirk et al., 2003; Davidson and Campbell, 2009). The result has been a tendency towards risk-averse practice leading to an overdependence on compulsory admissions at the expense of preventative approaches that would enable clients to be supported in alternative, less restrictive community settings (a point we made in Chapter 1). In addition, problems of multi-disciplinary working can frustrate attempts to use agreed holistic assessments that can protect the rights of service users and carers (Smith, 1991; Bowers et al., 2003; Fakhoury and Wright, 2004; Furminger and Webber, 2009). In these circumstances it is perhaps not surprising that stress and burnouts occur amongst mental health social workers (Huxley et al., 2005; Evans et al., 2006). Another important factor in the way that ASWs have carried out their functions is how they, alongside other mental health professionals, make decisions that affect particular groups and communities. We further explore this issue of discrimination and social exclusion in Chapter 4. It would appear that some sections of society are more likely to be subject to compulsory powers including women, young men, members of minority ethnic communities and those with schizophrenia, affective disorders and addiction problems (Hatfield and Mohamad, 1994; Hatfield et al., 1997; Fernando, 2001; Hatfield, 2007; Browne, 2009; Rogers and Pilgrim, 2009).

Working with new mental health laws

If anything these factors have been further highlighted by the introduction of new mental health laws to the UK in recent years. Mental health social workers now have additional responsibilities, often involving the use of coercion, for example in deciding whether compulsory care and treatment in the community is appropriate, and in terms of considering issues of capacity. It is important to note that, as a result of increasing devolution of political responsibilities to the four nations of the UK, mental health law and policy has become more heterogeneous, with consequent variations in the role of the mental health social worker.

Scotland was the first jurisdiction to introduce a new mental health law in the 2000s. Following the deliberations of the Millan Committee, the Mental Health (Care and Treatment) (Scotland) Act 2003 created new responsibilities for MHOs (www.scotland.gov.uk/Publications/2006/10/02095357/4): MHOs, with other professionals, became involved in the application and administration of a range of orders, including:

- a short-term detention certificate
- an interim Compulsory Treatment Order (CTO)
- a CTO
- an assessment order
- a treatment order
- an interim compulsion order
- a compulsion order
- a hospital direction
- a transfer for treatment direction.

The Act has been viewed as relatively successful so far because of the way safeguards were built into law and policy, for example in terms of funding community-based services, the establishment of advocacy services and tight scheduling of the permitted timetable for processes associated with compulsory powers and the use of tribunals. A recent review of the working of the legislation (www.scotland.gov.uk/Publications/2010/03/04155611/2) has recommended some changes to the operation of advance statements, mental health review tribunals, independent advocates and named persons. Mental health social work practice in this field is prescribed by a Code of Practice (Scottish Government, 2005) (www.scotland.gov.uk/Publications/2005/08/29100428/04289).

Whereas the reform of Scottish mental health law has been generally perceived in a favourable light by stakeholders, the protracted, contentious processes involved in changes to the law in England and Wales resulted in substantial amendments to the existing Mental Health Act 1983, implemented through the Mental Health Act 2007 (www.dh.gov.uk/en/Healthcare/Mentalhealth/DH_078743). The recommendations of the Richardson Committee were not fully adopted by the government and the debates which followed tended to focus on the overly inclusive use of definitions of mental disorder and what was perceived to be a preoccupation by policy makers about the need to manage risk in the community (Moncrieff, 2003). Unlike the other UK jurisdictions, a new, hybrid professional role was created for England and Wales, the AMHP, allowing other professionals (nurses, occupational therapists and psychologists) to also carry out statutory functions that were previously the sole domain of ASWs (Department of Health, 2008). The use of these powers is further discussed and analysed in Chapter 11. Social workers, however, will remain the most populous profession within this grouping. The AMHP, like their MHO counterpart, has considerable mandated powers to use if they believe that a person is at risk and suffering from a mental disorder. They can:

- along with the approved clinician, decide if someone should be compulsorily admitted to hospital for assessment;
- along with the approved clinician, decide if someone needs to be detained under a treatment order;
- participate in multi-disciplinary decisions that will lead to the establishment of a CTO;
- contribute to decision making in mental health review tribunals.

Unlike Scotland, and England and Wales, in Northern Ireland the older mental health law (The Mental Health (Northern Ireland) Order, 1986) is currently used but new legislation is planned, following the recommendations of the Bamford Review (www.dhsspsni.gov.uk/legislative-framework-for-mental-capacity.pdf). Until then ASWs in Northern Ireland can use a range of powers if they believe that someone is mentally disordered and at risk to themselves or others (Manktelow et al., 2002; DHSS (NI), 1993 Code of Practice). They can:

- make an application for someone's compulsory admission to hospital;
- along with other professionals, decide whether guardianship is an appropriate alternative to hospital care and treatment;
- contribute to decision making in mental health review tribunals.

The government in Northern Ireland is recommending combined mental health and capacity legislation and is also enhancing the role of the ASW. As in other jurisdictions ASWs will have a future role in the decision-making process leading to CTOs and will be involved in functions associated with the assessment of capacity.

Given these variations it is vital that you establish which mental health laws are relevant to your practice by considering the following Exercise.

Exercise 2.1

Consider the country in which you are working (England, Wales, Scotland, Northern Ireland). Describe the statutory functions of the mental health social worker as stated in mental health law in your jurisdiction and compare and contrast these functions with those of mental health social workers in other parts of the UK.

Hopefully you will discover quite a lot of variations, depending on the jurisdiction that you work in. For example, in England and Wales, unlike Scotland and the new law proposed for Northern Ireland, close relatives can still be involved in the use of compulsory powers. There are also differences in the prescribed periods in which compulsory admission and detention can take place that have to be adhered to by professionals. You should also be able to note the subtle nuances in the ways that mental disorders and the conditions for compulsory treatment are defined.

Mental health social work and community-based coercion

Debates about the complexity of the role of mental health social workers in the UK are intensifying in the light of these changes to mental health law across all jurisdictions of the UK (Campbell et al., 2006). In particular the introduction of CTOs has been challenging to mental health social workers whose key statutory function was, hitherto, more limited to using compulsory powers to seek admissions to psychiatric hospitals. The prospect of this increased suite of community-based powers potentially changes the traditional relationship the profession has with vulnerable clients. For this reason mental health social workers should be mindful of debates about the purpose and effectiveness of CTOs. In the most comprehensive review of the literature to date, Churchill et al. (2007) are critical of the evidence base, largely because of flaws in its study methodologies. A current randomized control trial in England is seeking to strengthen this evidence base (OCTET, 2010). Proponents of CTOs have argued that they may offer benefits such as increased quality of life, reductions in hospitalization, symptoms and violence, and greater compliance with medication (O'Reilly, 2004; Romans et al., 2004; O'Brien and Farrell, 2005). These are the types of outcomes that CTOs are expected to deliver. However, as those who are more critical of CTOs point out, there are also a variety of problems that they can bring as well, including threats to therapeutic relationships and a retreat to medication-only regimes as a result of poorly resourced community services (Brophy et al., 2003; Petrila and Christy, 2008). Early research into the use of CTOs in the UK suggests that they will only be effective if complemented by adequate community-based services and fit for purpose systems of legal and administrative arrangements (Lawton-Smith and Dawson, 2008). A range of problems and concerns has been highlighted (Lawton Smith, 2011). As in other jurisdictions, the number of people placed on CTOs has exceeded policy makers' projections with an over-representation of Black and Minority Ethnic (BME) communities in these figures. There are worries about over-use of medication and problems of inter-disciplinary communication as well as the use of second opinions. The voices of patients and carers are often not well heard, however where patient views are listened to they are more likely to be compliant with the CTO.

Mental health social work and capacity laws in the uk

The introduction of mental capacity laws in the UK will also have a major effect upon the work of mental health social workers across a wide range of settings. Amongst the many reasons for the introduction of these capacity laws was a primary concern that, following the case of *HL* v *UK* (Bournewood Judgment), a person should not be compulsorily held without a legal process and protections, even if they appear compliant. Subsequent mental health and capacity laws sought to bridge what has been described as the 'Bournewood gap' by ensuring that a capacity test is carried out by professionals, including mental health social workers, when concerns about capacity are presented to them. UK jurisdictions are now required to use law and guidelines to ensure good practice in this area. In Scotland, for example, there are overlapping responsibilities across the older Adults with Incapacity (Scotland) Act 2000 and the more recent Mental Health (Care and Treatment) (Scotland) Act 2003 (www.scotland.gov.uk/Publications/2005/07/1595204/52186). Similarly in England and Wales there are two separate interrelated statutes, the Mental Health Act 2007 and the Mental Capacity Act 2005 (www.dh.gov.uk/en/SocialCare/Deliveringadultsocialcare/MentalCapacity/MentalCapacityAct2005/index.htm). Unusually a single act (Dawson and Szmukler, 2006) is being proposed for Northern Ireland (www.rmhldni.gov.uk/legal-issue-comprehensive-framework.pdf).

Mental capacity refers simply to everyone's ability to work through all the processes necessary to make decisions, whether these are everyday routine decisions or very significant decisions about our care, where we live, handling our money and our lives in general. It is not about the decision itself which may be regarded by others as unwise or even irrational but the processes needed to make that decision. Section 2.1 of the Mental Capacity Act 2005 specifies that for intervention to be enabled the person has to be 'unable to make a decision for himself in relation to the matter because of an impairment of, or a disturbance in the functioning of, the mind or brain'. The Mental Capacity Act Code of Practice explains that this therefore requires a two-stage test. First it has to be established that the person has an impairment, temporary or permanent, of the mind or brain and then that this means that they are currently unable to make the specific decision. In assessing mental capacity, Section 3.1 of the Mental Capacity Act 2005 specifies that four factors must be considered: 'a person is unable to make a decision for himself if he is unable -

a to understand the information relevant to the decision,
b to retain that information,
c to use or weigh that information as part of the process of making the decision, or
d to communicate his decision (whether by talking, using sign language or any other means)'.

Under the Adults with Incapacity (Scotland) Act 2000, similarly, 'incapable' means incapable of: acting on decisions; or making decisions; or communicating decisions; or understanding decisions; or retaining the memory of decisions (Section 1.6).

When considering both mental health and capacity laws it may be helpful to think of a continuum of decision making (Brayley, 2009; Chartres and Brayley, 2010) which begins with autonomous decision making when the person has all the information they need for the decision and is able to make it on their own, moves through supported decision making when the person needs some form of support to make the decision, and then ends with substitute or proxy decision making when another person makes the decision based on what can be determined about the person's best interests. A crucial aspect of practice in this area is ensuring that all possible support has been provided to the person to make their own decision and so preventing the need for substitute decision making. This is implicit in mental health law but is more explicitly stated in mental capacity law, for example, Section 3.2 of the Mental Capacity Act 2005 states,

> A person is not to be regarded as unable to understand the information relevant to a decision if he is able to understand an explanation of it given to him in a way that is appropriate to his circumstances (using simple language, visual aids or any other means).

In Scotland there is specific guidance under the Adults with Incapacity (Scotland) Act 2000, *Communication and Assessing Capacity: A guide for social work and health care staff* (Scottish Government, 2008), to help ensure all practicable steps have been taken to help a person make the decision.The Department of Health (2007b) has also produced general guidance on supported decision making. Although supported decision making is a central aspect of mental health social work practice, capacity law may ensure this important role is further considered, researched and developed.

It is important that you understand the differences in respective laws across the UK, so consider the following exercise:

Exercise 2.2

Consider the country in which you are working (England, Wales, Scotland, Northern Ireland).

Describe the statutory functions of the mental health social worker as described by the capacity law in your jurisdiction and compare and contrast these functions with those of mental health social workers in other parts of the UK.

When you have completed this exercise we hope it becomes apparent that capacity laws imply that mental health social workers, alongside other professionals and stakeholders (in particular Independent Mental Capacity Advocates), have important responsibilities in ensuring that the rights of clients and their families are protected when issues of capacity are to be considered. In their comprehensive guide to The Mental Capacity Act 2005, Brown et al. (2009: 17) highlight functions of the Act. Of particular note are the five principles that underpin the application of the law:

1 That a person must be assumed to have capacity unless it is established that he lacks capacity.
2 A person is not to be treated as unable to make a decision unless all practicable steps to help him to do so have been taken without success.
3 A person is not to be treated as unable to make a decision merely because he makes an unwise decision.
4 An act done, or decision made, under this Act for or on behalf of a person who lacks capacity must be done, or made, in his best interests.
5 Before the act is done, or the decision is made, regard must be had to whether the purpose for which it is needed can be as effectively achieved in a way that is less restrictive of the person's rights and freedom of action.

Mental health social workers are one of a number of professionals who are involved in making decisions when concerns are raised about a client's capacity. In addition the law requires professionals to make decisions about Best Interests when a client lacks capacity. The Code of Practice sets out a checklist that should be used when Best Interests Assessments (BIA) are taking place. Brown et al. (2009: 26–8) summarize the key principles when using this checklist: it should be presumed that the person has capacity; there should be a clear understanding of how capacity and lack of capacity is defined and assessed; understanding and assessing the ability of the client to make a decision; assessing the client's capacity to make complex decisions (perhaps involving other professionals); all clients should be treated equally; clients should be encouraged to make decisions for themselves. In some circumstances mental health social workers will also be involved with Deprivation of Liberty Safeguards (DoLS), usually in the context of clients with dementia, learning difficulties and neurological conditions who are living in hospital or residential and nursing facilities. In order for DoLS to be implemented, there are six qualifying requirements, in terms of age, mental health, mental capacity, Best Interests, eligibility and no refusals. Eligible mental health social workers can be involved in assessing all of these DoLS requirements apart from mental health which has to be assessed by a doctor (Brown et al., 2009: 99).

The proposed legal decision-making frameworks for people who have impaired capacity are clearly intended to provide better and more consistent protection, but there are some uncertainties about how these complex processes work in practice. An initial issue is how accurately and consistently incapacity will be identified and assessed. Some research evidence suggests there is a high level of agreement between psychiatrists (Cairns et al., 2005) and between psychiatrists and nurses (Singhal et al., 2008) when assessing incapacity, but it is not yet known how well this is being done in the context of the processes required by the legislation and between all the people who are involved in these assessments. There is a range of audit tools available to evaluate the assessment of capacity and these are listed by SCIE at www.scie.org.uk/publications/mca/audits/index.asp. These include a tool specifically designed by the British Psychological Society and SCIE (2010) to consider the quality of formal assessments. The complexity of the new frameworks, particularly in England and Wales where the MCA, MHA and DoLS have considerable overlap, reinforces the importance of ongoing training for the professionals involved but also raises issues about how understandable and accessible the new provisions are for service users and carers (Manthorpe et al., 2009).

The current proposals in Northern Ireland, to no longer have specific mental health legislation and simply have one legal framework for everyone whose decision-making capacity is impaired, highlight a number of questions about how this would work in practice, but also about the appropriateness of separate mental health laws in the rest of the UK. The main argument for bringing these legal powers into one law is that it is less discriminatory (Dawson and Szmukler, 2006) and so potentially less stigmatizing. The impact of stigma and discrimination will be considered further in Chapter 4 but a single legal framework for all does seem like one way in which this could be addressed, although what the new legislation can achieve on its own without wider changes in attitudes, practices and policies should not be over-estimated (Appelbaum, 1994). The possible introduction of a single framework also highlights the need to consider whether the decision-making capacity of those who are currently compulsorily admitted and treated is necessarily impaired; and indeed whether those who are currently informally admitted to hospital may lack capacity. Owen et al. (2009) reported that from a sample of 200 patients 24 per cent had an informal status but lacked capacity and 6 per cent were detained but retained capacity. Under the proposed framework in Northern Ireland, it is therefore reasonable to speculate that some people (although it may be a relatively small proportion) who are currently detainable would not be under a single capacity-based framework.

Another potentially complex and controversial aspect of these laws is their impact on the use of advance statements and advance decisions. Advance statements can be understood in the context of a person who has decision-making capacity that enables them to set out their preferences for future health and welfare decisions, should they no longer have the capacity to make them. There is evidence that the use of advance statements, in the form of joint crisis plans, may reduce the need for compulsion (Henderson et al., 2004). Under proposed capacity laws, advance statements must be considered in making decisions about a person's care but they are not legally binding. Advance decisions, in contrast, are binding, and can specify the future refusal of specific medical interventions. The possibility of devising an advance decision was already available in the common law across the UK, but in England and Wales although not in Scotland advance decisions were included in the new capacity legislation. This area of law raises some difficult issues for mental health social workers and wider society. The central issue is perhaps whether society accepts, and so allows, the possibility of a rational suicide (Hewitt, 2010). This debate was intensified by the suicide of Kerrie Wooltorton, aged 26, who had used the provisions under the MCA to devise an advance decision refusing medical intervention to save her life. She then drank poison and called an ambulance, but gave the medical staff caring for her a written advance decision which specified she did not want to have medical intervention to save her life but only to ensure that she did not die alone and in pain. This case highlights some of the very complex, ethical dilemmas faced by professionals in this area.

A further area of complexity relates to how these legal frameworks apply to children (under 16) and young people (aged 16 and 17) and overlap specifically with children's law. In general, the mental health laws do apply to children and young people with some additional safeguards and most aspects of the capacity laws do not apply to children but do cover young people. Chapter 36 of the Mental Health Act 1983 Code of Practice (Department of Health, 2008) provides clear, detailed and helpful guidance on this area. It specifies that when decisions are being considered in this area the following should always be borne in mind:

- The best interests of the child or young person must always be a significant consideration.
- Children and young people should always be kept as fully informed as possible, just as an adult would be, and should receive clear and detailed information concerning their care and treatment, explained in a way they can understand and in a format that is appropriate to their age.
- The child or young person's views, wishes and feelings should always be considered.
- Any intervention in the life of a child or young person that is considered necessary by reason of their mental disorder should be the option that is least restrictive and least likely to expose them to the risk of any stigmatization, consistent with effective care and treatment, and it should also result in the least possible separation from family, carers, friends and community or interruption of their education, as is consistent with their wellbeing.
- All children and young people should receive the same access to educational provision as their peers.
- Children and young people have as much right to expect their dignity to be respected as anyone else; and
- Children and young people have as much right to privacy and confidentiality as anyone else (pp. 327–8).

Debates in this area often discuss the competence of children to make decisions, specifically around treatment. Competence is a legal term which refers to whether a child has the mental capacity to make the decision and so is legally competent to do so (Buchanan, 2004). Obviously there may be issues of maturity and development when considering the mental capacity of children to make decisions, but it could be argued that it is discriminatory that mental capacity law is not applied to children based on a somewhat arbitrary age limit. On the other hand it could be argued that retaining the decision-making framework for children within children's law may offer some protection against the potentially stigmatizing effects and/or long-term implications (both internal and external) of being subject to mental health and/or mental capacity law. At present, under children's law, those with parental responsibility for a child are the decision makers unless the child is assessed as competent to consent to treatment under the common law in England, Wales and Northern Ireland (often referred to as Gillick competency), and under the Age of Legal Capacity (Scotland) Act 1991, s2(4). Lefevre (2010) and Winter (2011) provide excellent guidance for how to effectively communicate with children and young people and this is obviously fundamental to assessing their mental health and capacity.

The Human Rights Act and international law

In addition to mental health and capacity laws, mental health social workers have to be mindful of the Human Rights Act 1998 (HRA) which came into force across the whole of the UK in 2000. Of particular note are the following extracts from Articles of the European Convention on Human Rights that were incorporated into the HRA (Bindman et al., 2003):

> **Article 2**: Everyone's right to life shall be protected by law
>
> **Article 3**: No one shall be subject to torture or inhumane or degrading treatment or punishment
>
> **Article 5**: ... No one shall be deprived of his liberty save in the following cases... (a) the lawful detention of a person after conviction by a competent court; ... (e) the lawful detention of persons for the prevention of the spread of infectious diseases, of persons of unsound mind, alcoholics or drug addicts, or vagrants ... Everyone who is deprived of his liberty by arrest or detention shall be entitled to take proceedings by which the lawfulness of this detention shall be decided speedily by a court and his release ordered if the detention is not lawful
>
> **Article 6**: In the determination of his civil rights ... everyone is entitled to a fair and public hearing within a reasonable period of time by an independent and impartial tribunal established by law
>
> **Article 8**: Everyone has the right to respect for his private and family life, his home, and his correspondence ... except ... such as is ... necessary for the protection of health ... or for the protection of the freedom of others.

Early reviews of the impact of the HRA indicated its minimal influence upon domestic mental health laws in the UK (Bindman et al., 2003), echoing concerns about how effective the ECHR had been in protecting the rights of European citizens with mental health problems (Prior, 2001). There is, however, a developing body of case law which has had a direct impact on clarifying, reinforcing and developing mental health law and social work practice in the UK. Article 5(2) of the ECHR states: '... everyone who is arrested shall be informed properly, in a language which he understands, of the reasons for his arrest and of any charges against him'. This reinforces the duty on service providers, and in particular mental health social workers, to inform people of their rights under mental health and human rights law, of the reasons for their detention and of their rights to challenge this. In *Van der Leer* v *The Netherlands* (1990) the person was not informed of the reasons for her confinement so 5(2) was violated (Prior, 2001).

There is an ongoing debate about whether Article 6, the right to a fair trial, entails that all compulsory mental health interventions should be considered by an independent body, usually the Mental Health Review Tribunal. This reinforces the principle that people must at least have access to a court or tribunal and that access should be speedy. How expedient this process should be has not been specified except that eight weeks was found to be too long (*R (on the application of C)* v *Mental Health Review Tribunal, London S & SW Region)* (Court of Appeal, 3 July 2001). It could be argued that Article 6 does entail that all compulsory interventions should automatically be considered by an independent body, and that placing responsibility for requesting this on a person whose decision-making capacity is impaired is unreasonable, but this has not yet been clearly established in case law. Another relevant case, *AR* v *Homefirst Community Trust* [2005] NICA 8 (16 February 2005), established that social workers must take people's human rights into consideration when making decisions about interventions that may impinge on these rights, and that these considerations must be documented.

A related development which is also of direct importance for mental health social workers' practice is the ruling by the High Court in 2005 that the Code of Practice for the MHA 1983 was wrong when it stated that 'Practicability refers to the availability of the nearest relative and not to the appropriateness of informing or consulting the person concerned' (2.16) and that an ASW, 'In determining whether it is practicable to consult and/or inform the nearest relative under sections 11(3) and (4), ASWs may (and should) consider whether doing so would lead to a breach of the patient's rights under Article 8 of the European Convention of Human Rights (right to respect for private and family life)'. The need to consider whether consulting the nearest relative and/or nominated person would breach the service user's Article 8 rights does perhaps need to be clarified further. This ruling refers to not consulting/informing rather than displacement by county court and so it could be argued it may deprive the service user of the potential benefit/protection of someone being consulted/informed – a possible infringement of Article 6 (fair trial).

As well as the HRA there are a number of key international human rights standards which should also be considered by mental health social workers. The United Nations' 25 Mental Illness (MI) Principles were 'the first step in providing a global set of minimum standards for protecting persons with mental illness and improving mental health care' (Maingay et al., 2002: 19). They are not formally binding but are an influential and important statement of the international standards expected of all jurisdictions (Gostin and Gable, 2004). They are therefore very useful but also necessarily general. The principles include the following: 'all persons have the right to the best available mental health care, which shall be part of the health and social care system' (1.1); that 'every person with a mental illness shall have the right to live and work, as far as possible, in the community' (3); and that 'every patient shall have the right to be treated in the least restrictive environment and with the least restrictive or intrusive treatment appropriate to the patient's health needs and the need to protect the physical safety of others' (9.1).

More recently the UN Convention on the Rights of Persons with Disabilities (2006) was ratified by the UK in 2009 and provides a further expression of the international human rights standards that should be considered, respected and promoted by mental health social workers. Article 19 establishes the right to live independently and be included in the community. Article 12 specifies that people with disabilities should have equal recognition before the law and have legal capacity on an equal basis with others in all aspects of life. It also requires states to take appropriate measures to provide access to the support people may need to exercise their legal capacity. This further reinforces the need to consider how decision making can be best supported in practice. Article 25 states the right to the highest attainable standard of health which is provided on the basis of free and informed consent.

Conclusion

This chapter has summarized and critically reviewed literature on some key statutory functions that UK mental health social workers are responsible for. It has not been possible to give full details of mental health and capacity laws for each jurisdiction (this is provided by other specialist texts such as Hale, 2010; Brown et al., 2009), but important overarching themes are discernible. The discussion highlighted how mental health social workers have to make judgements about when and how to use coercion where there are concerns about risk and capacity. The chapter also explained how salient aspects of international law have to be considered by professionals when powers of coercion are being used. In making such judgements, mental health social workers have a difficult task in balancing competing demands of the state, public opinion, clients and their families. We will be explaining how these laws can be used later on in the book (particularly Chapter 11), in order to illustrate how mental health social workers can fulfil their statutory functions whilst also preserving the rights of service users and their families.

Recommended reading

Archambeault, J. (2009a) *Reflective Reader: Social Work and Mental Health.* Exeter: Learning Matters. Chapter 3 provides a useful discussion of the role of the mental health social work in dealing with functions prescribed in laws for England and Wales.

Barber, P., Brown, R. and Martin, D. (2009) *Mental Health Law in England and Wales.* Exeter: Learning Matters. This provides an overview of new legislation and its relevance to a range of professional groups, including mental health social workers who are employed as AMHPs.

Brown, R., Barber, P. and Martin, D. (2009) T*he Mental Capacity Act 2005: A Guide for Practice.* Exeter: Learning Matters. This thoroughly describes the Act and its relationship to the Mental Health Act 2007.

3

Models of Mental Health and Illness

National occupational standards

This chapter will help you meet the following National Occupational Standards for Social Work.

Key Role 5: Manage and be accountable, with supervision and support, for your own practice. Unit 17: Work within multi-disciplinary and multi-organizational teams, networks and systems.

Key Role 6: Demonstrate professional competence in social work practice. Unit 18: Research, analyse, evaluate, and use current knowledge of best social work practice.

It will also help meet the following National Occupational Standards for Mental Health.

- Assess how environments and practices can be maintained and improved to promote mental health (SFHMH 66).
- Encourage stakeholders to see the value of improving environments and practices to promote mental health (SFHMH 67).
- Monitor and review changes in environments and practices to promote mental health (SFHMH 70).

Learning outcomes

1 To increase knowledge of the variety of models of mental health and the recovery approach.
2 To critically analyse theoretical ideas on this subject and apply them to social work contexts.
3 To consider aspects of professional power when such models are being used with service users and carers.

Introduction

Most practitioners in the mental health field regularly encounter competing paradigms that seek to explain the nature of mental health and disorder. It has been argued that discourses associated with biological or medical models appear to dominate others when decisions are made about the organization and delivery of services. In this chapter debates about the veracity of knowledge claims made by those who espouse this worldview will be critically examined. Although there appears to be some evidence about the explanatory potential of these models, there are also weaknesses, including an over-reliance on the perceived certainty of positivism and problems in assuming dichotomies between subject and object, exclusionary and inclusionary knowledge. It is argued that social workers should be critically aware of the diversity of paradigms that can help explain the mental health problems faced by their clients and approaches that can assist them with recovery.

This chapter will highlight existing theories that contribute to a more holistic understanding of mental ill-health and consequent views on how service users and carers can be helped. Some of these are drawn from the discipline of psychology, including behavioural, cognitive behavioural, humanist and analytical ideas. Theories from sociological traditions (including the concepts of social causation, construction and reaction) will also be outlined in order to explore the social factors and processes that contribute to mental health problems. The chapter will conclude with a discussion of increasingly influential debates about the recovery approach, which will be considered in greater detail in Chapter 5. Each model is presented in a relatively extreme or pure form which is rarely encountered in practice but we hope that we can help you understand these in terms of a range of social work interventions that focus on working with individuals, families and communities (these domains of practice will be further discussed in Chapters 7, 8 and 9). The key point to be made in this chapter is that single, grand or middle ranking medical, social or psychological theories cannot, on their own, explain the concept we usually describe as 'mental illness'. It is argued that, in the light of the range of relevant models, a more critical, eclectic view of mental health may enable a better understanding of service users and their subjective world.

Bio-medical model

The bio-medical model, also referred to as the disease, illness or medical model, remains dominant within mental health services, and is widely used by mental health social workers (Morely, 2003; Beresford, 2005). Its adherents view mental health problems in much the same way as they do physical illnesses. As a result there is a tendency to focus on, or search for, genetic, biochemical and physiological causes that can be diagnosed and treated by pharmacological and physical interventions, provided through hospital and other clinical settings. This paradigm reflects the optimism of the Enlightenment and the belief that science could deliver progressive alternatives to pre-modern, inhumane approaches to madness (Beecher, 2009). The paradigm shift from evil to illness is often illustrated by a famous painting of Dr Philippe Pinel removing the chains from women in-patients in Paris in 1795. The role of the doctor, in this model, is denoted by the expert who uses their exclusive knowledge to identify the problems and prescribe the solutions. The origins of the mental health social worker in the early nineteenth century involved a caring role as directed by the doctor and accepted by the service user who normally complied with professional judgements. A recent attempt to define the bio-medical model in mental health services is as follows: '... a process whereby, informed by the best available evidence, doctors advise on, coordinate or deliver interventions for health improvement. It can be summarily stated as "does it work?"' (Shah and Mountain, 2007: 375).

The bio-medical model has its strengths and can make a positive contribution to mental health care. For example medical expertise is essential when there may be underlying physical or organic causes for a person's difficulties, such as infection and neurological disorders. The bio-medical model should also promote the general physical health of people with mental health problems although this principle is sometimes neglected in mental health services (Harris and Barraclough, 1998). There is a comforting assumption that if at least some mental health problems have their origins in bodily causes, then well trained and trusted medics are ideally placed to deal with the needs of clients (Golightly, 2008). However reassuring the model appears to practitioners, service users and carers, particularly when mental health problems first become apparent, there are limitations and criticisms of this model.

Some of the most important critiques of an over-reliance on the medical model have come from within psychiatry itself. In the 1960s, what became known as the anti-psychiatry movement emerged and gained some credence. This was not a coherent movement, but rather consisted of a number of psychiatrists who proposed alternative ways of understanding mental illness. Perhaps most influential amongst them were R.D. Laing (1960) and Thomas Szasz (1960). Laing suggested that the unusual ideas and behaviours that were being diagnosed as psychosis were better understood in terms of patients' attempts to make sense of, and communicate their distress about, family and societal situations that appeared irrational or dysfunctional. He therefore suggested mental health problems were 'a sane response to an insane world'. Although Laing's ideas are now being seriously questioned, back then the kernel of an idea was sown. For example for some mental health professionals it is now increasingly accepted that, even where thoughts and behaviours seem bizarre, it is important and helpful to work with and try to understand the meaning of people's experiences (British Psychological Society, 2000). In addition, the more recent interest in the concept of 'hearing voices' is an example of this willingness to look beyond the medical model (Romme and Escher, 2000). Szasz was arguably more extreme in his criticism of psychiatry and distanced himself from the rest of the anti-psychiatry movement who, he argued, still accepted the idea of mental illness (Szasz, 2008).

He asserted that what was being called mental illness was not legitimately an illness but should more appropriately be understood as 'problems in living'. He therefore argued that these problems could not be used as justification by the state to control people and deprive them of their liberty, nor by individuals to imply they were not responsible for their actions. Szasz's work is perhaps most useful in its repeated challenges to the justifications for compulsory intervention and state control of the lives of people with mental health problems.

In the 1980s and 1990s another wave of psychiatrists began to question the dominant discourse. Described as critical psychiatrists, this grouping espoused a much more coherent and unified position than the anti-psychiatrists. They argued that in mental health systems there was an unwarranted over-reliance on the explanatory potential of the bio-medical model and questioned the centrality of drugs as the main treatment for mental disorders. It was proposed that ethical, cultural and social factors were involved in the way clients were treated and cared for. Critical or post-psychiatry does not propose a whole new way of understanding mental illness but does argue that mental health care should be democratized, that the service user should be listened to, and there should be a more considered understanding of these social contexts (Bracken and Thomas, 2001). It is also possible to critique the bio-medical model by analysing the centrality of the systems of psychiatric classification used by practitioners. It is worthwhile at this point to consider these systems briefly.

The *Diagnostic and Statistical Manual of Mental Disorders* (DSM-IV) (American Psychiatric Association, 1994) and the *International Classification of Diseases (ICD-10): Classification of Mental and Behavioural Disorders* (World Health Organisation, 1992) are the keystone to diagnosis, treatment and care in this field. In general terms, a system of classification offers a way of: organizing observations about mental health problems; communicating complex descriptions; identifying patterns; offering some predictions for how things may develop; and some guidance for treatment (Archambeault, 2009b). When working in mental health services it is important, regardless of your view of the strengths and limitations of diagnoses, to be familiar with the main terms used. Both Mind (www.mind.org.uk/help/diagnoses_and_conditions/mental_illness) and the Royal College of Psychiatrists (www.rcpsych.ac.uk/mentalhealthinfoforall.aspx) produce excellent, clear and accessible summaries of the main forms of mental health problems. There is a very wide range of possible diagnoses under the current classification systems and people may be given more than one diagnosis at a time and these may also vary over time. Here, only the most common diagnoses are mentioned very briefly.

Schizophrenia is perhaps the diagnosis that attracts the most controversy, misunderstanding and stigma. The conventional understanding is that it affects about one in 100 people at some time in their lives and has a range of symptoms that are often referred to as positive and negative symptoms (Royal College of Psychiatrists, 2011d). Positive symptoms refer to something that is there that shouldn't be rather than anything necessarily positive. These include: hallucinations, which are sensory perceptions without any external stimuli, most commonly hearing voices (auditory hallucinations) which often say negative things; delusions, which are fixed, false beliefs, not amenable to reason and not shared by your peers/community and may include frightening and paranoid ideas; thought disorder which makes concentration and communication more difficult; and feelings of your thought, body or actions being controlled. Negative symptoms are the lack of something that should be there such as motivation, interest, enjoyment, emotions, expressiveness and speech. These can sometimes contribute to people becoming more socially withdrawn and isolated, and/or being criticized by family and, at times professionals, for not fully engaging with whatever is recommended.

Bipolar affective disorder, or manic depression, is also thought to affect about one in 100 people (Royal College of Psychiatrists, 2011b) and is characterized by different combinations of periods of depression and mania or elation. Mania tends to involve people having a lot more energy, ideas and emotion than usual; it can include people hearing voices and sometimes people will behave in ways that will put themselves and others at risk and/or may cause more long-term difficulties such as engaging in reckless sexual behaviour, making excessive financial commitments and damaging important relationships.

Depression affects many more people, perhaps as many as one in five, at some point in their lives (Royal College of Psychiatrists, 2011c). When a person is depressed they may feel unhappy or have an absence of emotion most of the time and little interest in life; their patterns of eating and sleeping may change; they may feel tired all the time, have less self-confidence and self-esteem, be irritable and/or restless; have difficulty making decisions; and may feel life is not worth living (a risk of suicide should be checked out regardless of the specific diagnosis).

Anxiety, panic attacks and phobias are also relatively common, affecting about one in ten people at some time in their lives (Royal College of Psychiatrists, 2011a). Anxiety is part of everyday life but at times it can prevent people doing things that, in the absence of anxiety, they would be keen to do and, in the form of panic, can involve extremely frightening experiences.

It is argued that although the diagnostic approach works well with most physical health problems it should not be uncritically applied to mental health problems (Boyle, 2002; Bentall, 2003). This is because most mental health problems cannot be tested for and identified in the way that occurs in other medical disciplines; the suggestion is that such diagnostic categories in mental health are 'invented not discovered' on the basis of an ongoing discussion by psychiatrists (Bentall, 2009). Although specific mental health problems may reappear across generations, genetic causes are hard to establish and family interactions and contexts may be just as crucial (Rogers and Pilgrim, 2009). It is also argued that the dependence on this system of classification, especially the use of 'schizophrenia' as a diagnostic category, can have negative consequences for the lives of service users:

> The notion that 'mental illness is an illness like any other', promulgated by biological psychiatry and the pharmaceutical industry, is not supported by research

> and is extremely damaging to those with this most stigmatizing of psychiatric labels. The 'medical model' of schizophrenia has dominated efforts to understand and assist distressed and distressing people for far too long. It is responsible for unwarranted and destructive pessimism about the chances of 'recovery' and has ignored – or even actively discouraged discussion of – what is actually going on in these people's lives, in their families and in the societies in which they live. Simplistic and reductionistic genetic and biological theories have led, despite the high risks involved and the paucity of sound research proving effectiveness, to the lobotimizing, electroshocking or drugging of millions of people. (Read et al., 2004: 3)

The diagnostic approach also encourages the idea of a dichotomy between those who have or do not have a pathology – clients are either sick, and so diagnosed, or healthy. The bio-medical model does seem to encourage a focus on the problems or deficits (Pritchard, 2006) and is less focused on understanding the person's experiences, strengths and resources (Bentall, 2003). It has been argued that this misleading dichotomy reinforces the stigma and discrimination that people with mental health may experience as a result of labelling processes and the internalization of 'spoiled identities'(Goffman, 1963). The bio-medical model has also tended to promote the hospital as an appropriate setting for care which is consistent with approaching these issues as equivalent to physical illness. Goffman (1961) demonstrated the damaging impact of institutional care for people with mental health problems. He found that psychiatric hospital care involved: an almost total loss of control; restrictions on decision making and choice; a lot of time spent doing nothing; stigma and discrimination; a lack of privacy; and an absence of ordinary relationships. The impact of institutionalization was also highlighted by Wing and Brown (1970) who confirmed the negative effects on people's motivation, mood and behaviour. As a way of illustrating some of these points we want you now to consider the following seminal experiment by Rosenhan (1973) which highlighted the way in which the systems of assessment and diagnosis failed and demonstrated how professionals behaved when immersed in the practices of the institution. Here is a summary of the paper:

> Eight people who didn't have mental health problems were recruited for the study and instructed to attempt to gain admission to 12 different hospitals, in five different states in the USA. These pseudo-patients telephoned the hospital for an appointment, and on arrival at the hospital complained that they had been hearing voices. They said the voice, which was unfamiliar and the same sex as themselves, was often unclear but they thought it said 'empty', 'hollow', 'thud'. The pseudo-patients each gave a false name and job, but all other details they gave were true including their major life events, relationships, and general social history. After they had been admitted to the psychiatric ward, the pseudo-patients stopped simulating any symptoms of mental health problems. They took part in ward activities and spoke with other patients and staff. When

asked how they were feeling by staff they said they were fine and no longer experienced symptoms. Each pseudo-patient had been told they would have to leave the hospital by their own devices by convincing staff they were sane. The pseudo-patients spent time writing notes about their observations. Initially this was done secretly although as it became clear that no one was bothered by this the note taking was done more openly. None of the pseudo-patients was detected and all but one were admitted with a diagnosis of schizophrenia and were eventually discharged with a diagnosis of schizophrenia in remission. The pseudo-patients remained in hospital for 7 to 52 days (average 19 days). In a follow-up study, staff of a teaching and research hospital, who were aware of the first study, were falsely informed that during the next three months one or more pseudo-patients would attempt to be admitted into their hospital. Around 10 per cent of their admissions were judged by one psychiatrist and another staff member to be pseudo-patients.

Now that you have read this summary, consider a situation from your own practice where institutional care was being provided and answer the following questions.

Exercise 3.1

1. What were the differences in power between you and the clients?
2. How much of the clients' thoughts and behaviours had their origins in biological processes and how many were socially caused or constructed?
3. To what extent did professionals and clients behave independent of institutional expectations about how they should act?

A further issue with the bio-medical model is that, by focusing on proposed biochemical and physical causes, there is often an overdependence on the use of medication at the expense of other forms of care and treatment. Unfortunately, it seems the drugs do not always work, or certainly not very well, despite the huge investment in pharmacological research (Whitaker, 2002; Moncrieff, 2008). It may even be the case that drugs are a factor preventing cure in this field; for example, outcomes for schizophrenia tend to be better in developing countries where drug treatment is not widely available and where these citizens tend not to be excluded or stigmatized in the way they are in industrial countries (Warner et al., 2004). In conclusion, the bio-medical model may be of benefit but only if important personal, familial and social circumstances are incorporated into the assessments and interventions (Rogers and Pilgrim, 2009).

Psychological models

There is a wide range of psychological models that offer further possible perspectives on understanding mental health problems. The two main psychological approaches that will be considered here are psychodynamic and cognitive-behavioural. Psychodynamic models have their origins in the work of Sigmund Freud. Payne (2005) separates out Freud's theoretical ideas into three parts: his theory of human development; his ideas about personality and mental health problems; and how these should be treated. Freud's theory of human development is based on a series of psychosexual stages defined by where the child is seeking gratification: oral (baby), anal (toddler), phallic (pre-school), latency (until puberty), then genital (puberty). At any stage the child may experience difficulties and disapproval and this may cause anxiety which may have long-term implications for the child's future personality and mental health. Freud suggested that the personality was made up of the id (innate basic drives for physical gratification), the ego (which develops in the early years, what people usually mean by 'I') and the super-ego (which are the internalized values of society). The ego manages relationships and interactions with people and things, also referred to as object relations. The ego also has to attempt to hold together the competing and sometimes conflicting demands of the id and super-ego. Mental health problems arise, it is argued, when the ego struggles to manage these conflicts. Freud insisted that we are not consciously aware of all our thoughts and that we defend ourselves against those that are too difficult and frightening through processes of repression, removing them from our conscious mind, but they still will affect us unless made conscious. The role of the mental health social worker is therefore to provide the expert skills and knowledge that will enable these developmental and unconscious issues to be accessed.

It can be argued that Freud's theory of development is, ironically, perhaps too fixated on sexual development but the central idea, that there may be psychological issues that a person may not be fully aware of and may need some facilitation to access, does seem very useful to contributing towards understanding mental health problems. It has been suggested that psychodynamic approaches are of limited use to service users as the intervention, similar to the bio-medical model, is focused on notions of illness and pathologies (Pritchard, 2006). In addition research about how effective interventions based on Freud's work can be remains an area of debate and controversy (Roth and Fonagy, 2005). Freud nonetheless has had a substantial influence on ways of understanding mental health problems and his ideas have influenced many other important theorists and practitioners. These include Erikson, who developed Freud's theory of development beyond sexual development and towards a framework for understanding the issues and tensions that people may be struggling with throughout their lives (Sudbery, 2009). Bowlby was also influenced by Freud; attachment theory is increasingly considered in research as a potential important explanatory framework for adult mental health problems

(Ma, 2006; 2007). He argued that to have good mental health 'the infant and young child should experience a warm, intimate, and continuous relationship with his mother (or permanent mother substitute) in which both find satisfaction and enjoyment' (Bowlby, 1951: 13). Difficulties with important early attachments can then impact on relationships, how people interact and their mental health in later life. In contrast to Freud's pessimism about the human condition, Rogers conceptualized people as instinctively trying to develop, to reach their full potential, and his humanist or person-centred approach has been very influential in social work training and education. He proposed that if people are provided with approval and positive regard then they will develop, a position that has resonance with mental health social work practice (Dryden, 2007).

The other main psychological approach which will be considered here is cognitive-behavioural. As the name suggests this has developed through a combination of behavioural and cognitive perspectives that are applied to our understanding of mental health problems. The behavioural paradigm suggests that behaviour can be learned and unlearned, or modified, through classical (Pavlov's dogs) and operant (Skinner's box) conditioning or learning (Richards, 2007). Classical conditioning is based on the notable finding that if you introduce an unrelated cue (such as ringing a bell) to a cue that produces an instinctive physiological response (food producing saliva) then eventually the unrelated cue (bell) will alone produce the now conditioned response (saliva). Operant learning emphasizes the importance of the consequences of behaviour in determining whether it is likely to be repeated or not. Behaviours can be shaped through positive (providing something pleasant) or negative (removing something unpleasant such as withdrawal symptom) reinforcement and/or through punishment (which can be active and/or with-holding).

Cognitive therapy developed in response to the psychodynamic focus on the unconscious internal world and behavioural approaches that focus on the external responses (Moorey, 2007).Cognitive ideas suggested that how people understand and interact with the world is important, and that feelings and behaviours are affected in the way they think about or interpret the world (Beck, 1976). Our interpretations of the world may be affected by how we are taught to do this, Our experiences and the beliefs we develop about ourselves, other people and the world. Cognitive behavioural approaches to understanding mental health problems, then, combine the understanding that cues or triggers can produce physiological responses, that behaviour can be modified, and that how people think about or interpret the world is influential in how they feel and behave. Cognitive-behavioural therapy is today being widely promoted as an effective, evidence-based response to a wide range of mental health problems (Department of Health, 2001a).

The central limitation of psychological approaches is that their focus tends to be on the individual and so there is a danger that the individual, even in situations where the causes are well beyond their control, will feel blamed. Models that offer some understanding of the wider social and contextual issues will be considered next.

Social models

There are a number of different social models of mental health which offer potential insights into our understanding of mental health issues. The main models that will be discussed here are social causation, social construction and societal response (Rogers and Pilgrim, 2009). Social causation implies a relationship between social disadvantage and mental health problems. For example, in their influential study of the origins of depression in women Brown and Harris (1978) suggested that there was an increased risk of depression when young mothers were isolated, relatively poor and, often because of childcare responsibilities, were subject to many stressors. The Department of Health (1999: 14) has also identified a range of factors that may be significant to understanding some of the relevant social issues in mental health:

- unemployed people are twice as likely to have depression as people in work;
- children in the poorest households are three times more likely to have mental health problems than children in well off households;
- half of all women and a quarter of all men will be affected by depression at some period during their lives;
- people who have been abused or the victims of domestic violence have higher rates of mental health problems;
- people with drug and alcohol problems have higher rates of mental health problems;
- between a quarter and a half of people using night shelters or sleeping rough may have a serious mental disorder, and up to half may be alcohol dependent;
- some black and minority ethnic communities are diagnosed as having higher rates of mental health problems than the general population – refugees are especially vulnerable;
- there is a high rate of mental health problems in the prison population;
- people with physical illnesses have twice the rate of mental health problems compared to the general population.

This notion of social causation suggests that the stress that people encounter due to factors such as poverty, unemployment and social exclusion in general, has a negative impact on their mental health. It may be that other structural causes are at play, for example in terms of wider levels of social deprivation in communities, but there seems very limited evidence to suggest that social drift (the theory that people with mental health problems drift down the social classes and so are over-represented in more deprived groups and areas) is a factor in explaining the higher levels of mental health problems associated with social exclusion (Fox, 1990). Warner et al. (2004) argue that demand for workers and therefore access to employment can have a dramatic impact on the identification and outcomes of people who have mental health problems and their perspective focuses on the wider political and economic factors involved in the social causation of mental health problems. By examining studies of recovery from schizophrenia he found that the state of a country's economy appeared to be linked to mental health outcomes and that recovery rates were lower when the economy was not doing so well. He suggests that gainful employment has many positive mental health benefits and that economic stress and unemployment have a negative impact on people's mental health. Another interesting and relatively recent development within the social causation model is the evolving and compelling evidence that more unequal societies have poorer mental health and this affects everyone, not just those who are relatively deprived (Wilkinson and Pickett, 2009).

The concept of social constructionism offers alternative ways of viewing mental health problems. The idea here is that social forces, processes and contexts contribute to our ideas about mental health and illness. In particular social constructionists highlight the central part that power plays in the creation of ideologies and discourses by groups (Laurence, 2003; Rogers and Pilgrim, 2009). Social constructivist approaches apply these ideas to individuals and seek to analyse the processes by which they develop meaning and learn ideas through their interactions with others (Rogers and Pilgrim, 2009). Pritchard (2006) has suggested that, although sociological approaches may help provide a better understanding of the context, they have less to offer to direct work with service users. This view will be challenged in Chapters 7, 8 and 9 which describe work with individuals, families and communities using some of these perspectives to inform practice. An important aspect of the social work role should entail a consideration of these wider issues in providing service users with information about the possible influences that may be directly affecting them. It also involves campaigning at local and national levels to encourage change to address the oppressive aspects of a society which may cause, or at least add to, the distress people are experiencing. Tew (2005: 16) argues that social perspectives approaches require 'an end to them and us thinking ... a commitment to a holistic approach ...[and] a commitment to hear and take seriously what people say'.

We will now consider a final discrete model, one that focuses on how society reacts to mental health problems. One influential explanatory concept, labelling theory (Scheff, 1966), suggests that society reacts to behaviours that do not fit with its socially constructed norms by labelling these as deviant, in this case as mental illness. This then affects both what other people expect of them, and what the labelled person thinks and expects of themselves; in other words, they come to fulfil the expectations, usually negative, of the label. In Scheff's original work it was suggested that the labelling process effectively caused people to be ill, but Link et al. (1989) have modified this claim to suggest that, although labelling may not on its own cause mental illness, its effects can certainly have very negative social and psychological consequences for clients. These may include the undermining of the self-esteem of the labelled person who responds to the perceived stigma of the label by withdrawing from social support networks and employment. Adverse media portrayals of mental health problems, especially the focus on the relatively very small number of people with mental health problems who pose a risk to others, have also been identified as reinforcing the negative societal responses (Laurence, 2003). These arguments connect with the issues around diagnosis discussed earlier and which will be pursued further in the next chapter.

Integrated approaches

The final section in this chapter considers three approaches that, mirroring the views of those involved in critical psychiatry, do not necessarily offer a new and different perspective on mental health but aim to combine various aspects of the main models to provide a more holistic, and so more effective understanding and response to mental health problems. These are the bio-psychosocial model, the stress-vulnerability model and the recovery approach.

Gould (2010) advocates for a bio-psychosocial model, underpinned by general systems theory. This implies that the individual level can only be understood by reference to the other levels of relevant social systems. This was first applied to the field of mental health by Meyer (1952) and elaborated on by Engel (1980) who confirmed the idea that trying to explain mental health problems by referring to, or focusing on, only one aspect of the person's biological, familial and social system would inevitably fail. Such an approach was judged to be incomplete and reductionist – in other words, it would be attempting to explain the multi-factorial complexity involved in mental health problems by referring solely to a relatively simple aspect without reference to the others. Pilgrim (2002) has suggested that, as criticisms of the narrow biomedical model are increasingly accepted, the bio-psychosocial model, supported by service users and other constituencies, may re-emerge. Most modern mental health services and professionals would probably characterize their theoretical foundation as the bio-psychosocial model although it is important to acknowledge that there may be a wide range of different emphases and power imbalances within this.

Read et al. (2008) also argue for a renewed consideration and application of an older model which is consistent with the bio-psychosocial model: Zubin and Spring's (1977) stress-vulnerability model. In this model, vulnerability to stress may be related to a range of factors, including a genetic disposition and childhood traumas. It also acknowledges that the level of stress that people are exposed to may vary for a wide range of reasons, so it is the combination of vulnerability to and exposure to stress that may lead to a person developing mental health problems. This model is supported by Read et al.'s (2005) work identifying the very high levels of childhood trauma among adults with mental health problems.

The final perspective which will be briefly mentioned as potentially helpful in providing a positive, inclusive, umbrella for the bio-medical, psychological and social models is the recovery approach. This will be discussed in depth in Chapter 5, but it is important to at least outline the approach here and acknowledge its potential to provide a framework that can integrate the diverse range of perspectives that may inform our understanding of mental health. In this approach 'Recovery is about building a meaningful and satisfying life, as defined by the person themselves, whether or not there are ongoing or recurring symptoms or problems' (Shepherd et al., 2008: i). Andresen et al. (2003) identify the essential components of the process of recovery as: finding and maintaining hope; the re-establishment of a positive identity; building a meaningful life; and taking responsibility and control. This approach does seem to have generated considerable interest, support, and even some optimism.

Now that we have completed this overview of some of the key theoretical perspectives that can inform mental health social work practice, complete the following, final exercise.

Exercise 3.2

- What theoretical models do you use to understand your own, and others', mental health?
- What is the dominant theoretical model underpinning your own and your colleagues' current practice?
- How might a broader range of theoretical ideas be incorporated into how you understand and respond to people with mental health problems?

Conclusion

This chapter has examined some of the main theoretical models that inform our current understanding of mental health and illness. These were grouped into bio-medical, psychological and social theories. The strengths and limitations of each perspective were considered and it has been argued that no one perspective can provide a holistic and balanced understanding of the complexities of mental health problems. Some integrated approaches were also considered: the bio-psychosocial model, the stress-vulnerability model, and the recovery approach, although this will be returned to in more depth in Chapter 5. It is important to acknowledge that the bio-medical model has traditionally been the dominant model in mental health services in the UK and that the medical profession and pharmaceutical industry have considerable vested interests in protecting this power and resources imbalance. Nonetheless the bio-medical model is an important aspect in understanding mental health and unnecessarily dismissive and/or divisive approaches to these theoretical debates may not contribute to the better understanding of mental health and so to positive developments in more effective care and support. In the next chapter the focus is on addressing discrimination, stigma and social exclusion, which are key factors in the social component of people's experience of mental health problems.

Recommended reading

Care Services Improvement Partnership, Royal College of Psychiatrists and Social Care Institute of Excellence (2007) *A Common Purpose: Recovery in Future Mental Health Services.* London: Social Care Institute for Excellence.

Read, J., Loren, R.M. and Bentall, R.P. (eds) (2004) *Models of Madness: Psychological, Social and Biological Approaches to Schizophrenia.* Hove: Brunner-Routledge.

Rogers, A. and Pilgrim, D. (2005) *A Sociology of Mental Health and Illness* (third edition). Maidenhead: Open University Press.

Warner, R. (2004) *Recovery from Schizophrenia*, (third edition). Hove: Brunner-Routledge.

Recommended websites

Critical Psychiatry Website: provides an overview of critical psychiatry, a wide range of interesting articles and links to other relevant websites. www.mentalhealth.freeuk.com/

Social Perspectives Network: provides discussion, events and in-depth reports on the role of social factors in mental health problems and recovery. www.spn.org.uk/

4

Addressing Discrimination

National occupational standards

This chapter will help you meet the following National Occupational Standards for Social Work.

Key role 1: Prepare for, and work with individuals, families, carers, groups and communities to assess their needs and circumstances. Unit 2: Work with individuals, families, carers, groups and communities to help them make informed decisions.

Key Role 6: Demonstrate professional competence in social work practice. Unit 21: Contribute to the promotion of best social work practice.

It will also help meet the following National Occupational Standards for Mental Health.

- Challenge injustice and inequalities in access to mainstream provision for people with mental health needs (SFHMH 43).
- Project manage action targeted at addressing mental health issues (SFHMH 89).
- Enable people with mental health needs to access and benefit from services (SFHMH 2).

Learning outcomes

1. To develop knowledge about the stigma, discrimination and oppression that people with mental health problems may face.
2. To increase skills to challenge and address stigma, discrimination and oppression at personal, interpersonal and structural levels.
3. To understand the types of interventions that can be effective at these levels.

Case study

Sean and Annie Murphy live in a working-class community in Northern Ireland. Sean was caught up in an indiscriminate bombing that occurred 35 years ago.

(Continued)

(Continued)

This has him with severe physical injuries that have resulted in a permanent disability to his left leg and arm. As a result he has been dependent on disability benefits for most of his adult working life. In addition Sean experiences flashbacks about the bombing and his two-month stay in hospital. He has been seen by psychiatrists over this period and they have diagnosed post traumatic stress disorder. Sean has been attending a local mental health day centre and has asked for a social worker to visit him and his wife at home to help him deal with these past traumas.

Introduction

People with mental health problems face many forms of discrimination. This chapter will use a multi-layered approach to describe and explain why this occurs, and how practitioners can challenge discrimination. The World Health Organisation has highlighted why this area of practice is so important:

> Discrimination, stigma and social exclusion have enormous social and economic costs for individuals, their families, and society. The cost to society includes the loss of the skills and talents of people with mental health problems because discrimination excludes them from contributing and participating. (2008a: 7)

The concept of stigma is considered first because it involves the process of separating and devaluing people with mental health problems; this in turn forms the basis for the stereotyping and prejudices which lead to discriminatory behaviour. Disablist ideas about people with mental health problems often combine with other forms of discrimination. For this reason the chapter draws upon the literature on inequalities in gender, race, age, sexual orientation and religion, to identify the complexities of discrimination in society that are reflected in mental health systems. We will be arguing that economic inequality is a central factor in causing, exacerbating and maintaining the discrimination that people with mental health problems experience. The oppressive consequences of discrimination and inequality are then explored using a framework for helping to understand the processes involved. The chapter will then go on to describe how this knowledge base can inform practice interventions, at various levels (individual, group, structure), using the case study about Sean and Annie Murphy.

Stigma

We introduced you to the important concept of stigma in the previous chapter. According to Goffman (1963) this originated with the Ancient Greek practice of burning or cutting a sign or stigma into the bodies of people, such as slaves and criminals, who were devalued and should be avoided. People with mental health problems can sometimes be physically distinguishable, usually as a result of the side-effects of medication (Novak and Svab, 2009), but generally they are not visibly unwell and sociological ideas about stigma are more broad and complex than physical signs or marks. Goffman's original concept of stigma, as characterized by negative assumptions about personhood and identity, continues to be an important contribution to our understanding of mental health and illness. He defined stigma as 'an attribute that is deeply discrediting' which has the effect of reducing or distinguishing the marked person 'from a whole and usual person to a tainted, discounted one' (1963: 3). Link and Phelan (2001) have further developed the concept in relation to mental health problems and have emphasized the role of social, economic and political power in how difference is identified and valued. They argue that stigma arises through four processes:

1 People, with relative power, identify and label characteristics they view as different.
2 They then link these labels to negative stereotypes.
3 This facilitates the process of separating the labelled people into a separate category – them and us.
4 Finally the labelled people lose status and are excluded.

The stigmatization of people with mental health problems is based on ignorance, misunderstanding and fear about mental health and enables attitudes or prejudices which lead to damaging behaviours such as discrimination and oppression. It is important for mental health social workers to understand these processes in order that they can help their clients. Take a moment to think about the following exercise.

Exercise 4.1

1 Have you ever been subject to stigma?
2 In your practice as a mental health social worker can you identify the process described by Link and Phelan?
3 What do you think can be done to challenge stigma in this field?

It is likely that you will have experienced some form of stigma, and this self-understanding can help you begin to realize the difficulties faced by clients who have mental health problems. As we discussed in Chapter 1, policy makers, agencies and practitioners are required to develop strategies to combat the stigma and discrimination that service users experience. The Social Exclusion Unit (2004) reported that, for people with mental health problems, the greatest barriers to social inclusion were not their mental health problems but the stigma and discrimination associated with them. It also highlighted that stigma and discrimination could reinforce and compound people's mental health problems, could inhibit recovery and also create difficulties after their mental health problems had been resolved. The (2008) *Time to Change* campaign (www.time-to-change.org.uk) surveyed people with mental health problems and found that 87 per cent had been affected by stigma and discrimination with more than two thirds prevented from acting because of stigma. It also identified the diverse impacts of stigma; respondents reported that it affected all aspects of their lives including work, education, relationships, their social life and their willingness to talk about their difficulties.

The annual *Attitudes to Mental Illness* survey (Department of Health, 2008) reveals some of the prejudices that lead to the stigmatization of mental health problems. It found that one in eight people would not want to live next door to someone who has a mental health problem and that nearly six out of ten people described a person with a mental health problem as 'someone who has to be kept in a psychiatric or mental hospital'. One factor in the development of these attitudes is how mental health problems are portrayed in the media. The Social Exclusion Unit (2004) reported that two thirds of press and television coverage included an association with violence, and that between 40–50 per cent of tabloid articles about mental health used derogatory terms such as 'nutter' and 'looney'. Some examples include *The Sun*'s headline from 23 September 2003, following the detention of Frank Bruno, 'Bonkers Bruno Locked Up', and *The Belfast Telegraph*'s article on 4 September 2009, 'Pyschiatric [sic] outpatient ate brain of his victim' is an example of the focus on sensational and bizarre aspects of tragedies. Even the misspelling of the work 'psychiatric' adds to this sense of neglect and ignorance. Finally *The Daily Mail*'s 4 May 2010 'Grandmother killed by schizophrenic in random stabbing' is an example of both the generalizing and dehumanizing of 'the schizophrenic' as though the individual had no other forms of identity. It is little wonder then that the wider population will often over-associate mental health problems with a risk to others.

As a practitioner it is crucial that you critically engage with the commonsense ideas that create often such unjust and inaccurate stereotypes. Laurence (2003), for example, has suggested that the killing in 1992 of Jonathan Zito by Christopher Clunis marked a shift in media reporting and public attitudes that moved away from a concern about the welfare of people with mental health problems towards concerns and fears about the very small numbers of people with mental health problems who pose a risk to the public. Christopher Clunis had a diagnosis of paranoid schizophrenia and was not taking his prescribed medication before he, without warning or provocation, stabbed Jonathan Zito, a person unknown to him who was standing on an Underground platform in London. Laurence (2003) argues that distorted perceptions of people with mental health problems associated with a high risk of violence to others have greatly reinforced stigma and fuelled the debate about the process of deinstitutionalization. Taylor and Gunn (1999) examined the evidence for these concerns and found that in England and Wales between 1957 and 1995, when many of the large psychiatric hospitals were closed, there was little change in the numbers of people with mental health problems committing homicide and a small relative decline as the overall numbers of homicides increased. This was a point we made in our discussion on policy and risk in Chapter 1 and will return to in Chapter 11. The escalation of rates of homicide has been demonstrated to be correlated with the social exclusion and inequalities affecting young men in general (Shaw et al., 2005). Between 1997 and 2005, however, the National Confidential Inquiry into Suicide and Homicide by People with Mental Illness (2010) reported an increase in the numbers of homicides committed by people with mental health problems (from 22 cases in 1997 to 48 cases in 2005). This increase appears to be associated with wider increases in the use of alcohol and/or drugs and may not be continuing.

Another important aspect of considering the impact of stigma is its effect on how a person with mental health problems may view themselves. The wider prejudices of society are often internalized by people with mental health problem, undermining their sense of status, worth and self-esteem (World Health Organisation, 2008b). This is usually referred to as self-stigma and can lead to people losing hope, feeling worthless and withdrawing from society (Social Exclusion Unit, 2004). On the other hand, stigma can also inspire righteous anger (Corrigan and Watson, 2002) in people with mental health problems and initiate efforts to address the injustice and unfairness that it generates.

Discrimination

It was argued above that the work of Goffman and later sociologists was helpful in highlighting the disadvantages faced by people as a result of stigma. The related concept of discrimination is a much broader idea that tends to focus on the effects of socio-economic structure and behaviour. In this context, discrimination is associated with negative behaviour towards people with mental health problems often based on stigmatizing beliefs and prejudices about mental health. Discrimination may be intentional or unintentional but it involves the unfair restriction or denial of people exercising their rights and opportunities in the same way as everyone else (World Health Organisation, 2008b). People with mental health problems may encounter discriminatory behaviour and responses in all aspects of their lives but three main areas will be highlighted here: social networks, employment and within mental health services. Erikson (1968), building on Freud's work, identified the ability to love and work as being central to mental health but people with mental health problems experience additional obstacles in these areas due to discrimination.

In terms of social networks, the National Mental Health Development Unit (NMHDU) reports that:

> two thirds of people with mental health problems live alone – four times more than the general population; more than 50% of people with mental health problems have poor social contact, as defined by the Oslo Social Support Scale, compared with six per cent of the general population; people with mental health problems see fewer friends regularly – between one and three in an average week, compared with the four to six friends reported by the general population. (2010a: 3)

The Social Exclusion Unit (2004) also provides more research findings that highlight this issue. They reported that: people with mental health problems are more likely to have an unmet desire to participate more in family and social activities; people with a psychotic disorder are three times more likely to be divorced; and in one survey the social networks of four out of ten people were restricted to mental health service users and professionals. Crisp et al. (2000) discussed the way that popular beliefs about mental illness and health were created and reinforced. These included assumptions that people with mental health problems are hard to talk to, feel differently and are unpredictable. These assumptions can contribute to some of the social isolation that people encounter. The manner in which mental health services are planned and delivered can also lead to discrimination in this field. Current professional interventions are often focused on the direct treatment of mental health problems through specialist mental health services; these can be necessary but often not sufficient if full citizenship rights are to be realized for mental health service users. It is commonplace that organizations and their staff are more focused on supporting and sustaining the person's relationships with family and friends but less successful in promoting their engagement with mainstream social and recreational activities. The isolation and segregation involved in prolonged hospital admissions may also disrupt social networks and make accessing and maintaining education and employment more difficult.

For many people employment provides a valuable source of social contact, structure, income, status, identity, purpose and support (Perkins et al., 2009). Research has established that work is good for our physical and mental health and, logically, that unemployment can damage our health (Sainsbury Centre for Mental Health, 2009). Unfortunately, people with severe mental health problems are less likely to be employed than any of the other main groups of people with disabilities but are the most likely to want to be working (Social Exclusion Unit, 2004). Approximately 21 per cent of people with mental health problems are in paid work compared to 47 per cent of all people with disabilities, and rates for people with more severe difficulties are even lower and have fallen over the past 40 years (NMHDU, 2010a). Employers acknowledge they tend to be more discriminatory in this field, with only four in ten being willing to consider employing a person with mental health problems compared to six in ten for someone with a physical disability (NMHDU, 2010a). It is important to accept that mental health problems can, at times, greatly impair a person's ability to work and that fluctuations in mental health may be difficult to predict: however, with the appropriate support and work environment these obstacles can be overcome (Perkins et al., 2009).

In parallel with the beliefs associated with self-stigma is anticipated discrimination. This is the idea that people with mental health problems will stop doing or not attempt things because of their fear of discrimination, rejection or exclusion. One survey found that almost three quarters of people with mental health problems had stopped doing something they wanted to, not because they had experienced discrimination but because they anticipated or feared discrimination (NMHDU, 2010a). Mental health services themselves may also discriminate against people with mental health problems. In addition mental health professionals may share some of the stigmatizing views of wider society as well and, as a result, will try to maintain a sense of 'them and us', overestimate risk, have very low expectations about what people can achieve and so effectively undermine their hope and recovery (Social Exclusion Unit, 2004). Other forms of stigma and discrimination may also contribute to this; the service response to childhood trauma provides an example here. There is a growing body of research that has established the associations between childhood trauma and mental health problems in adulthood. Read et al. (2005) reviewed 46 studies of women using mental health services and found the majority (69 per cent) had been subjected to physical and/or sexual abuse. A review of 31 studies of men found 59 per cent had experienced physical and/or sexual abuse. Despite this, childhood trauma and adversity is not routinely screened for, assessed and responded to by adult mental health professionals. This may be partly explained by the ongoing dominance of the medical model (see Chapter 3) and its focus on physiological causes, but professionals' reluctance to ask about and discuss childhood abuse may also be an important factor. Discrimination on the basis of mental health may therefore be compounded by and interact with discrimination on the basis of other factors and some more of these will now be explored.

Gender

Sexism in society means that women are disproportionately exposed to stressors such as poverty (Wetzel, 2000), caring responsibilities and various forms of abuse (Read et al., 2005), including domestic violence (Humphreys and Thiara, 2003), which may then have a direct impact on their mental health. Women are also over-represented in some specific forms of mental health problems, for instance rates of anxiety and depression are between 1.5 and 2 times those for men and rates of self-harm are 2 to 3 times higher (NMHDU, 2010b). Women may also experience sexism within mental health services, for instance when assumptions based on sexist stereotypes are made or when the woman's social context is not sufficiently considered. It is also important to note that certain groups of women and men are over-represented in admissions to psychiatric hospitals (Hayes and Prior, 2003). The Sainsbury Centre for Mental Health (1998) found that women in in-patient settings had concerns about levels of privacy, and safety and sexual harassment and assaults on wards remain an ongoing concern (Lawn and Mcdonald, 2009). Although safer services are developing, single sex wards are not yet available to all. There are also important gender issues when considering addressing discrimination in men's mental health. Approximately three quarters of suicides are by men, they are less likely to seek help, three times more likely to be alcohol dependent and twice as likely to be detained (NMHDU, 2010b). A Mind survey in 2009 concluded that,

> Men's mental distress is a hidden problem. An examination of the evidence suggests that gender and the way we are socialised into different cultural norms could be having a big impact on the way men interact with mental health services. The image of the tough, resilient male who hides emotion is deeply ingrained in society and may affect men's help-seeking behaviour. (2009: 29)

It therefore recommended that services should be considering how best to engage men, as is the case with all groups for whom there may be barriers to accessing the support needed.

Race, ethnicity, culture and religion

Discrimination on the basis of race, ethnicity, culture and/or religion also has been demonstrated to be of concern in mental health provision as well as in society in general (Fernando and Keating, 2009). As with gender, the processes by which these forms of discrimination impact on mental health and may interact with other forms of discrimination are complex and varied but research findings demonstrate some of the issues. The Social Exclusion Unit reported that:

> people from ethnic minority groups are six times more likely to be detained under the Mental Health Act than white people; rates of diagnosed psychotic disorders are estimated twice as high among African Caribbean people than white people, although they are three to five times more likely to be diagnosed and admitted to hospital for schizophrenia; South Asian women born in India and East Africa have a 40 per cent higher suicide rate than those born in England and Wales. The prevalence of common mental health problems is fairly similar across different ethnic groups, although rates are higher for Irish men and Pakistani women and lower for Bangladeshi women. (2004: 16)

The independent inquiry following the death of David Bennett while he was being restrained in hospital suggested that, often because of a fear and mistrust of mental health services, young black men's mental health problems tended to be exacerbated by not accessing services at an early stage, and therefore receiving inadequate or inappropriate diagnosis and treatment (Blofeld, 2003). It was concluded that 'At present people from the black and minority ethnic communities, who are involved in the mental health services, are not getting the service they are entitled to. Putting it bluntly, this is a disgrace' (2003: 58). Concerns have also been expressed about the high levels of involuntary admissions of people from black and ethnic minority (BME) communities to psychiatric hospitals, an issue we raised in Chapter 2 and will raise again in Chapters 7 and 10.

Age

Ageism is also an important aspect of discrimination within society and mental health services. It has been estimated that one in four older people in the community have symptoms of depression but only a third of those will ever discuss it with their GP. Only half are diagnosed and treated; when this occurs the primary intervention is the use of anti-depressants and there is less chance of referral to specialist mental health services than is the case with the wider population (Age Concern, 2007; NMHDU, 2010b). Age Concern (2007) have identified the need to address discrimination as the first priority for policy makers particularly as it occurs in the immediate and widespread problems with access to appropriate services for older people.

Sexual orientation

Mind (2010) reports that, although this is not a well researched and monitored aspect of discrimination, the available evidence shows that lesbians, gay men and bisexuals are at a significantly higher risk of experiencing suicidal feelings, self-harm, drug or alcohol misuse and mental health problems. Again, it is important to acknowledge the complexities of how discrimination in wider society, usually referred to as homophobia, and the general bias in society in favour of heterosexuals, may be internalized, and interact with other forms of discrimination and other important stressors on mental health. Although the quite recent pathologizing of homosexuality and open discrimination in mental health services is now relatively rare, a recent survey (Warner et al., 2004) still identified problems of knowledge, empathy and understanding amongst professionals about these issues.

Economic inequality

There is a developing and convincing body of evidence that explains the incidence of mental ill-health in relation to levels of social and economic inequalities (Wilkinson and Pickett, 2009). For example, the Marmot Review states;

> There is a social gradient in health – the lower a person's social position, the worse his or her health. Action should focus on reducing the gradient in health. Health inequalities result from social inequalities. Action on health inequalities requires action across all the social determinants of health. (2010: 15)

Once a country is reasonably affluent, then how unequal it appears to help predict health outcomes rather than overall income. There are a number of possible explanations for this phenomenon. One of the most plausible is that experiences of inequality can be anxiety-provoking and stressful for everyone, not just those who are at the poor end of a steep social gradient. Wilkinson and Pickett (2009) have summarized some other explanations. The first, which has been proposed by Oliver James (2007), uses the metaphor of the 'affluenza' virus which involves placing a high value on the acquisition of material goods and how we appear to others which then undermines our self-esteem and trust in others. Alain de Botton (2004) has also suggested 'status anxiety' as a way of describing the unhealthy competitive approach to social interactions and hierarchy which tends to make people feel unfulfilled and at times ashamed of themselves and bitter towards others. This constant striving for more has been described by Richard Layard (2005) as our 'addiction to income'. The next section will consider the how stigma, discrimination, inequality and their oppressive consequences may be challenged by mental health social workers.

Challenging stigma, discrimination and oppression

We have, in this chapter, described and analysed the negative attributions associated with stigma, the excluding impact of discrimination and the oppression experienced by users of mental health services. Thompson (2003) offers a simple but extremely useful model of three concentric circles to facilitate our understanding of how these processes work across the different levels and aspects of society. At the centre is the personal level and, whilst prejudices and discrimination operating at this level need to be addressed, they cannot be fully understood without reference to their context which is provided by the next two levels – cultural and structural. The cultural level encompasses the meanings and values shared by groups which may be taken for granted, without question, but still discriminatory. The structural level refers to the social, political and economic structures which include key factors such as power and inequality.

The PCS Model also facilitates an understanding of the range of levels and methods that may be needed to address stigma, discrimination and oppression. As Sayce has argued,

> There is no single solution to discrimination, but different elements to potential 'solutions' exist. What is needed is to bring different strands of work together. In particular it would be helpful to force a stronger synthesis between, on the one hand, securing legislative improvement and enforcement and, on the other, promoting universal benefits of a more inclusive society. Each complements the other. (2003: 625)

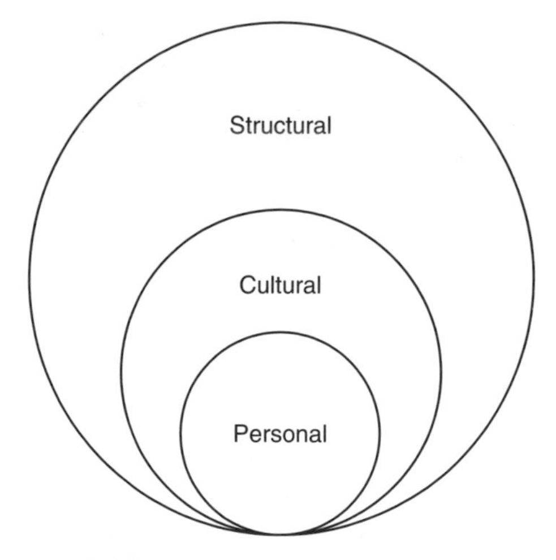

Figure 4.1 Thompson's PCS Model

Source: Neil Thompson (1998) *Promoting Equality*. Reproduced with permission of Palgrave Macmillan.

The (2008) *Time to Change* campaign identified four key components of a comprehensive approach to addressing discrimination. The first is sustainability which accepts that the ignorance and fear which provide the basis for discrimination may take years to break down. The second component highlights the need for a multi-layered approach that reinforces key messages for change. Having people who are directly affected by the discrimination and oppression in society at the centre of planning and delivering anti-discrimination initiatives is next recommended. Finally, there is a need to understand and target the circumstances in which people are more likely to think and behave in discriminatory ways. Using the PCS levels some possible strategies for addressing discrimination in practice will now be explored.

For mental health social workers, an understanding of 'the personal' is the starting point for addressing thoughts and beliefs about discrimination; self awareness and appropriate supervision are important in this respect. The process of critical reflection which begins at qualifying level must continue into post-qualifying practice in order to identify any prejudices that may negatively influence the therapeutic relationship and decision-making processes. Supervision should provide the time and safe space for this to routinely happen but it seems reasonable to suggest that this may not always be the case. If supervision is not providing this benefit, or is not even happening, then the individual social worker has a professional responsibility to ensure this process of examining their own attitudes and responses is protected and to raise the lack of supervision within their agency and, if need be, as a professional issue. Critical awareness is particularly important in situations where there may be personal, cultural or structural factors that will increase the likelihood of 'obedience to authority'. This may occur, for example, in a crisis situation where another professional is strongly advocating one way to proceed or where a very experienced consultant psychiatrist is proposing an intervention which you are concerned about. Stanley Milgram's (1974) obedience to authority experiment established that most people (65 per cent) can do things they would not usually contemplate (in the experiment, administering a lethal voltage of electricity) if instructed to do so by a perceived expert who is claiming to take responsibility for the consequences. This also highlights the potential difficulties of directly challenging prejudices and discrimination in group settings, such as on a ward or as part of a team, where you may be the only person raising concerns. Interventions at this level may also be planned such as providing education and information on the relevant issues and processes. Community integration is an important intervention as well that covers all three levels as it has been found that the strongest evidence-based intervention for reducing stigmatizing attitudes is direct social contact with a person who has mental health problems (Rose et al., 2007).

At the cultural level tackling negative media portrayals may be a key intervention and there have been positive examples internationally where this has been successfully achieved (Commonwealth of Australia, 2009), and to some extent in the UK (Mind Out for Mental Health, 2007). There have also been a number of large-scale anti-stigma and discrimination campaigns that have aimed to directly inform, challenge and change attitudes, such as the current *Time to*

Change campaign in England and the ongoing *See Me* campaign which began in Scotland in 2002. An interim evaluation (Myers et al., 2009) of the *See Me* campaign concluded that,

> National surveys and surveys commissioned by 'see me' over the period 2002–2006 revealed positive shifts in mental health awareness and in attitudes towards mental health problems. The number of other related initiatives over this period make it difficult to determine 'see me''s specific contribution, but the data may suggest the value of a number of different initiatives working in parallel to effect change. (2009: 9)

At the structural level, mental health social workers can, and should, individually and collectively be lobbying decision-makers at all levels to address discrimination, develop services and reduce mental health inequalities. The potential for equality legislation to help with this process should also be fully explored. The introduction of the Equality Act 2010 (www.equalities.gov.uk) which covers England, Wales and Scotland, should provide a unified and more accessible legal framework for challenging discrimination. Similar provisions are in place in Northern Ireland and are also supported by the Equality Commission (www.equalityni.org). Challenging discrimination at all levels is not only necessary to address social injustice, it is also in everybody's interests. The World Health Organisation has stated that 'Societies in which there is less discrimination, and therefore less marginalisation of various groups tend to be more healthy as well as more just societies ... Changes in legislation, policy and resource allocation can result in substantial improvements in the mental health of all citizens' (2008a: 7).

The application of theory to practice: working with Sean and Annie Murphy

We will now apply some of these ideas on discrimination to the circumstances of Sean and Annie Murphy. Sean and Annie live in a society that has suffered from 40 years of political conflict. Inevitably there are contested histories about this conflict, but what seems clear is that a particular form of discrimination, that of sectarianism, is a pervasive characteristic of Northern Irish society. Sectarianism functions at a variety of levels, where discrimination on the basis of religious and national identity (Protestants and Catholics, Unionists and Nationalists) determines the life chances of individuals and the way that social divisions are maintained and reproduced. The conflict in Northern Ireland, however, is more than just an age-old religious war between two divided communities; the causes of sectarianism can be traced to the colonial history between Britain and Ireland, and more recently, to the involvement of these states alongside the international community in attempting to resolve the conflict (Campbell, 2007). What is often missed in the analysis of the conflict in Northern Ireland is the adverse impact upon working-class and other disadvantaged communities (Pinkerton and Campbell, 2002). As in other impoverished areas of the UK, there is relatively high unemployment and poverty, poor health and rising levels of suicide, particularly amongst young men (Leavey et al., 2009). In recent years, particularly following the Belfast Agreement (1998), governments and a range of statutory and voluntary agencies have increasingly focused on the needs of victims and survivors of the conflict. This has led to more funding for organizations, particularly those in the voluntary sector, in order to deliver more targeted services to a population with substantial unmet needs as a result of the conflict in Northern Ireland (Dillenburger et al., 2008). Over 3,700 people have died during these four decades of political violence, and many tens of thousands have been physically and psychologically traumatized. These are the contexts that have shaped the lives of Sean and Annie Murphy. You may feel that this case example is only relevant to Northern Ireland, but you might also be able to draw upon other experiences of working with clients who have suffered from the effects of political conflict at home or abroad (Ramon, 2008; Guru, 2010). How then could you, as a mental health social worker, intervene to help this family, using your knowledge and understanding of the concept of discrimination discussed so far in this chapter?

Level 1: personal and interpersonal

Whether you are practising in Northern Ireland, the rest of the UK, or for that matter elsewhere in the world, when faced with families traumatized by political violence, stigma and discrimination, it is important to consider how your own identity has been formed and shaped by your knowledge of political and social conflict and the processes of discrimination that precede and follow such circumstances. Mental health social workers are just as likely as the wider population to make judgements about the causes and solutions to conflict, division and inequality that may involve the types of stereotyping described earlier in this chapter. To begin with here have a think about your own identity and how this might affect the way you view discrimination caused by political and social conflict. Then consider the questions posed in the following exercise.

Exercise 4.2

1 Have you or your family suffered because of social or political conflict and inequalities?
2 Have you had to deal with families who have suffered as a result of social or political conflict?
3 How might your understanding of your identity formation affect the way you may intervene to help families in these circumstances?

It should be the case that, when you answer these questions, some challenging thoughts will come to you, either because you or your family have been affected by conflict and inequality, or because you have views about what the causes and solutions to political conflict and discrimination will be (regardless of where you practise in the UK).

In your initial visit with Sean and Annie, you should tune into your thoughts about the political context; is it inevitable that you will hold a position on the rights and wrongs of the conflict, depending on your national identity and views on the causes and solutions to the problems of this society? In our discussion of the causes of discrimination in this chapter, we have argued that a non-judgemental attitude to work with people with mental health problems is crucial; this is particularly important for those who have been traumatized as a result of political and inter-communal conflicts. Fundamentally it is important for the victims of such conflicts to be given space to tell their stories in a safe environment, and that is something you can offer on your first visit. A variety of accessible counselling styles are available to you when helping people who are traumatized in this way (Kapur and Campbell, 2004; Stewart and Thompson, 2005; Duffy et al., 2007). Key to working with Sean and Annie is helping them gain trust in you, not just as part of the helping process, but in order to overcome the potential stigma and discrimination they face as victims of political conflict. Practical support, for example with social benefits, and the provision of information, for example about Post Traumatic Stress Disorder, may also be important at this level and facilitate engagement.

Level 2: engaging with wider social networks

A positive attitude combined with good interpersonal skills and an informed understanding of practice interventions will help many people who have been traumatized by such conflict. Numerous individuals and families, however, will need more than this, and you, as a mental health social worker, are well positioned to engage in community solutions to discrimination. It is crucial in mental health social work not to collude with or even reinforce messages or interventions that ignore the context of a person's mental health problems and so essentially 'blame the victim'. With Sean and Annie, interventions at this level could include identifying, accessing or even helping establish relevant support groups. Possible opportunities in mainstream activities, education, training and employment opportunities could also be explored. This should involve considering any possible practical or psychological obstacles to accessing these. As has been mentioned, one of the most effective means of addressing stigma is direct contact. Exploring these opportunities could certainly benefit Sean's mental health and address any self-stigma, but could also help challenge stigma and break down barriers for others. Sean may even choose to become involved in anti-discrimination initiatives or campaigns at the community level.

Level 3: asserting the political role of social work

There may be opportunities for Sean and Annie to engage with organizations and groups that are campaigning for structural changes, perhaps for the provision of better resourced, more appropriate mental health services. Equality legislation might provide a possible means of challenging and overcoming any obstacles Sean encounters. There could also be wider political issues about how the benefits system may inhibit people with disabilities returning to work, or about the general levels of inequality in our society. Sean and Annie may not wish to become involved in these activities but as a mental health social worker you can and should still be raising the general issues through engaging with politics and campaigning.

Conclusion

We hope this chapter has encouraged you to think more critically about these issues of stigma, discrimination and social justice. Focusing on the importance of stigma, discrimination and inequality does not mean that directly addressing the presenting problems service users bring to mental health social workers should be neglected. It does suggest, however, that if the focus is only on a person's symptoms and these wider social processes are ignored then intervention may be less effective and recovery may more difficult. The growing research evidence on the extent and impact of stigma and discrimination (Social Exclusion Unit, 2004) does strongly support the need to base our practice on the integrated theoretical models discussed in Chapter 3 and to intervene beyond the individual level. Efforts to challenge and overcome stigma, discrimination and oppression need to be sustained across the personal, cultural and structural levels and are core to the mental health social work role.

Recommended reading

Social Exclusion Unit (2004) *Mental Health and Social Exclusion*. London: Office of the Deputy Prime Minister. Available to download at www.socialinclusion.org.uk/publications/SEU.pdf

Thompson, N. (2006) *Anti-discriminatory Practice*, (fourth edition). Basingstoke: Palgrave Macmillan.

World Health Organisation (2008a and 2008b) *Stigma: Guidebook for Action, and Stigma: An International Briefing Paper*. Both are available to download at www.supportproject.eu/news/stigma/stigmatoolkit.htm

(Continued)

(Continued)

Recommended websites

Mind's Mental Health Media Awards which celebrate the best portrayal or reporting of mental health issues www.mind.org.uk/mediaawards

See me anti-stigma campaign in Scotland www.seemescotland.org.uk

Time to Change anti-discrimination campaign in England www.time-to-change.org.uk

5

Listening to Service Users' Needs

National occupational standards

This chapter will help you meet the following National Occupational Standards for Social Work.

Key role 1: Prepare for, and work with individuals, families, carers, groups and communities to assess their needs and circumstances. Unit 3: Assess needs and options to recommend a course of action.

Key Role 3: Support individuals to represent their needs, views and circumstances. Unit 10: Advocate with, and on behalf of, individuals, families, carers, groups and communities.

It will also help meet the following National Occupational Standards for Mental Health.

- Enable people to recover from distressing mental health experiences (SFHMH 94).
- Work with individuals with mental health needs to negotiate and agree plans for addressing those needs (SFHMH 20).
- Enable people with mental health needs to participate in social, economic and cultural activities and networks (SFHMH 42).

Case study

You are a manager in a large, traditional, voluntary sector mental health agency with responsibility for a number of supported housing and day care units. There is constant pressure to accept referrals from different sources, both professionally and organizationally. A large proportion of the people who use these services have had long periods of hospitalization and you are struggling to keep pace with these competing demands, the pressures for fuller assessments of

(Continued)

(Continued)

new referrals and reviews of existing client need. For many years the organization has championed the idea of user empowerment and the notion of recovery, but somehow this rhetoric scarcely matches the reality of service user experiences in the units you are responsible for. A newly qualified social worker has just been employed in the organization. She seems to be enthused about new ways of enabling service users to have their voices heard. This seems like an obvious opportunity to speak to the new person to discuss what she thinks, but a worry from a manager's perspective is the sort of damage such changes might do to relationships with more established colleagues and even the clients themselves.

Learning outcomes

1. To become aware of the shifting debates about the concept of empowerment and the competing models about how this can be realized in the mental health field.
2. To be able to contextualize the emerging literature on the recovery model, and explore its relevance to your practice.
3. To develop an understanding of the skills and values needed to work, using a recovery approach, with mental health service users and survivors.

Introduction

It is only in the last decade that health and social care organizations have taken seriously the prospect of engaging with service users when planning and delivering services. This is perhaps surprising as there is a range of convincing arguments for listening to service users and involving them in most aspects of mental health care. These arguments can be grouped into three main themes: values-based; pragmatic; and rights-based. Service user involvement is supported by the traditional social work values of: individualisation; acceptance; non-judgemental attitudes; client self determination; confidentiality; respect for persons; and unconditional positive regard. The developing emancipatory values of equality, social justice, partnership, empowerment and citizenship rights also fit with these perspectives (Thompson, 2005). Mental health social workers should also integrate ideas of service user empowerment at different levels of intervention – individual, community and societal (Thornicroft and Tansella, 2005). The pragmatic arguments for service user involvement tend to focus on what are the most effective methods to achieve positive mental health outcomes. The most effective approach to engagement, assessment and planning with people with mental health problems involves the core value of respect, where practitioners are prepared to listen and act upon service users' views and needs. These pragmatic arguments apply even when compulsion is used, as demonstrated by the research on procedural justice (McKenna et al., 2000; Galon and Wineman, 2010). This issue is further discussed in Chapter 11 regarding the role of the AMHP. The rights-based argument for service user involvement may be underpinned by values associated with the pragmatic theme, but is legally required by governments and agencies. It has been argued, however, that policy, even the legal compulsion that requires service user involvement, is insufficient to ensure that empowerment happens, particularly when other organizational and government priorities take precedence (Lewis, 2005).

This chapter will describe and critically analyse the theory and practice of empowerment and service user involvement in the context of the case study described above. It will also highlight why, to date, organizations and professional groups have generally failed to match practice with the aspirations of empowerment that characterize policy in this area. The chapter will draw upon an expanding literature to identify the knowledge base which practitioners can access in order to re-examine relationships of power, and identify the skills needed to enable service users to have more control of their lives. The related and overlapping concepts of advocacy, consumerism, person-centred planning, personalization and strengths-based approaches will also be considered. A particular focus in the second part of the chapter will be the emerging literature on the recovery approach, alluded to earlier in Chapter 3. The recovery approach is becoming the stated ethos of many organizations, but problems remain about how effectively recovery principles are being translated into practice. There will be a description of these principles – where service users have the central role in choices made about their own lives including their care, treatment and the services they use. The recovery approach involves a paradigm shift in terms of what the priorities of mental health social work should be, moving away from an over-emphasis on symptoms, deficits and risk towards priorities informed by service users, including relationships, employment and hope for the future. As discussed in Chapter 4, a critical component of this approach is the need to acknowledge and address the role of stigma and discrimination, including within mental health services, which often impoverishes the lives of people with mental health problems. First, the concepts of service user involvement and empowerment will be examined.

Definitions of service user involvement and empowerment

Service user involvement can mean a wide range of activities, from partnership working at the individual care level, to inclusion in the planning, evaluation and research of services (Tait and Lester, 2005). Arnstein's (1969) ladder of participation represents these processes in terms of a series of rungs from non-participation which includes manipulation and therapy, through tokenism in consultation and providing information, to empowering partnership and service user control. Peck et al. (2002) have suggested that, in order to understand the full scope of user involvement, it is useful to consider both the type of interaction (from receiving information through being consulted to influencing or having control) and the level of interaction (from between service users to involvement in policy formation). Faulkner (2009) also recommends that it may be helpful to consider a range of domains of user involvement which include: individual care; specific services; whole organizations; service evaluation and research; policy development; and education and training.

The concept of empowerment, on the other hand, is much wider and more contested. Masterson and Owens (2006) have argued that an understanding of the concept can be captured through two main interpretations: collectivist social action and individualistic consumerism. The notion of empowerment has its origins in the United States in the 1960s where it was used to highlight the way that individuals and communities had been oppressed, leading to collective action to redress this. In the 1980s and 1990s, however, the concept of empowerment became used to argue for greater choice and/or consumerism within mental health care. In this chapter the focus is on how service users can and should be involved in the planning and delivery of mental health services, highlighting the relationships between power, inequality and oppression in this discussion.

Development of service user involvement

The theoretical context for service user involvement and empowerment was provided by the philosophical and political ideas around freedom, autonomy and oppression in the eighteenth and nineteenth centuries (Traynor, 2003). It was not until after the Second World War that the demand to protect the human rights of all was enshrined in the Universal Declaration of Human Rights (General Assembly of the United Nations, 1948). The social movements that then developed in the 1950s and 1960s sought to promote empowerment and civil rights across many areas involving issues of gender, race, disability, religion, sexual orientation and mental health. In 1967 Martin Luther King declared that 'the deep rumbling of discontent that we hear today is the thunder of disinherited masses, rising from dungeons of oppression to the bright hills of freedom... All over the world like a fever, freedom is spreading in the widest liberation movement in history' (King et al., 2010: 179).

It was not until the mid 1980s, however, that these broad societal discourses led to effective organization and campaigning by mental health service users which in turn resulted in much greater involvement at various levels in the system (Black, 1992; Campbell in Heller et al., 1996; Campbell in Bell and Lindley, 2005). The 1980s saw the establishment of Patients' Councils in hospitals, many grassroots organizations, user-led groups, and wider networks such as Survivors Speak Out, the Hearing Voices Network and the UK Advocacy

Network (Faulkner, 2009). Although service user organizations have been central to these processes, it should be acknowledged that the user movement is heterogeneous and contains what can be conflicting views about the forms of involvement of professionals and service users in service development (Rogers and Pilgrim, 1996). Nevertheless, service user involvement is now a central component of most mental health policy and practice (Lewis, 2005) and there have been some attempts to provide an evidence base in this field which will now be discussed.

Benefits of service user involvement

Tait and Lester (2005) have summarized the potential benefits of user involvement in three main areas: information, effectiveness and service development. They argue that service users can be viewed as experts about their own mental health and lives and so can provide unique information and perspectives which are central to assessment and care planning. They also suggest that this involvement may be therapeutic in itself and may have direct benefits for social inclusion and so promote more positive outcomes. A final justification for service user involvement is that listening to service users will increase our understanding about mental health problems and facilitate the development of new and alternative approaches to responding to people's needs. There have also been some attempts to empirically investigate the impact and effectiveness of user involvement. At the individual level a very clear example is the research finding that the use of joint crisis plans can reduce the need for compulsory admissions (Henderson et al., 2004). A systematic review (Simpson and House, 2002) reported that involving users as workers led to their greater satisfaction and less hospital use. It also found that involving service users as trainers improved the attitudes of providers towards users.

Complexities of service user involvement

There has been some scepticism about the real impact of user involvement that has occurred in the last two decades. Early studies quickly reflected a sense of pessimism about the pace of change. For instance, Brandon (1991a: 1) described such involvement as 'innovation without change' and also argued that 'all of this will be mainly cosmetic unless there is a complete redistribution of power so that service users have much more control over their own lives' (Brandon, in Barker and Baldwin, 1991b: 11). Rogers and Pilgrim (1991: 144) also expressed the view that perhaps opportunities for user involvement were only a side effect of the introduction of consumerism which was not primarily intended to increase the power of users and carers but was instead aimed at reducing the power of the professionals. Faulkner (2009) has identified some of the complexities and potential barriers to these approaches. The first is that the different stakeholders in any process of service user involvement may have different agendas, priorities, even understandings of the purpose, process and goals. This may then create tensions, especially if the user groups involved are funded by the service provider. A further possible concern is that involvement could, to some extent, replicate services by not making sufficient efforts to include under-represented groups. The existence of a very small number of service users in the whole of an organization's activities would also raise concerns about how representative these people could be, and the potentially damaging impact of their relative isolation and the stressful roles that might be expected of them. This relates to another concern that, if involvement is a policy requirement but this has not been incorporated into the organizational culture, then a few service users may be exploited as token representatives without any shift in the power imbalance. All of these concerns and complexities can be overcome if there is the will and resources to do so.

Implementing service user involvement

The case study at the beginning of the chapter reflects the distance there can be between organizational and policy statements about user involvement and the realities of practice. In this case the manager is concerned that increased service user involvement may create difficulties for both the more established staff and some of the service users. Tait and Lester (2005) identify four main barriers to implementing service user involvement. The first is a lack of information. Staff and service users who have become used to paternalistic forms of care may not yet have the necessary knowledge, resources or training to develop a more empowering, participative way of working. For example, at the individual or service planning level, it may not be possible for a service user or member of staff to consider and comment on possible service developments without in-depth information about what those developments might be like. Without this knowledge the proposed change could be threatening, anxiety provoking and, for staff, viewed as a criticism of their current practice. In practical terms there are also financial and time implications which, if not addressed, could further deter involvement. A further barrier identified by Tait and Lester (2005) is that there may be concerns expressed, especially regarding involvement, at planning and policy levels, about how representative the individuals involved are. Ironically this is not a concern that is usually expressed about professionals; however, it does reinforce the need to avoid tokenism by enabling opportunities for involvement at all levels and across all staff and service users, not just those who are immediately willing and able to be involved. The final possible barrier may be that not all service users and staff are fully convinced that service users do have a central role as experts in their own care and in the development of mental health services and policy. This barrier again highlights the importance of preparing everyone involved when service user empowerment is attempted.

Hanley and Staley (2005: 12) have provided good practice guidance on what is needed to prepare an organization for involvement, which would be extremely useful for the manager in this case:

- Be clear about why you want to involve service users and carers.
- Develop a strategy for an involvement in partnership with stakeholders.
- Be clear about who you want to involve.
- Ensure you have all the appropriate policies and procedures in place.
- Identify the resources required to support user and carer involvement.
- Be ready to constructively challenge people's attitudes and beliefs.

What do you think are the issues the manager would have to consider for the process of involvement from the perspectives of service users, staff and carers?

Hanley and Staley (2005) also provide some recommendations for the process of involvement:

- Give service users and carers a choice about how, when, where and how often they get involved.
- Think about the level of involvement you want – consultation, collaboration or user control.
- Ensure you involve a wide range of people – make special efforts to involve people who may often be marginalized.
- Provide training and support for service users, carers and staff – think about expenses and payment, training, access issues, information, involvement in meetings and emotional support.
- Ensure user and carer involvement has an impact.
- Keep all stakeholders informed of the success of user and carer involvement.
- Involve service users and carers in measuring the impact of user and carer involvement (p. 26).

In this case it would be particularly important for the manager to support and encourage the newly qualified social worker and ensure that their enthusiasm and ideas are nurtured and supported rather than viewed with suspicion and cynicism and then dismissed. It will also be crucial to consider the possible barriers to involvement for staff, service users and carers. These may reflect anxiety about what the process may entail and lead to, but should be addressed through careful preparation, clear and open information and keeping everyone involved from the start. Service user involvement should benefit all but how it is implemented will determine if this happens.

Faulkner (2009: 24) has also summarized what effective involvement needs:

- adequate resources;
- payment for involvement;
- transparent and clear goals and objectives;

(Continued)

(Continued)

- benefits for everyone involved;
- adequate practical and emotional support;
- training in relevant skills for service users and staff/professionals;
- equal access and accessibility;
- involvement of diverse communities and marginalized groups;
- respect for everyone;
- good communication and feedback about progress and results.

Empowering practice

There is a range of related concepts and approaches that have developed from theories of service user involvement to offering other opportunities to listen to service users. These include advocacy, consumerism, person-centred planning, personalization and strengths-based approaches. We will now consider these.

Advocacy

An important aspect of the social work role is to advocate for the service users you are working with by listening to and representing their views and arguing for the services needed to meet their needs. It is crucial to acknowledge that this is different from types of independent advocacy because the social work role may involve important conflicts of interest, for example in representing the state in the use of powers of compulsion (see Chapters 2 and 11) or in the general use of professional authority. Henderson and Pochin (2001) distinguish between various forms of advocacy including self, peer, citizen, volunteer, professional casework and legal, but perhaps the key distinguishing characteristic is their relative independence from mental health service providers. This independence may be compromised to some extent as many advocacy providers are also part of a larger service provider organization and/or are at least partly funded by trusts and/or local authorities. The funding organizations should not attempt to influence the practice of the advocates in any way but in that context complete independence may be harder to achieve. Nonetheless advocacy can play a key role in ensuring that service users are listened to. We argue that mental health social workers should be informing service users of the availability of advocacy services and positively engaging with all forms of advocacy.

Consumerism

It has already been mentioned that the concept of empowerment can be captured by two, sometimes conflicting, themes: collective social action to address social injustice and the idea of service users as consumers (Masterson and Owen,

2006). The second theme is most closely associated with broader New Right or neo-liberal ideas of consumer choice and self-responsibility which have been transferred to health and social care contexts. Choice and autonomy are certainly extremely important principles to be promoted, but the imposition of a consumer model on aspects of society where people may not have the material or psychological resources to make choices, or indeed, where there may be little or no real choices available, seems inappropriate. The consumerist approach to listening to the service user does put a positive emphasis on the need to provide flexible care that meets individual needs. Political ideas that underpin this aspect of empowerment, however, tend to include the desire to reduce public spending by shifting the responsibility for welfare from the state to the individual (Ferguson and Woodward, 2009).

Person-centred planning

This approach has developed over the past 25 years in North America and the UK. It has been used widely in working with people with learning disabilities but has more recently been applied across adult services, including in mental health. Although it echoes the consumerist appeal for individually tailored services, its origins are in the person-centred counselling theory of Carl Rogers and the deinstitutionalization process (Dowling et al., 2006). This has therefore made it more attractive to health and social care agencies and professionals as well as viewed with less suspicion. It has been defined as

> a way of discovering what people want, the support they need and how they can get it. It is evidence-based practice that assists people in leading an independent and inclusive life. Person-centred planning is both an empowering philosophy and a set of tools for change, at an individual, a team and an organisational level. It shifts power from professionals to people who use services. (Department of Health, 2010: 3)

This form of planning overlaps with the ethos of the other approaches discussed above but it also provides some very specific tools for working with people, focusing on their strengths and interests and developing their independence. The specific approaches within person-centred planning include: Essential Lifestyle Planning (ELP); Planning Alternative Tomorrows with Hope (PATHS); Making Action Plans or the McGill Action Planning System (MAPS); and Personal Futures Planning. These may be used in combination and each has a range of tools which will facilitate the planning process and will tend to use more accessible and inclusive ways of assessing, communicating, recording and planning than traditional interviews and forms (Department of Health, 2010). As with the consumerist approach, person-centred planning has been criticized for: focusing too much on the individual and so not enough on societal responsibility and interdependence; promoting autonomy over all other values; and assuming that independent living in the 'community' is, in all circumstance, preferable to more collective approaches (Dowling et al., 2006).

Personalization

This is a more recent approach to listening to service users' needs and has been defined as

> thinking about care and support services in an entirely different way. This means starting with the person as an individual with strengths, preferences and aspirations and putting them at the centre of the process of identifying their needs and making choices about how and when they are supported to live their lives. (Carr, 2010: 3)

It was formally introduced in *Putting People First* (HM Government, 2007) as a new approach to social care. Again, this concept overlaps with the other approaches considered here but personalization has an explicit focus on self-directed support, personal budgets and direct payments. This focus involves the service user arranging and managing their care and controlling the budget for it. This has been promoted as potentially revolutionary, as finally achieving the transfer of control to the service user, but there are also concerns that it could transfer all the responsibility as well – this may not be appropriate for everyone, and there is uncertainty about how it will translate into everyday practice (Mental Health North East, 2009). There is also uncertainty about the most effective role for social work within this process. Leece and Leece obtained the views of 66 people with disabilities about the role of social work within personalization. They concluded that

> it was clear that people valued their autonomy; respondents questioned the necessity for the provision of social services and social work, stressing that people were able to do things for themselves. Overwhelmingly, respondents said they wanted brokerage and advocacy systems that were independent and this appeared to relate to issues of power and autonomy. (2011: 219)

Social workers have often criticized the medical profession for its reluctance to address the power imbalances in mental health care but developments in personalization may challenge social workers to also more actively address these power issues themselves.

Strengths-based Approaches

Strengths-based approaches to listening to service users' needs have been developed since the 1980s by Rapp (1998) and Saleeby (2006), amongst others, at the University of Kansas. They devised the strengths model of social work which takes the view that 'clients are most successful when they identify and use their strengths, abilities and assets' (Rapp in Saleeby, 2006: 129). The approach has been criticized for its almost exclusive focus on strengths (Test, 1999) although it can be applied to situations even when coercion and compulsion are needed.

The original tenets of the strengths model are: to focus on strengths and not symptoms or problems; the community and social interactions are viewed as an oasis of resources; intervention should be based on self-determination and so voluntary; the relationship between social worker and service user is of central importance; working with people in the community is preferable to hospital settings; and people with mental health problems continue to learn and change (Rapp, 1998). It also emphasizes the importance of building hope and confidence to enable people to move towards fulfilling their potential and so fits well (McCormack, 2007) within what has become the most influential paradigm in mental health over recent years – the recovery approach. We will now spend some time describing and analysing this most recent attempt to empower mental health service users and their families.

The recovery approach

It is important to clarify that the recovery approach does not provide another competing theoretical model of understanding mental health but instead it challenges, using a range of arguments, traditional services and public attitudes to mental ill-health that are viewed as stigmatizing, discriminating and excluding. The meaning of 'recovery' within this approach is not the conventional sense of getting better, being cured, having no symptoms, or even getting back to how everything was before (Pilgrim, 2008). Slade (2009) helpfully contrasts 'clinical recovery' with the meaning attributed to 'personal recovery' in using this approach. There is no single agreed definition of recovery, but it is referred to in various ways including as a set of principles or processes or outlook or vision (Surgeon General, 1999). A commonly used definition about recovery is stated in terms of,

> a deeply personal, unique process of changing one's attitudes, values, feelings, goals, skills and roles. It is a way of living a satisfying, hopeful and contributing life, even with the limitations caused by illness. Recovery involves the development of new meaning and purpose in one's life as one grows beyond the catastrophic effects of mental illness. (Anthony, 1993, quoted in Shepherd et al., 2008: 1)

Roberts and Wolfson (2006: 18) distil this down to recovery as 'a personal process of how to live, and how to live well, with enduring symptoms and vulnerabilities'. Central to understanding this approach is the idea that people should not be defined or unnecessarily restricted by their mental health problems. It also recognizes that for many people with mental health problems, due to their experiences of services and society, it may be necessary to re-build their self-esteem and restore hope and meaning. Davidson (in Fardella, 2008: 120) suggests the essence of recovery is 'a renewed sense of self as a whole person, despite or incorporating one's illness, along with a redefinition of one's illness as only one aspect of a multidimensional self'. The Mental Health Commission (2005) in Ireland has identified some common themes in the various definitions of recovery and these include: the idea of 'living well' despite ongoing mental health problems; social inclusion; respect for autonomy; the importance of self-management; person-centred services; and hope. How the recovery approach has developed over time is considered next.

History of the recovery approach

It has been argued that the recovery approach has its roots in a range of important historical developments in mental health services. Fardella (2008) suggests that the approach originates in a combination of the rational humanism of Philippe Pinel, and the therapeutic approach or religious humanism of William Tuke who founded the York Retreat in 1796. The York Retreat was, in effect, a therapeutic community with staff and patients living and working together with an emphasis on meaningful activity, interaction and personal responsibility. Shepherd et al. (2008) also trace the roots of the recovery approach to therapeutic communities in the UK which were part of the deinstitutionalization process following the Second World War, and progressive aspects of rehabilitation within psychiatry. There were also influential developments outside mental health services, perhaps most clearly represented in the civil rights and empowerment movements in the 1960s, and the growth of self-help and disability rights in the 1970s (Roberts and Wolfson, 2006). In the 1980s in the USA and in the 1990s in the UK service user movements were becoming increasingly influential and there were also increasing numbers of people writing personal accounts of their own experiences of mental health problems and how they responded to them (Care Services Improvement Partnership (CSIP) et al., 2007). As discussed at the beginning of this chapter, although the underlying philosophies may have been very different, there was also a convergence of campaigning to promote the involvement and rights of people with mental health problems coinciding with the development of more consumerist approaches to health and social care (Pilgrim, 2008). In recent years, in some countries, recovery has become the approach advocated within mental health policy. This has been most clearly evidenced in New Zealand (Mental Health Commission, 1998), the USA (Department of Health and Human Services, 2003), Australia (Australian Government, 2003), Ireland (Mental Health Commission, 2005) and Scotland (Scottish Executive, 2007).

Implications for practice

Now that you have read this background discussion about empowerment and recovery, consider the following exercise.

Exercise 5.1

What implications do you think these ideas may have for the voluntary organization described in the case study in terms of the support provided, the day care services and how the organization is managed?

Andresen et al. (2003) identify the essential components of the process of recovery in practice as: finding and maintaining hope; the re-establishment of a positive identity; building a meaningful life; and taking responsibility and control. The Sainsbury Centre (2009: 1) has identified the ten key organizational challenges for implementing this approach:

1. Changing the nature of day-to-day interactions and the quality of experience.
2. Delivering comprehensive, service user-led education and training programmes.
3. Establishing a 'Recovery Education Centre' to drive these programmes forward.
4. Ensuring organizational commitment, creating the 'culture'.
5. Increasing 'personalization' and choice.
6. Changing the way we approach risk assessment and management.
7. Redefining service user involvement.
8. Rransforming the workforce.
9. Supporting staff in their recovery journey.
10. Increasing opportunities for building a life 'beyond illness'.

These challenges not only demonstrate the extent of the changes this approach requires but also the overlaps with the other approaches discussed in this chapter. The recovery approach, with its emphasis on the person and their story, also links with the role of social history within mental health social work, which will be discussed in Chapter 7, and overlaps with calls for more general narrative approaches in mental health services (Roberts, 2000) and within social work in general (Roscoe and Madoc, 2009). Roberts and Wolfson (2006) have highlighted the power shifts required in relationships between service users and professionals, moving towards greater openness, trust and an acknowledgement of mutual learning. Borg and Kristiansen (2004: 504) in attempting to identify the key ingredients of recovery in practice concluded that 'a central and greatly valued support from the professionals was finding ways to convey optimism, encouraging the person's belief in him/herself, and in general, keeping hope alive'. A very specific application of the recovery approach in practice is the use of Wellness Recovery Action Plans or WRAPS (Copeland, 1997). This has aspects of person-centred planning and involves a structured process which enables service users to identify their own wellness tools and resources, and to develop a written plan to support recovery and respond if crises occur (Mental Health Commission, 2005). Although the recovery approach does appear to incorporate many of the most positive aspects of efforts to listen to and respond to service users' needs, a number of concerns have been expressed about it.

Concerns about the recovery approach

An initial issue is about the use of the word 'recovery' which sometimes denotes the end of the client's mental health problems; this idea has been criticized as being misleading and possibly creating unrealistic expectations (CSIP, 2007). Oyebode (in Roberts and Wolfson, 2006) has argued that the unusual use of 'recovery', especially when supported in policy, suggests this may be more about politics than individual mental health. Campbell (in George, 2008), a service user and leading author on the service user movement and involvement, has argued that he does not find it useful to view either his past or future life in terms of recovery. Fernando (in George, 2008) has echoed the criticism of the more consumerist perspectives on this subject by asserting that the recovery approach is too focused on the individual level and so neglects the wider social, political and economic context. Davidson et al. have attempted to list the concerns expressed about the recovery approach:

> recovery is old news, recovery-oriented care adds to the burden of already stretched providers, recovery involves cure, recovery happens to very few people, recovery represents an irresponsible fad, recovery happens only after and as a result of active treatment, recovery-oriented care is implemented only through the addition of new resources, recovery-oriented care is neither reimbursable nor evidence based, recovery-oriented care devalues the role of professional intervention, and recovery-oriented care increases providers' exposure to risk and liability. (2006: 640)

Pilgrim (2008) has also argued that it is important to acknowledge the role of anxiety about risk in any consideration of the recovery approach, and that professionals, despite their stated support for greater involvement, may still hold assumptions about service users being irrational or not fully capable. These are perspectives that he believes need to be challenged. Perhaps most of these concerns about the recovery approach would be eased if it could be demonstrated that it improves the lives of people with mental health problems.

Research on effectiveness

Research on the recovery approach is in relatively early stages and its implementation seems to have been supported because it resonates to service users, carers and professionals (Mental Health Commission, 2005). Given the emphasis on the need for care to be based on the individual's needs and preferences it would seem to be extremely difficult to attempt to isolate any critical ingredients (Shepherd et al., 2008) but there are ongoing efforts to research practice and services that are based on the recovery approach. One user-led tool is the DREEM (the Developing Recovery-Enhancing Environments

Measure) (Ridgway and Press, 2004; Allotte et al., 2006) which concentrates on identifying where people are in their process of recovery and how recovery-orientated their services are. It has also been argued that, given the individualized nature of the approach, narrative research might be the best strategy (Roberts, 2000, 2006; Shepherd et al., 2008) and some excellent examples of this are emerging (Brown and Kandirikirira, 2006). A key aspect of the development of the recovery approach may be if it can be demonstrated to work effectively even with people who are reluctant to engage with services and/or compelled to do so (CSIP et al., 2007).

Conclusion

This chapter has discussed the importance of ensuring that the service user's voice is central at all levels of mental health care. This seems an obvious position but service users have certainly not always been listened to enough and more progress is needed here . The historical development of involvement was traced from the radical social movements of the 1960s and the benefits of service user involvement were outlined before some of the complexities were acknowledged. There is now a very useful body of literature about the barriers to involvement and how these may be overcome so some of this guidance was summarized. Different approaches to empowering practice were examined in the second half of the chapter – advocacy, consumerism, person-centred planning, personalization, strengths-based approaches and the recovery approach. A common theme runs through all these approaches and it is that the person themselves should lead. As has been acknowledged in Chapter 2, people often need considerable support to make decisions but the aim should be to do everything practicable to enable people to identify their own priorities and pursue their hopes for the future rather than those imposed by mental health services. In the next chapter the importance of also listening to carers will be explored.

Recommended reading

Care Services Improvement Partnership (CSIP), Royal College of Psychiatrists (RCPsych), Social Care Institute for Excellence (SCIE) (2007) *A Common Purpose: Recovery in Future Mental Health Services*. London: SCIE. Available online at www.scie.org.uk/publications/positionpapers/pp08.pdf

Hanley, B. and Staley, K. (2005) *User and Carer Involvement: A Good Practice Guide*. London: Long-term Medical Conditions Alliance. Available to download at www.twocanassociates.co.uk/pdfs/CarerUserpractice.pdf

Slade, M. (2009) *100 Ways to Support Recovery*. London: Rethink. Part of a series of reports on recovery by Rethink and available to download at www.mentalhealthshop.org/document.rm?id=8914

(Continued)

(Continued)

Recommended websites

The Centre for Mental Health has a range of reports on implementing involvement and recovery – www.centreformentalhealth.org.uk/

The Mental Health Foundation is developing an audit tool for involvement and you can follow its progress at www.mentalhealth.org.uk/our-work/all-adults/service-user-involvement-audit-tool/

The Scottish Recovery Network's website at www.scottishrecovery.net/ includes an excellent narrative research project, and a link to the Scottish Recovery Indicator was initially based on a tool called the Recovery Oriented Practices Index (ROPI).

6

Listening to Carers' Needs

National occupational standards

This chapter will help you meet the following National Occupational Standards for Social Work.

Key Role 3: Support individuals to represent their needs, views and circumstances. Unit 10: Advocate with, and on behalf of, individuals, families, carers, groups and communities. Unit 11: Prepare for, and participate in decision-making forums.

It will also help meet the following National Occupational Standards for Mental Health.

- Empower families, carers and others to support individuals with mental health needs (SFHMH 9).
- Determine the concerns and priorities of individuals and families in relation to their mental health and mental health needs (SFHMH 62).
- Support families in maintaining relationships in their wider social structures and environments (SFHMH 12).

Case study

Lucy is a 24-year-old woman who was recently diagnosed with bipolar disorder. There is a family history of mental health problems on her father's side and her parents divorced when she was 14 after which she lived with her mother and older brother. Lucy's father was verbally and physically abusive to his wife and children but since the divorce has had little contact with them and has provided virtually no support. Lucy left school aged 16 with five GCSEs and has had several low-paid part-time and/or casual jobs since then but lost her last job when she became unwell. Lucy lives with her mother, Mrs McDonnell, on a large housing estate and has some contact with neighbours and friends but rarely goes out socially. Her mother is increasingly desperate and is asking mental health services to do something to prevent her daughter becoming more ill.

Learning outcomes

1. To understand the needs of informal carers and their rights.
2. To develop skills in negotiation, conflict resolution and responding to crises.
3. To be aware of the professional and value dilemmas in working with carers of people with mental health problems.

Introduction

Carers of people with mental health problems play significant, if often unrecognized roles which underpin and complement formal mental health services in the UK. This chapter will begin by highlighting the legal and policy requirements that mental health social workers, alongside other professionals, should adhere to when working with carers. Despite these policy commitments, we will explain how and why services to carers often fail. This is partly because of issues of organizational and professional discretion, but also because of inadequate systems of information and access to services. A critical understanding of these complexities, it is argued, will enable mental health social workers to engage more productively with carers and those they care for. The chapter then focuses on two complementary perspectives, one from a carer and the other from a mental health social worker. Although there is some divergence of views in these accounts, we argue that there are important overlapping principles that should inform mental health social work practice. These include the use of active listening skills, awareness of the potential conflicts between service users and carers and the need for a more holistic understanding of the carer's needs. The chapter concludes with an application of the guidelines outlined in NSF Standard 8 to the case material described above.

The policy context

As a qualified mental health social worker you will encounter many situations where the actions of carers will make a significant contribution to the well-being of service users; for this reason you are required to provide as much support to carers as possible. Although informal caring is crucial for many clients, it is only in the last few decades that successive governments in the UK have made sustained attempts to recognize this caring role across client groups (Twigg and Atkin, 1994). Apart from your statutory obligation to involve carers in decision making when using compulsory mental health laws (see Chapters 2 and 11), a number of other pieces of legislation outline professional responsibilities in this area. In England and Wales the following laws are relevant.

The NHS and Community Care Act 1990

This introduced principles of care planning in health and social care services, including more comprehensive assessments involving service users and carers.

The Carers (Recognition and Services) Act 1995

This made provision for a separate assessment of carers' needs.

The Carers and Disabled Children Act 2000

This introduced a special grant to help provide more responsive services to carers, partly mirroring the direct provision available to service users.

The Carers (Equal Opportunities) Act 2004

This required assessing practitioners to consider carers' needs beyond the caring role, for example paid employment and other opportunities.

Exercise 6.1

Take a moment to consider the laws that are described above. Then answer the following questions:

What laws inform social work practice with carers in your devolved region of the UK?

How do they help you provide support for the carers of your clients?

What are the weaknesses and strengths of these laws and how might they be improved?

In answering these questions you will probably come to the conclusion that there has been limited success in delivering support and services to carers in your part of the UK. Despite the intentions of these Acts (and accompanying policy documents: DH, 1999a; DH, 2001b), to require health and social care organizations to assess and meet the needs of carers, criticisms of these policy initiatives remain (Carers UK, 2007). Seddon et al. (2007) reviewed the research literature to explain why, despite the intentions of successive governments to support carers, services in this field are at best piecemeal and often inadequate.

Local and health authorities may be legally required to act in accordance with such laws and policy directives, but the way professionals assess 'regular' and 'substantial care', Seddon et al. (2007) suggest, tends to adversely affect the level of services provided to carers. This sense of restriction is compounded by research findings that carers are not being informed about their legal right to an assessment of their needs, despite the fact that it is a statutory duty of the local authority and the professional to provide this information and service. Seddon et al. (2007) in their discussion of the literature also suggest that there is a need for a much broader understanding of carers' needs, beyond the conventional, usually conservative notion of caring applied by professionals, and that a more systematic appreciation of outcomes would help deliver more appropriate interventions. As a conclusion to this section, take a moment to reflect upon the reasons for the success, or lack of it, in policies for carers. Have any of the views summarized by Seddon et al. (2007) helped you to understand the problems that you face, as a mental health social worker, when you are engaging with carers in your everyday work?

Debates about the caring role

Even if there was a more comprehensive approach to meeting the needs of carers by social workers and other professionals, a number of conceptual difficulties arise when we consider the caring role, and therefore how an assessment of need and intervention should take place. Importantly, some of the assumptions that are often made about the caring role by practitioners and policy makers in this field have been subject to critical analysis by a number of writers. Burton (2004), in his review of literature in this field, challenges the assumption made by policy makers and professionals, as well as some carer organizations, that carers constitute a fairly homogeneous group with definable needs. He argues that such 'politically powerful' constructions that have informed the policy-making process in recent years do not always reflect the lived reality of the caring role. For example, carers often frame roles for themselves and some may not even wish to be identified as carers. In addition, most of the evidence used to justify policies is based on studies of carers who are already in receipt of services or particular client groups. It may be the case that the findings from these studies may not be transferable to other, hidden carer groups. Once these generalizations are disaggregated in this way, then more critical debates can take place about relationships of power and inequalities. For example, Hepworth's (2005) qualitative study of Asian carers living in England found that there was a high dependence on support from local ethnic minority workers, supplementary to the professional help that was available, and that they, like many other carers, remained unsure about their legal entitlement to assessment and services. Much has also been written about the gendered assumptions often made by service providers in this area. Williams (in Tew, 2005), points out that women are particularly disadvantaged because they often accept, and are expected to take on, the caring role. The negative effects on health and mental health, alongside restricted access to the labour market and income, often outweigh the positive experiences of caring for loved ones. Some men who are full-time informal carers will also encounter these disadvantages (Arber and Ginn, 1990).

These debates about carers' rights and differentiated experiences, it can be argued, are not fully recognized by policy makers. It may even be the case that laws and policies can generate perverse outcomes. Critics of the modernizing agenda undertaken by UK governments since the election of the first New Labour administration in the 1990s have challenged personalization strategies that appear to adversely affect relationships between service users, carers and professionals (see Chapter 5). It may be that some strategies that enable service users and carers to gain more control of decision making in health and social care services can be effective (Duffy, 2008), although inevitably forms of resistance do take place, often amongst agencies and organizations (SCIE, 2007). As we pointed out in Chapter 5, discourses on personalization mask broader neoliberal policies that are corrosive of collectivist approaches to health and social welfare (Ferguson and Woodward, 2009). In conclusion a concern is that government policies at times champion service user and carer strategies that may not, in fact, lead to empowerment and the control of resources, but will contribute to the commodification of health and social welfare services, with few gains for already disadvantaged citizens.

Carers' needs and mental health services

So far we have restricted the discussion of carers' rights and needs to the context of a generic policy background that all social workers should be mindful of. For the rest of this chapter we will focus on mental health services and the specialist role of the mental health social worker when intervening to support carers. Let us start with the point made at the end of the last section, on power and inequality, and consider how these ideas can be applied to the situation of carers of people with mental health problems. In the previous chapter we analysed the literature on service user empowerment in mental health services and how mental health social workers can engage, critically, in partnerships with clients to achieve good outcomes. Carers' needs, we believe, should also be viewed in a separate, but complementary way, as part of a holistic approach to mental health social work. This point about potentially competing, sometimes conflicting needs between service users and carers is not always made clear in social work policy and practice, where there is a tendency either to conflate the two areas, or to relegate discussions about carers to a relatively minor aspect.

Although this point about different sets of needs and perspectives is not necessarily confined to mental health practice (similar perspectives can be assumed for other client groups), the relationships between carers and clients are particularly nuanced in mental health social work. Tew (2010) helpfully unpacks many of the conventional assumptions made about the relationships between a person who is mentally distressed and those who care for them. What should be avoided is the way some mental health professionals oversimplify these roles and relationships. Thus people with mental health problems often have important caring responsibilities and, as we have discussed above, carers themselves can become mentally unwell. Tew (2010) suggests that a reframing of the term 'carers' would lead to a broader understanding of these roles; the neutral concept of 'allies' might lead to more holistic understanding of informal and formal helping strategies. In dismissing rather dated, simplistic explanatory theories which tend to label and pathologize families and carers in terms of the aetiology of mental disorders or causes of relapse, he appeals for a broader, contextual approach to understanding mental health problems in families, a position that we support in Chapter 8 on 'Working with families'. Tew also touches upon difficult situations when the rights and needs of service users and carers appear to be in conflict. Henderson's (2002) study of service user and carer experiences of compulsory admission to hospital reveals the very real ethical dilemmas that carers face when they ask professionals to compulsorily admit relatives to psychiatric hospital. This issue is discussed by other authors in this field:

> Carers can sometimes feel that they are the sole person responsible for identifying relapse and referring service users back into services, often when they are seriously ill. This can place the carer in a dilemma, in that s/he can be the person who instigates admission, perhaps against the user's wishes, thereby impacting on the relationship with his or her user's wishes, thereby impacting on the relationship with his or her relative or friend. (Pearsall and Yates, in Ryan and Pritchard, 2004: 235)

It is very important that mental health social workers, when carrying out statutory functions (see Chapters 2 and 11), support carers during these difficult and emotionally charged processes – before, during, and after admission to hospital. Carers in Henderson's (2002) study describe how they had to rebuild relationships with the person they cared for, after their discharge from psychiatric hospital. Issues of loss and grief for carers have been recognized in other studies of this process (Jones, 2004). There is a clear role for the mental health social worker, alongside other professionals, in ensuring that, where possible, positive family relationships are maintained to prevent another crisis and possible relapse.

In summarizing this section, we have argued that mental health social workers have key responsibilities in supporting carers of people with mental health problems. This role is sometimes made complex by the intricacies of the relationship between the carer and service user, especially at times of crisis when compulsory powers are being considered.

Working with carers of people with mental health problems

By now it will be apparent that, although there is considerable interest and intention by policy makers, agencies and professionals in valuing the role that carers play in the lives of clients, there are complicated problems of definition and interpretation of need that tend to complicate and undermine supporting interventions. Mental health social workers are required to adhere to the requirements of law and policy described above; these are generically applied to the carers of all the client groups that would be familiar to social workers. Mental health social workers should also be mindful of additional, client-specific policies that affect decision making. For example the Mental Health Carers Strategy (DH, 2002a) identifies gaps in services to carers of people with mental health problems and highlights the need for more strategic approaches to support. A key document that attempts to shape policy and practice in supporting and addressing the needs of rights of carers in this field is the National Service Framework for Mental Health (DH, 1999b). Standard 6 outlines a care planning approach that should be adhered to by mental health social workers and other professionals. The Standard includes guidelines on how mental health professionals should address carers' needs using care plans:

Care plans (reviewed annually) should include:

- information about the mental health needs of the person for whom they are caring (including medication and potential side effects);
- action to meet defined contingencies;
- information on what to do and who to contact in a crisis;
- what will be provided to meet their own mental and physical health needs, and how it will be provided;
- action needed to secure advice on income, housing, educational and employment matters;
- arrangements for short-term breaks;
- arrangements for social support, including access to carer's support groups;
- information about appeals or complaints procedures. (DH, 1999b: 7)

Later in this chapter we will apply these Standards to the case study, but in the meantime consider the following question.

Question 1: The National Service Framework is over a decade old: how well do you think it (or similar policies) has been adhered to in your region of the UK and what are the impediments that prevent its use in working with carers of people with mental health problems?

We ask this question because, as we have alluded to earlier in the chapter, it is sometimes difficult to operationalize policies and to make sense of them in the interests of carers. However, we want to be positive in our intention to explore how mental health social workers can be effective despite problems of professional and organizational intransigence and restrictions on community based resources that, too frequently, characterize the health and social care landscape in the UK. We are now going to explore how the needs and rights of carers of people with mental health problems might be addressed from two perspectives – the carer's and the mental health social worker's.

The views of carers

Pearsall and Yates (2004) have set out what they believe are the central concerns of carers in dealing with mental health services. As we have suggested above, although these views have been recognized in successive laws and policies, they are often ignored or neglected by mental health professionals, including social workers. They argue that a professional value base, that underpins principles of partnership, is fundamental to good working practices: 'Professionals can demonstrate regard for carers as co-clients or co-workers, each producing distinct and separate approaches. Each can benefit the cared-for and cared, but importantly must be recognized, negotiated and agreed by all stakeholders for relationships to work positively' (2004: 229–30). Like many well intentioned statements, most mental health professionals would be likely to agree with these sentiments, but we need to examine the rationale behind Pearsall and Yates' views. A thoughtful, engaged approach by mental health social workers can achieve a great deal in a number of areas.

As we have discussed earlier, caring responsibilities often raise many emotions, negative as well as positive. In the mental health field professionals can help carers deal with anxiety, guilt and fears using good communication and counselling skills. This can lead to a positive, secondary effect by helping carers contain and process these emotions and preventing an overspill into the lives of those being cared for. In their appeal to professionals, Pearson and Yates also echo other writers' views about acknowledging the complexity of identities that carers carry with them, above and beyond their caring responsibilities. It is crucial that mental health social workers can see beyond the sometimes suffocating caring role and help the carer to expand their social networks and lifestyle opportunities. Mental health social workers should also reflect upon their knowledge of mental health problems and systems of mental health care to enhance the lives of carers and those they care for. For example, when conflicts between a carer and service user occur, or where compulsory admission to psychiatric hospital is necessary, there may be opportunities for a referral to patient and carer advocates or other professionals; these supporting networks might help to alleviate potential distress for both the carer and the person who is being cared for. The mental health social worker should also take a rights-based approach to their intervention with carers, for example by informing carers of their rights to an assessment of need and act as a guide for access to resources and information. Pearson and Yates return to a key point throughout this account – that successful interventions are only possible if professionals take their roles seriously in providing a skilled, value-based approach to ensuring that carers' views are listened to and their rights are consistently respected.

The Views of a Practitioner

Having learned about a carer's expectations of mental health professionals, we thought it would be a good idea for you to hear about an alternative perspective, that of the mental health social worker. The following account was written shortly after the NSF was introduced (Hervey, 2001). The author begins by discussing the opening stage of a carer's assessment, highlighting key skills and values that prepare the ground for a more developed engagement later on in the professional–carer relationship. He recommends that mental health social workers should be explicit in their advice to carers about their right to receive a carer's assessment. If the carer wishes to continue with the assessment then an appointment should be made in an appropriate, private place, in good time. The principle of partnership is one that mental health social workers should aspire to in their relationships with service users and carers (Davis et al., 2008). For this reason, if a care plan can be agreed then a signed copy should be kept by both parties. Hervey (2001) then summarizes the characteristics of what he believes would constitute a good-quality assessment. It should include an initial perception of the situation facing the carer; a key to this initial aspect of the assessment is some understanding of the relationship between the carer and those cared for, strengths as well as weaknesses. An important part of the assessment is to establish the nature of the caring role and its physical and psychological impact upon the carer. As we mentioned above, it can often be the case that conflicts arise between the carer and those cared for; these conflicts need to be explored and understood. Most significantly carers must be allowed to express their hopes and aspirations for roles beyond caring, a point already emphasized by Tew (2010) earlier in the chapter. Finally any cultural contexts should be considered in the overall assessment, for example, care must be taken in avoiding an excessively Eurocentric approach in working with BME families and communities.

Hervey (2001) suggests a number of interventions that, he feels, will enhance the lives of carers in these situations. These might include individual counselling provided by the mental health social worker, particularly where there are experiences of stress, grief and loss associated with the caring role (Henderson, 2002). When necessary, more specialist, family-based interventions might be appropriate, particularly where there are situations of stress and conflict between the carer and service user. For example this may involve other mental health professionals engaging with families in information-giving sessions on mental health and ill-health. The provisions of the *Carers and Disabled Children Act 2002* encourage mental health professionals to access grants to fund respite care services, a crucial source of help for some carers, and one that should be considered by the mental health social workers as part of the care plan. Finally, the mental health social worker should always be mindful of wider social and professional systems that can be used to address the needs of carers. There may be opportunities to refer carers to specialist community-based support groups, and, in situations of crisis, carers should be made aware of specialist mental health teams who can be quickly contacted when relapses in the mental health of service users occur.

In our discussion so far we acknowledge that there are many real and potential difficulties in this area of mental health social work practice. Historically systems of health and social care have generally not adequately addressed carers' needs, and these needs are complex and sometimes difficult to establish. In addition there is sometimes professional ignorance and resistance in working with carers. Bearing all these factors in mind we feel that there is considerable overlap in the aspirations and objectives of the two accounts. We conclude, and hope that you do as well, that many carers' concerns and needs can be at least partially addressed by a skilled, listening practitioner who views the caring role holistically, has a commitment to ensuring rights enshrined in law and policy are adhered to, and is willing to access resources outside of the immediate family and caring network to support this fundamental caring role.

Application of theory to the case study

It is now time to draw these ideas together and apply them to the case study we have chosen for this chapter.

Beginning stages

So far we have emphasized the importance of taking carers' view seriously, not just in terms of legal and policy commitments, but also by recognizing the profession's value base when dealing with what are often substantial levels of unmet need amongst carers. As we have alluded to in our earlier discussion, policy and practice in this field have tended to misunderstand, or even ignore, the needs of carers. Mental health social workers should be aware of such pitfalls and assess and intervene with carers and their families in non-judgemental and empowering ways.

Having received the referral described in the case material, you should take some time to reflect upon the family, the sets of existing and missing relationships, and the recent diagnosis of Lucy's serious mental health problem. There might be a temptation to read too much into the aetiology of the illness and even find some sort of historical pattern of behaviours that you might attribute to pathological family traits. Our view, reflected in Chapter 3, and later in Chapter 8 on working with families, is that the lived reality of having a mental disorder, and the experiences of carers, require mental health social workers to take a holistic approach to assessment and intervention (Bailey, 2009). In particular we need to avoid generalizations based on unfounded assumptions about families and mental health/ill-health (Tew, 2010). It may be that Lucy has experienced a childhood trauma that has led to this first onset of a bipolar disorder; there is evidence to support the claim that a proportion of adults who experience psychoses have experienced traumatic incidents whilst growing up (Davidson et al., 2009), but there may also be more immediate social and individual stressors at play that might explain what could be a one-off episode (Ramsey, 2001).

Instead of being overly preoccupied with thoughts about causal factors, mental health social workers should be more focused on how Mrs McDonnell might feel about another distressing event in the life of her family. It is likely that she is very concerned about her daughter's behaviour and thought processes. There is little evidence that she is aware of any formal systems of advice and support and it is a worry that she has few informal social contacts in the community to share her concerns with. On the other hand you should be mindful of not being overly pessimistic about the family's situation. Using a strengths-based approach there are positive aspects that you would hope to build on, including Mrs McDonnell's long-standing commitment to Lucy's well-being and the hope that Lucy's behaviour may be temporary and socially contextualized.

Assessment

Mental health social workers should be rightly mindful of their statutory responsibilities, including those associated with a duty of care for carers of people with mental health problems. We discussed, earlier in this chapter, how professional mental health practice across all jurisdictions of the UK is subject to sets of legal requirements and policy standards. For example, Barber et al. (2009: Chapter 11) helpfully outline the range of responsibilities towards, and complex judgements about, the Nearest Relative (NR) when compulsory powers are being used in mental health law in England and Wales. The NR will usually be identified by the AMHP during an MHA assessment, although the NR may not be the same as the next of kin. The NR can contest professional decisions about the application and discharge and there is a new ground to replace the NR if they are judged to 'be unsuitable'. A key aspect of the mental health social work role in all jurisdictions in the UK is to engage with NRs and carers when these significant legal powers are being used.

These principles should inform your involvement with Mrs McDonnell and her family. For example, you should view Mrs McDonnell's right to a carer's assessment as essential; the purpose and processes involved in such an assessment should be set out, using non-jargonized language. Although there is a need to be realistic with carers about what an assessment can deliver, bearing in mind Seddon et al.'s (2007) overview of the limitations of carer policies in the UK, you should be prepared to invest time and effort in exploring with Mrs McDonnell the level of care she is providing and the effects this is having on her well-being.

Intervention

After two interviews carried out with Mrs McDonnell in her home, the following care plan is agreed and the following interventions are carried according to the National Service Framework for Mental Health Standard 6:

1 Information about the mental health needs of the person for whom they are caring (including medication and potential side effects)

You are in the fortunate position to be a well-established member of the local CMHT with a good deal of experience in this field. You arrange for Lucy to have an appointment made with a consultant psychiatrist; this reassures

Mrs McDonnell that a specialist assessment will help her understand what has happened to Lucy. Following this assessment, Lucy agrees to a time-limited use of major tranquillizers which will help reduce some of the racing thoughts she has experienced recently. As part of this formal care, Lucy and her mother receive a number of visits from the team's CPN to explain the potential side-effects of the medication as well as information about bi-polar type illnesses.

2 Action to meet defined contingencies

Your role as an experienced community mental health social worker should encompass work within the family unit and the wider, external social system. This requires a difficult balancing act (Bailey, 2009) in seeking to meet the needs of both the service user (Lucy) and carer (Mrs McDonnell). You agree to meet each family member every other week to explore their concerns and hopes, but where necessary you should access other services where there may be a conflict of interest. For example, your CPN colleague could take the lead role with Lucy whilst you concentrate on helping Mrs McDonnell. Lucy might also benefit from contact with a local peer-led advocacy service which helps young people with first episode psychosis deal with their needs. Whatever way these contingencies develop you must, in a skilled manner, demonstrate a sense of commitment and trust by ensuring that you attend home visits on time and also demonstrate an empathic listening approach in your communication with the family.

3 Information on what to do and who to contact in a crisis

One of the reasons for Mrs McDonnell's referral to you was her worries about Lucy's strange behaviour and thought processes which gradually emerged over the period of a fortnight. Fortunately the combination of the appointment with the psychiatrist, information-giving, and regular visits appears to have assuaged Mrs McDonnell's anxieties, to some extent. Nonetheless, there are still inevitable unpredictabilities about the situation, particularly at weekends when Lucy appears more stressed because she has lost contact with friends she used to socialize with. Although there are many variations in the design and operation of community mental health teams across the UK (see Chapter 10), a well-established crisis response team exists in your area. You explain its purpose to Mrs McDonnell, and, with her agreement, liaise with the team leader, so that she can avail of this service if necessary in an emergency situation, for example if Lucy's mental state deteriorates over a weekend when normal services are not available.

4 What will be provided to meet their own mental and physical health needs, and how it will be provided

An important aspect of the work with Mrs McDonnell will be to assess her emotional needs. As we pointed out earlier, carers in this field often experience feelings of guilt, stress and loss. In this case Mrs McDonnell may feel somehow responsible for Lucy's mental health problems because of the poor relationship with her former husband, or lack self-esteem because of her experiences of domestic violence. There are a number of interventions available to you as a practitioner. You have already established a good working relationship with Mrs McDonnell, so an individualized, counselling approach may be sufficient to allow her to express these concerns, and this experience, alongside the educational inputs, could eventually reduce her feelings of guilt and remorse.

5 Action needed to secure advice on income, housing, educational and employment matters

Our earlier review of the research literature on the needs and rights of carers highlighted differentiated experiences and a wide range of unmet needs, often ignored by policy makers and professionals. It is evident from Mrs McDonnell's social circumstances that she is disadvantaged across a number of areas, including poor housing and social isolation. Many carers face discrimination and inequalities directly or indirectly as a result of their responsibilities and commitment to the caring role. Mrs McDonnell has had little employment opportunities as a lone parent, and later as carer of a daughter with a mental health problem. Mental health social workers are in a good position to access community-based services and resources, a point we make in Chapter 9. Given Mrs McDonnell's poor housing circumstances and unemployment, you could carry out a review of her welfare rights and advocate with your local authority either to attend to her poor housing circumstances, or to arrange a possible move to more appropriate housing for her and Lucy.

6 Arrangement for short-term breaks

Given the early stage of Lucy's mental health problems, Mrs McDonnell will want to be near to her, to help her recover as best she can. However if Lucy's mental state were to deteriorate and become long term, then you, as a mental health social worker, should consider applying for funding for respite care. Such care should be carefully planned for maximum benefit for both Mrs McDonnell and Lucy.

7 Arrangements for social support, including access to carers' support groups

As an alternative to individual work with Mrs McDonnell you could consider the option of a referral to one of a number of peer-led carer groups who would very much welcome her joining one of their self-support groups.

8 Information about appeals or complaints procedures

Finally, all clients are entitled to access to appeals or complaints about services. Although it has been argued that Personal Public Involvement (PPI) policies may encourage citizens to unfairly criticize already overstretched public sector agencies, thus fulfilling a right-of-centre political agenda (Ferguson and Woodward, 2009), you are obliged to inform the family about these processes.

Conclusion

In this chapter we have explained some of the complexities that mental health social workers experience in engaging with carers and their families. Mental health social workers can inform their practice by, as we suggest, considering the generic policy context that requires all social workers to be sensitive to carers' needs, and in doing so, to fully recognize the substantial contribution that they make to the overall mental health care in the UK. In addition, experienced mental health social workers should be confident enough to develop this background knowledge and apply it to the specific arena of mental health and care services. These particularities bring with them a number of complex, sometimes contradictory practice scenarios. We have highlighted some of these. For example, mental health social workers should be mindful of the differentiated experiences of carers and their diverse identities, including issues of class, ethnicity and gender. They also need to recognize and explore the inevitable tensions that arise when the rights of carers and those they care for conflict, particularly when compulsory powers are being used. Ultimately, however, our message is to think positively and engage in ways that encourage partnership and holistic approaches to problem solving with carers and family members.

Recommended reading

Manthorpe, J., Rapaport, J. and Stanley, N. (2009) 'Expertise and Experience: People with Experiences of Using Services and Carers' Views of the Mental Capacity Act 2005', *British Journal of Social Work*, 39 (5): 884–900.

This is one of the few journal articles that has examined carers' and service users' experience of the Mental Capacity Act 2005, which applies in England and Wales.

SCIE Report 40: Keeping personal budgets personal: learning from the experiences of older people, people with mental health problems and their carers: www.scie.org.uk/publications/reports/report40/index.asp

This is an up-to-date review of the use of personal budget across a number of carer groups, including those caring in the mental health field.

7

Working with Individuals

National occupational standards

This chapter will help you meet the following National Occupational Standards for Social Work.

Key role 1: Prepare for, and work with individuals, families, carers, groups and communities to assess their needs and circumstances. Unit 1: Prepare for social work contact and involvement.

Key Role 2: Plan, carry out, review and evaluate social work practice, with individuals, families, carers, groups, communities and other professionals. Unit 5: Interact with individuals, families, carers, groups and communities to achieve change and development and to improve life opportunities.

It will also help meet the following National Occupational Standards for Mental Health.

- Work with individuals with mental health needs to negotiate and agree plans for addressing those needs (SFHMH 20).
- Maintain active continuing contact with individuals and work with them to monitor their mental health needs (SFHMH 22).
- Enable people with mental health needs to develop coping strategies (SFHMH 45).

Case study

Anita is a single, 29-year-old woman who lives with her parents in a middle-class suburban Indian community. Her GP has referred her to the local community mental health team and you have been allocated the case. Details of the referral are patchy but it would appear that Anita has not been feeling well for about a year following the breakdown in a three-year relationship with her boyfriend. Since then her GP has prescribed medication to deal with anxiety, panic attacks and depression. Her family are particularly concerned because she has become increasingly reluctant to leave her house.

Learning outcomes

1 To develop knowledge of the process involved in individual work and the range of possible interventions.
2 To develop the skills necessary for developing a positive therapeutic relationship.
3 To be aware of the practice and values dilemmas which arise when working at the level of the individual.

Introduction

In this chapter the process of working with an individual with mental health problems is discussed. The reader will be helped to analyse the process of referral, collecting information, assessing needs, using social histories, care planning, intervening and evaluating. In the course of this discussion a variety of approaches available to practitioners at the individual level will be highlighted. These include practical support, information and involvement, and therapeutically informed interventions using a range of theories – for example non-directive counselling, dealing with loss, cognitive behavioural techniques. Mental health social workers routinely intervene at the level of the individual, but, as the next two chapters (on working with families and working with communities) will highlight, it should not be the sole focus. The issues that need to be addressed may not be at the individual level and to concentrate exclusively on this could neglect opportunities for effective interventions at the family/group and community/societal levels and also risk 'blaming the individual' for systemic and societal issues.

The structure of the social work process will be used to explore working with individuals and to apply relevant theory and research to practice and the case study. At the initial assessment stage key processes will be described and analysed, including dealing with the referral, gate-keeping, engagement and the use of social histories. The care planning stage will focus on the range of possible interventions, being mindful of existing research that helps us understand effectiveness. The intervention stage will include a discussion of relationships, continuity of care and the importance of ongoing reflection. Finally the evaluation stage will identify the fundamental importance of endings, measuring outcomes and performance management.

Assessment: referral, gate-keeping, engagement and social histories

A critical understanding of the referral process is key to post-qualifying social work, a point we make later in Chapter 10 on multi-disciplinary working. The starting point for a mental health social work intervention is usually a referral from another professional. Some mental health teams will still accept self-referrals but, with increasing pressure on resources, it is more likely that you will mostly receive referrals from primary care professionals, usually GPs, and/or other mental health teams. As an experienced mental health social worker it is important to consider whether the referral information you have been provided with is sufficient. In the case study, the details as described are patchy and so it would be both appropriate and necessary to contact the referrer to confirm the reasons for referral, any relevant background information, any other services that are currently or previously involved, and what they feel would be the most effective intervention. The referrer should have discussed the referral with the service user but this should also be confirmed. It would also be appropriate to locate any records of previous assessments or contacts with services. Once sufficient referral-level information has been obtained it will be necessary to decide whether this is an appropriate referral, in particular because the threshold or eligibility criteria may vary between providers. This process may involve a discussion with the referrer and/or the team/service manager and is necessary to ensure that specialist resources are protected for those with the highest level of need and that the team has the necessary skills and expertise to respond effectively. If it is judged that this is not an appropriate referral then at the least information should be provided about what the best alternative services would be – this is sometimes referred to as signposting:

> Although assessment has been recognised as a core skill in social work and should underpin social work interventions, there is no singular theory or understanding as to what the purpose of assessment is and what the process should entail. Social work involvement in the assessment process may include establishing need or eligibility for services, to seek evidence of past events or to determine likelihood of future danger; it may underpin recommendations to other agencies, or may determine the suitability of other service providers. In some settings assessment is considered to begin from the first point of contact and may be a relatively short process, whereas elsewhere it may be a process involving several client contacts over an extended period of time. (Crisp et al., 2003: v)

Exercise 7.1

Consider your initial thoughts and emotional responses to the following range of possible referrals to you:

- A young man with alcohol and drug problems who has recently assaulted his mother.
- An older woman who lives alone and, according to her daughter, has stopped eating.
- A young mother who is experiencing depression and difficulties coping with looking after her children.
- A middle-aged man with a diagnosis of schizophrenia who is reluctant to comply with his recommended treatment plan and is keen to get into some form of employment.
- A young woman who has a diagnosis of bipolar affective disorder, is an in-patient in hospital, and has recently been assaulted by another service user.

We have used these examples to illustrate the range of quite complex referrals that mental health social workers can receive. It is essential that there is a flexible and individualized approach to all referrals that engage, not just with our knowledge about mental ill-health in these circumstances, but also with how we feel about these situations and contexts. Once it has been determined that mental health social work involvement is appropriate (by you or in discussion with your team and supervisor) then you should consider how to prepare for engagement with the client, in terms of knowledge, skills, values and self-awareness. Douglas (2008: 382) provides a structure for this process of preparation or tuning-in at this early, assessment stage of the social work process:

Consider the following:

(a) Legislation

- What provides a mandate for intervention?
- What about statutory roles, responsibilities and requirements?

(b) Policy and procedures

- Which agency policies and procedures are relevant?
- How do these impact on, or direct, this intervention?

(c) Theoretical considerations

- Relating to this situation.
- Relating to the method(s) of intervention.

(d) Previous knowledge

- As held by the agency/others.
- Experience of similar situations should be drawn on.

(e) Tuning-in

- To one's own feelings relating to this situation (self-awareness).
- To the client's possible feelings, re. the agency, the student, the situation (preliminary empathy).
- To a strategy for intervening in the situation (purpose, beginnings, contracting).

(f) Skills

- Which skills may be most relevant?
- What are the degrees of competence and confidence in using these?

(g) Values

- What are the values and ethical issues within this situation?
- What are the implications for practice?
- Consider anti-oppressive practice issues.

In the case study we are using for this chapter there are specific theories about anxiety, panic attacks, depression and possible cultural and power issues that will help you understand Anita's situation. It is crucial in this context to be as culturally competent as you can to avoid making Eurocentric assumptions about causal factors and need; you should also be aware of the supporting knowledge base in this respect. Burr (2002: 835) argues that 'Low rates of treated depression and high rates of suicide in women from some South Asian communities are evident in epidemiological studies in the UK ... explanations for these apparent differences are likely to be located in stereotypes of repressive South Asian cultures.' It has also been found that people from BME communities are less likely to be referred for psychological therapies (Fernando and Keating, 2009). Harrison and Turner (2011) have also highlighted that there may also be organizational and systemic factors that will inhibit a culturally competent and responsive approach.

As already mentioned, interventions that focus exclusively on the individual may be limited in scope, reinforce stereotypes about mental health and illness and reproduce racism and discrimination. McLaughlin summarizes the contexts in which these relationships of power are played out:

> social work is both political and personal. It is political in that social workers are gatekeepers to societal resources and have power over their clientele.
>
> However, in the sense that it is about fostering individual personal change and enforcing a new moral consensus from above, the anti-oppressive social worker is well placed for personally policing, not politically empowering the disadvantaged. (2005: 300)

At this stage of the process it is also important to bear in mind these factors in your work with Anita. The recent onset of her mental health problems, the loss of a relationship with her boyfriend and the concerns of her parents and possibly her community appear to be important to her. How you prepare and initially approach Anita may determine how effective your work with her will be. This should involve being clear about your role and the scope of your intervention, and exploring her expectations of your work together. This can form an important part of the engagement and assessment process. Engagement is a key aspect of mental health social work and so will now be considered in some depth. This concept can be thought of in relatively broad terms to describe the therapeutic or working alliance or relationship between a service user and social worker. The literature on engagement tends to include not only the level of collaboration but also, conversely, how reluctant the person is to have any contact with services, the level of contact with services that is achieved and the extent of their adherence to all forms of treatment including medication (Meaden et al., 2004). Bale et al. offer a comprehensive description and analysis of the term:

> At its most basic, it is used to indicate that patients are in contact with a service. It is also used to reflect this contact being regular, rather than intermittent. A less clear definition incorporates the idea of contact with the service and the individual

> agreeing with and participating in the treatment. 'Engagement' is also used to describe a process that occurs in the development of the relationship between patient and clinician, and to indicate, specifically, the development of a trusting relationship. (2006: 257–8)

The Sainsbury Centre pointed out that there may be issues with engagement from both the service user and service perspectives. They suggested that people:

> fail to engage with services for a variety of reasons, some due to individual experience or characteristics, others due to the inappropriate nature of services. Many are suspicious of statutory services because of their upbringing, life experiences or attitudes. They may feel that services have little to offer or may have experienced negative staff attitudes ... Services may find it difficult to engage because they are too focused on immediate outcomes or on medical treatment alone, or because they lack the staff with the appropriate skills and time or resources to achieve engagement. (1998: 8)

Services may also actively exclude people from their care and this is perhaps clearest around the issues of personality disorder and substance misuse, but may also exclude people by not facilitating access. Anita appears to be reluctant to engage with services, but at least, in this situation, it is possible to test your initial assessment that this may be associated with a loss in her life that has led to her retreat from society, rather than a long-standing serious mental health problem. Priebe et al. (2005) also investigated the processes of disengagement with standard services and engagement with assertive outreach by collecting qualitative data in interviews with service users. Respondents appeared to disengage with standard services for the following reasons: a desire to be independent; because they felt they were not being listened to; having a poor relationship with their workers; negative experiences of hospitalization; and the loss of control due to medication and its side-effects. They also found that the main reasons why people then engaged with assertive outreach services included the following factors: assertive outreach workers tended to have more time and demonstrated more commitment to their care; there was an emphasis on social and practical support rather than just medication; they felt more actively involved in their care; and it was possible to build up trusting relationships. The authors conclude that people are more likely to engage with services if they feel that they are being listened to, if their views have an effect on the care offered, and if they do have some power to make decisions about the services they use. They suggest that assertive outreach may ease some of the tensions involved in these negotiations as the approach encourages clients and workers to interact around a comprehensive range of issues, not just a compliance with treatment. The support provided on practical issues also allowed clients to build up a greater sense of control which helped them feel they were more involved in making decisions about their care. Priebe et al. (2005) report that this process can also be enhanced by involving people in planning for what happens if they do become unwell. This may involve working on the signs of relapse and possibly agreeing a crisis plan.

Gillespie et al. have speculated about other possible factors affecting engagement:

> it is possible that clients who have experienced secure attachments in their early life may be more able to form attachments with staff, and subsequently, more likely to engage with services. Clients' recovery style could also help explain clients' level of engagement with services ... It is likely there are many other factors which play a part in engagement which require investigation, such as previous experiences with mental health services, expectations of the benefits of engaging with services, feelings of shame and stigma. (2004: 447)

If a person is reluctant to engage and states they would prefer not to use mental health services, and there are no concerns about their capacity to make decisions and/or the level of risk to themselves or other people then their decision should be respected. If they are willing to engage, or if concerns about impaired decision-making capacity and/or risk require it, then an initial assessment should be completed (we develop these ideas further in Chapter 11). Most teams will have a standard format for this assessment which includes a consideration of risk but it is important to discuss critically any issues within this format and consider, for example, whether it is focused on facilitating the service user, to consider what is important to them and what they want to work towards. It may also be appropriate to involve the person's carer/s as discussed in Chapter 6.

Although carrying out social histories used to be more of a core component of the mental health social work role, it still has its uses, particularly when clients are less well known to services, as in Anita's case. Social histories are used to obtain a comprehensive and in-depth account from the service user and/or their carers of the potentially important aspects of their development, experiences, social circumstances and context which may inform the care planning process. A traditional format for the social history is as follows:

- Name: Date of birth: Address: Telephone: Marital status: Ethnic origin.
- Carer's details.
- Source of referral.
- What circumstances/events have led to the service user's recent/current contact with mental health services?
- Personal history to include: Family composition; Childhood; Adolescence; Education; Employment; Interests.
- Physical health history (including hospitalization).
- Past mental health history (include mental health history of extended family if applicable).
- History and current relationships.

(Continued)

(Continued)

- Dependents (if children, their needs and arrangements must be considered. Also consider potential impact of parental mental health problems on children).
- Forensic history (if applicable).
- Substance abuse (if applicable).
- Home circumstances (include financial situation).
- Personality (including any perceived changes).
- Conclusion (summary of issues and proposals for care planning and intervention).

A notable omission from the traditional social history is any explicit focus on strengths, resources and, crucially, what the service user views as their issues, priorities and hopes for the future (we hope you can reflect on the discussion on recovery in Chapter 5 to help you think about how you could adjust your practice in this respect). It also does not explicitly state that any history of trauma should be explored. Research on the association between childhood trauma and adversity and adult mental health problems (Davidson et al., 2010) suggests that this may be a very important area to explore and also that traditionally mental health services have not routinely asked about it. For example, the Adverse Childhood Experiences (ACE) Study, in San Diego, one of the largest studies conducted on adult health and well-being, found that 'Persons who had experienced four or more categories of childhood exposure, compared to those who had experienced none, had 4- to 12-fold increased health risks for alcoholism, drug abuse, depression, and suicide attempt' (Felitti et al., 1998: 245). Min et al. (2007: 833) also report that 'as many as 62%–81% of adult women in drug treatment have been victimized by childhood abuse and neglect . . . compared to general population rates of 26%–30%'. In considering the association between childhood sexual abuse and adult depression, Whiffen et al. (2000) suggested that the main mediating factor may be interpersonal problems. In other words, it could be the interpersonal or relationship difficulties that people who experienced childhood sexual abuse may develop, which increase the risk of depression (Davidson et al., 2009: 373).

Assuming that the initial and any subsequent in-depth and multi-disciplinary assessment suggest that some form of intervention is needed then the care planning process begins. It may also be important to keep in mind what research has suggested service users value from social workers:

> Being alongside individuals and tuning into their lives and aspirations; Listening to what service users say; Hearing what service users say; Assessing service users needs holistically; Advocating for service users in respect to their needs; Empowering service users to actively engage with their difficulties; Helping service users in practical ways to address the problems they face. (Beresford, 2007; Davis, 2008)

In carrying out the social history it is important that you engage with Anita using this listening approach. It becomes clear that she is feeling very down and anxious and this may be related to the loss of the relationship with her former boyfriend. With Anita's permission you could share the social history with her GP or any other appropriate professional involved in her care and then engage in the care planning process.

Care planning – the range of interventions

The care plan should be informed by the individual assessment and devised with the service user and, if appropriate, the carer/s, multi-disciplinary team and other service providers. It should detail the identified needs and how and when these are going to be met, as well as who has responsibility for whatever action is needed. Mental health social workers are required to address the care planning process with diligence. The Department of Health (1999) have highlighted the key components of the care plan:

- arrangements for mental health care, including medication and access to services 24 hours, 365 days a year;
- an assessment of the nature of any risk posed and the arrangements for the management of this risk to the service user and to others including carers and the wider public; including the circumstances in which defined contingency action should be taken;
- arrangements for physical health care;
- action needed to obtain accommodation appropriate to the service user's needs;
- arrangements to provide domestic support;
- action needed for employment, education or training;
- arrangements for adequate income;
- action to provide cultural and faith needs;
- arrangements to promote independence and sustained social contact, including therapeutic leisure activity;
- date of next planned review.

As discussed, some service users may be reluctant to be fully involved in this process for a wide range of reasons but there should be ongoing efforts to develop engagement. One possible approach to this is to initially concentrate on providing practical support which the service user has identified would be of benefit. There may be immediate issues around poverty, debt and accommodation impacting on their mental health and also barriers to addressing any other issues. Fitch et al. (2009: 4) reinforced the need to consider these issues:

> All health and social care professionals should ask patients about financial difficulties in routine assessments and, to enable action to be taken, they should

ensure good referral links exist with the money advice sector. *Why?*: population surveys indicate that nearly one-in-four adults with mental disorders are in debt.

Addressing accommodation needs may be another area of practical support and a means of developing a working relationship with the service user. It may also present very clear difficulties with accessing the most appropriate services:

> Consumers consistently reported that they would prefer to live in their own house or apartment, to live alone or with a spouse or romantic partner, and not to live with other mental health consumers. Consumers reported a strong preference for outreach staff support that is available on call; few respondents wanted to live with staff. Consumers also emphasized the importance of material supports such as money, rent subsidies, telephones, and transportation for successful community living. (Tanzman, 1993: 450)

Unfortunately it may not always be possible to facilitate a person's accommodation preferences and if this is because of resource limitations then, as with any other aspect of unmet need, it is the mental health social worker's responsibility to highlight this and advocate for the resources required to address it. Another consideration is that the move may not always be in the direction of independence. Service users may need higher levels of support and, again, sometimes an appropriate place will not be available:

> The literature reveals that there has tended to be an assumption that patients will progress from high(er) to low(er) levels of supported accommodation over time thereby marginalising the needs of a core of patients with particularly challenging behaviour who require long term, permanent accommodation with high levels of support. Over time these patients have been defined as 'difficult to place' and it is argued here that this is not because their behaviour is necessarily difficult to manage but rather that existing models of supported accommodation have failed to take account of their needs, based as it is on an assumption that patients will inevitably progress and require fewer services over time. (O'Malley and Croucher, 2003: 1)

The mental health social work role may also involve case management or having responsibility for co-ordinating all the services needed. The evidence base for this way of working has been reviewed by Dieterich et al. They examined the research comparing intensive case management (ICM) (caseloads less than 20), non-intensive case management and standard care (less clear responsibility for co-ordination) and reported that,

> When ICM was compared to standard care, those in the ICM group were significantly more likely to stay with the service, have improved general functioning, get a job, not be homeless and have shorter stays in hospital (especially when they had had very long stays in hospital previously). There was also a suggestion that it reduced the risk of death and suicide. If ICM was compared to non-ICM, the only clear difference was that those in the ICM group were more likely to be kept in care. There are no trials comparing non-ICM with standard care. (2010: 3)

Other key aspects of the care plan may include a joint crisis plan and advocacy as discussed in Chapter 11 on the role of the AMHP. As discussed in Chapter 4 on discrimination, priorities for the service user may include accessing education and employment and/or developing their social network and/or finding a partner but there may be considerable societal barriers to working towards these goals. The care plan offers an opportunity both to raise awareness of these wider structural issues as well as to consider the most constructive ways of working towards the service user's objectives.

Intervention

Let us now consider Anita and her circumstances. It is apparent from your assessment that she lives in fairly comfortable circumstances and the more systemic approach, described above, to meeting the needs of many other mental health service users is less relevant to her. The cause of Anita's mental ill-health, it now appears, is directly related to a lost relationship. It is important, therefore, to consider the range of possible therapeutic approaches that may be included in the care plan. Mental health social workers will have different levels of training, experience and capacity to provide therapeutic interventions. We argue that this aspect of the role is as important as the case management function that characterizes much contemporary practice.

A developed skills base in this area, it can be argued, will enhance other aspects of the mental health social work role. There is a wide range of therapeutic approaches available to experienced mental health social workers, but the four main approaches are: cognitive behavioural therapy; psychodynamic/psychoanalytic psychotherapy; systemic and family therapy; and humanistic psychotherapies (DHSSPS, 2010a). Deciding which is the best, or which is the best combination of approaches, should be done according to the evidence base for which type of approach is most effective for a service user's issues (Roth and Fonagy, 2005). Mental health social workers should be mindful of any relevant guidance (from the SCIE or NICE for example) and also engage in a discussion with the service user about their preferences. The current NICE (2009a) guidance for mild depression suggests that guided self-help based on CBT, computerized CBT and/or a structured group physical activity programme should all be considered. It also suggests that, unless the depression is moderate or severe, then anti-depressants should not be routinely used. If the depression is thought to be moderate or severe then anti-depressants in combination with CBT or interpersonal therapy are recommended. It will be important for the mental health social worker to consider whether they have the appropriate level of training and skills to provide these psychological interventions or whether a referral to another provider would be more appropriate. Houghton and Saxon (2007) also propose large group CBT psycho-education for anxiety and the research evidence for the range of approaches is continually developing. A more person-centred or humanistic approach (Reeves and Dryden, 2008) may also be appropriate to explore possible issues around attachment, relationships and loss.

It has been decided that, in Anita's situation, a person-centred approach should be taken. As we have alluded to above, engagement is crucial, and core to interventions with clients with mental health problems in ensuring a containing and empowering therapeutic relationship: 'the quality of the therapeutic relationship between social worker and individual or family is critical to achieving successful outcomes' (Scottish Executive, 2006: 27).

The focus on the relationship between client and worker as an important factor in mental health care originated in Freud's early work on psychoanalysis. He argued that 'the first aim of the treatment consists in attaching [the client] to the treatment and the person of the physician' (Freud, 1913, in Bale et al., 2006: 256). In recent years the importance of relationships in work with people with severe and enduring mental health problems has been increasingly recognized and researched:

> Research into the care of individuals with severe mental illness has generally neglected the therapeutic alliance despite an expanding literature on treatment compliance and recognition that the 'doctor–patient' relationship is a strong determinant of such compliance. The alliance has gradually become of increasing interest in psychiatric services research, however, although the implications of using the concept in a psychiatric context have been explored only recently. (Bale et al., 2006: 257)

It has been argued that there are three reasons why the therapeutic relationship is so relevant in this field: 'its role first as an independent predictor of treatment outcome, second as a mediating factor that captures significant variance in the outcome of treatment interventions ... such as pharmacological therapies and finally as an outcome criterion in its own right ...' (in McCabe and Priebe, 2004:125). In social work, 'in the past, the relationship between clients (service users) and social workers was seen to be at "the heart of social work"' (Collins and Collins, 1981: 6) and essential to good practice. In recent years, however, its importance and value have become 'confused and ambivalent' (Howe, 1998: 45 in Trevithick, 2003: 163). Hewitt and Coffey conclude that:

> People who experience a relationship as being therapeutic appear to have better outcomes. A consistent finding of a number of meta-analyses is that therapeutic relationships characterised by facilitative and positive interpersonal relationships with the helper have in-built benefits, and that this is an important element of advanced techniques ... Therapeutic relationships are necessary but not sufficient to enable change when working with people with schizophrenia. (2005: 561)

The factors that are identified as influencing the formation of a positive therapeutic relationship have been described as follows: 'self-awareness, sensitivity, warmth and a positive non-blaming attitude are advocated as essential characteristics for effective helpers ... Gamble (2000) has argued that the ability of the helper to appear "ordinary" and approachable, with a sense of fair play and humanity, promotes affinity between client and practitioner' (Hewitt and Coffey, 2005: 563).

Person-centred or humanistic theory emphasizes the workers' use of empathy, congruence (genuineness/honesty) and respect. The different characteristics of clients, such as age, sex, diagnosis, ethnicity, marital status, current accommodation and employment status, also need to be considered. Although such variables are usually researched in this field, it is less common for the characteristics of workers to be examined. This is a delicate and potentially difficult issue to research for a variety of reasons. For example, some workers may be more able to form positive relationships with clients, or certain clients, than others. If, as the literature implies, it is vital that engagement is achieved, such issues should be identified and discussed openly in teams. On the other hand, where professionals feel that they have deficits, or perceived deficits in this important area of their practice, they may be less willing to have these examined by researchers. The characteristics and life experiences of the client are also crucial, as are the quality and the nature of their previous relationships with others, including other health and social services workers (Hietanen and Punamaki, 2006).

An obvious potential component in the establishment of therapeutic relationships is that of continuity of care and continuity of worker. It appears almost self-evident that a crucial part of establishing, building and maintaining a trusting relationship between a service user and a social worker would require the latter to continue to be the same person. On the other hand, staff turnover is a regular feature of mental health services. There has been some research specifically aimed at examining the impact of this phenomenon on outcomes for people with mental health problems. Adair et al. (2005) developed a measure of continuity and followed 411 people with severe mental health problems for about 17 months. They found 'consistent, positive relationships between continuity of care and quality of life, community functioning, and service satisfaction' (2005: 1068).

Anita's current difficulties have been identified as anxiety, panic attacks, depression and being increasingly reluctant to leave the house. It has been suggested that these may be related to the ending of a relationship one year previously. Anita has agreed to a series of one-hour weekly meetings with you to discuss her problems. Initially the arrangement is contracted on a two-month basis. Egan's (2009) three-stage helping model offers a structure for understanding how the process of person-centred intervention with Anita may develop. In the first stage the focus is on enabling Anita to identify and clarify what is going on in her life. This may involve her exploring issues that may have been too painful or difficult for her to explore in the past. In order for Anita to feel sufficiently safe to do this it will be central to demonstrate that you respect her, care about her, and can respond in a non-judgemental and constructive way to the difficulties she communicates. Key to this process will be your use of social work skills, how you demonstrate that you respect and care for her, how you actively listen to her, and how you reflect on what she is saying and your responses to it. The second stage may involve exploring what Anita would like to be different – maybe not feeling so anxious, being able to leave the house without feeling panicky, and perhaps some of her hopes and aspirations for the future. It is very important to be working with her on what she wants to be working towards even if you may not share these goals or even initially think they may be unrealistic. The third stage is working with Anita to plan how to work towards this preferred scenario. This is finely balanced work so although it is important not to set entirely unachievable goals that may undermine her efforts, it is almost always possible to find some initial steps that are building towards whatever a person would like to achieve.

Evaluation – endings, outcomes and performance management

The final aspect of the social work process with individuals is evaluation and ending. Evaluation should be an ongoing process of critical reflection which helps us to examine 'our effectiveness and can help us to improve it, can increase our accountability to users and clients, develops our knowledge and identifies gaps in knowledge, and helps us develop new models of practice and service delivery' (Lishman, 1998: 101). It 'must address practice and process evaluation including needs assessment, reflection on and evaluation of process, empirically led theorizing about practice, and evaluation which leads to critiques of the political context in which practice and programmes develop and are provided' (Shaw and Lishman, 1999: 4). Increasingly service providers are using very structured performance management systems: 'Performance management is about the arrangements organizations make to get the right things done successfully. The essence of performance management is the organization of work to achieve optimum results, and this involves attention to both work processes and people' (Walters, in Burnham, 2006: 36). How these are implemented and perceived may vary depending on the amount of administrative work they require and any direct usefulness to the social worker involved.

Endings may happen at any stage in the process, for example in the referral or initial assessments it may be identified that another organization may be better suited to meeting the person's needs, so endings may be signposting or refering someone on to the appropriate service. There may be unplanned endings due to unexpected death, suicide, disengagement or sometimes the social worker is unwell or moves job. Sometimes endings may be forced due to resource limitations and other times, hopefully most of the time, the service user will have made sufficient progress to no longer need a social work intervention. Ideally anticipation of the ending will begin with your initial contact when the scope and objectives of your involvement should be clearly agreed. Clear and measurable indicators of progress in the care plan will enable an ongoing discussion and review of how things are going and form the basis of the decision about when to end. Ending the intervention with Anita should be part of what was initially agreed with her in the assessment process. Ideally this will be a joint decision based on agreed indicators of progress. This aspect of your involvement is important as it offers the opportunity to reinforce any positive progress, consider what were the difficult aspects of the process for both you and Anita, and assess the need for any further work and/or a plan if difficulties reoccur.

Conclusion

This chapter has focused on working with an individual with mental health problems and work on this level may form the majority of mental health social work. All aspects of individual work can be complex and offer opportunities for positive intervention: from an initial engagement and assessment through planning and agreeing what is needed, working therapeutically with people, reflecting on this process and preparing for ending. The next two chapters focus on working with families and communities, but these levels of working are not mutually exclusive and the theory, skills and research discussed at each level may also inform and influence interventions on the other levels.

Recommended reading

Dryden, W. (2007) *Dryden's Handbook of Individual Therapy*, (fifth edition). London: Sage.

Roth, A. and Fonagy, P. (2005) *What Works For Whom? A Critical Review of Psychotherapy Research*. New York: Guilford.

Recommended websites

Cochrane and Campbell Collaborations – www.thecochranelibrary.com and www.campbellcollaboration.org/library.php

National Institute for Health and Clinical Excellence – www.nice.org.uk

Social Care Institute of Excellence – www.scie.org.uk

8

Working with Families

National occupational standards

This chapter will help you meet the following National Occupational Standards for Social Work.

Key Role 2: Plan, carry out, review and evaluate social work practice, with individuals, families, carers, groups, communities and other professionals. Unit 7: Support the development of networks to meet assessed needs and planned outcomes. Unit 8: Work with groups to promote individual growth, development and independence.

It will also help meet the following National Occupational Standards for Mental Health.

- Determine the concerns and priorities of individuals and families in relation to their mental health and mental health needs (SFHMH 62).
- Enable individuals and families to identify factors affecting, and options for optimising, their mental health and social well-being (SFHMH 39).
- Plan and review the effectiveness of therapeutic interventions with individuals with mental health needs (SFHMH 23).

Case study

Angela is a 44-year-old woman with a history of depression. Her depression has returned and she is currently engaged in a confidence-building course at her local community centre. Some family and friends are supportive but others respond to her with frustration and anger. She is keen to return to work but was last in paid employment 20 years ago before the birth of her three children who are now aged 20, 17 and 12. Her husband, Winston, has not had a job for eight years. The family are dependent on income support and housing benefit. The community centre has asked you to work with the family because they are concerned that her depression is beginning to affect the well-being of the whole family.

Learning outcomes

1 To develop knowledge of the theory and implications of thinking of families as systems.
2 To develop skills in family work, including mediation, education and inter-agency working.
3 To develop awareness of the importance and complexity of the interface between adult mental health services and child care services.
4 To be aware of practice and values dilemmas, in terms of balancing competing rights, empowerment and protection.

Introduction

In this chapter three of the main aspects of working with families will be considered. The first is informed by thinking of families as systems in which each member interacts with, influences and affects all the other members. The theoretical ideas underpinning this approach will be outlined before its application to practice is explored. This can range from formal systemic family therapy to informing and influencing even brief social work contact with families. The case study will be used to illustrate this way of thinking about and intervening with families where there is a family member with mental health problems. The second aspect of working with families that will be discussed in this chapter is family work. Although this may overlap with systemic family therapy the focus tends to be more on psycho-education with first episode psychosis. The final aspect is the interface between adult mental health services and child care services and will reinforce the importance of the SCIE's (2009) guide for working with parental mental health and child welfare: *Think Child, Think Parent, Think Family*.

Families as systems

An important initial point is to acknowledge the socially constructed and evolving nature of what we mean by 'the family'. Traditionally inclusion in a family system was by birth, adoption or marriage but these ideas are now insufficient to reflect the realities of society and so a more pluralistic view is needed which includes people who spend their lives together, regardless of legal or biological ties (Goldenberg and Goldenberg, 2004). In this section the historical development of the theoretical ideas underpinning ways of working with families as systems will be outlined first. The relevance of these ideas to current mental health social work practice will then be explored by reference to the competences needed for systemic work, the processes involved in systemic practice and some of the specific techniques used within this approach. This approach will then be applied to the case study.

Historical development

Dallos and Draper (2005) argue that systemic theory and therapy with families developed from a range of theoretical and contextual sources. The context, especially from the 1950s onwards, included: a growing debate about the effectiveness of traditional psychodynamic approaches; developments in guidance work with families and group approaches in general; and concerns about the level of resources needed for long-term, past-focused individual work. The theoretical origins of viewing families as systems derive from a range of disciplines but the focus here will be on general systems theory, cybernetics and ecological approaches (Goldenberg and Goldenberg, 2004; Becvar and Becvar, 2006). These early, overlapping ideas will each be briefly explored before their current relevance to family therapy practice is considered.

General systems theory was developed by Ludwig von Bertalanffy (1950), a biologist, who aimed to provide a theoretical model that could be used to understand all living things. Rivett and Street (2009) explain these ideas by using the example of a rural field to demonstrate the complex interdependence at all levels of the systems and subsystems within this glimpse of the natural world. This example also reinforces the ideas that boundaries between and within systems are permeable, although the degree of openness varies, and, over time, the ongoing interactions or exchanges of information between them tend to be escalating/positive or balancing/negative. In the case of the natural world it is suggested that the direction of these interactions or feedback will tend to be towards trying to maintain equilibrium or balance, and this tendency is referred to as homeostasis, although systems are also continually changing.

Ideas from the study of communication and control form the next historical pillar of thinking of families as systems. These ideas were developed from the study of the processes and patterns by which living things and machines regulated themselves. Norbert Weiner (1948), a mathematician, was the first to use the term 'cybernetics' which focused on the feedback mechanisms within systems (Becvar and Becvar, 2006). The possible impact of the observer has also been included within these ideas and is sometimes referred to as second order cybernetics or second order systems theory (ibid.). Gregory Bateson (1972), an anthropologist, applied these ideas to the family as a system which involves patterns and processes of feedback, although he also importantly acknowledged that no one can ever perfectly describe a system as any view of it will always be, to some extent, subjective (Keeney, 1983; Rivett and Street, 2009). Bateson also developed the idea of different levels of communication, recognizing that it is necessary to consider the non-verbal and metacommunication (or underlying messages) which will accompany what is being said in families (Carr, 2006).

The final component of the historical development of this way of thinking that will be considered here emphasizes the role of the wider systems and is usually referred to as the ecological perspective or bio-ecological systems theory (Bronfenbrenner, 1979; Teater, 2010). This approach highlights the ongoing interactions between the person and their environment which is made up of other individuals, families, groups, communities, cultures, physical spaces and political systems. It therefore attempts to understand all aspects of the person's or family's environment that may be supporting or inhibiting them achieving their potential (Gitterman and Germain, 2008). A final recurring idea that occurs in theories of family therapy is the notion of circular causality. The next section will explore how the application of these theoretical ideas can be applied to your work with families.

Current relevance to practice

The important influence of these theoretical ideas is immediately evident in the recently devised competences required to deliver effective systemic therapies (Pilling et al., 2010). In order to further demonstrate the current relevance of these ideas their application throughout the process of working with a family will now be considered (Carr, 2006) and within this more specific influences on understanding family structure and rules, systemic hypothesizing, feedback and circular questions (Vetere and Dallos, 2003; Goldenberg and Goldenberg, 2004). Some of the research findings about how social workers can be effective in translating these ideas into therapy will also be outlined.

Carr (2006) breaks down the processes in family therapy into planning or preparation, assessment, treatment or intervention and disengaging or recontracting. In each of these the influence of systemic theory can be seen. During the planning or preparation stage it must be determined who should be invited and what initial questions might be asked. Thinking of families as systems clearly suggests that the individual's perspective may be insufficient to understand the complexity of what is going on and so it is usually important to invite the views of people who are within the person's immediate systems. The direction of the questions asked by social workers will also be informed by these theoretical ideas so some probing may be necessary about such issues as the interactions within and between the immediate and wider systems, the nature of the boundaries of these systems, the types and purposes of communication, how negative and positive feedback may have developed and work in these systems, any other patterns that may have developed, and the importance of the wider contextual factors for what is going on within the family system.

Preparation

In terms of the case study it is therefore important to consider how to make initial contact with the family and who should be involved. A systemic approach would suggest the involvement of the whole family, although not everyone may be willing to engage initially. It would also be helpful to think about what could be the important questions to ask of them. These could involve gathering information and perspectives on the family structure and its rules, asking about how people view current issues, how feedback works in the family, the various relationships within the family and any relevant issues in the wider community and societal systems.

Assessment

In the assessment stage, using this perspective, one suggested opening would be to acknowledge that everyone involved will have a view on what is going on in the family, and that the social worker will want to understand each person's view. These theoretical ideas also reinforce the need to understand all the relationships within and beyond the family, and this process is often facilitated by using genograms and ecomaps which will include the wider systems. Goldenberg and Goldenberg draw explicitly on cybernetics to suggest that an important part of trying to understand a family is to consider its structure and rules. As they put it, 'A family is a cybernetically rule-governed system. The interaction of family members typically follows organized, established patterns, based on the family structure; these patterns enable each person to learn what is permitted or expected of him or her as well as others in family transactions' (2004: 73–74). Carr (2006) suggests that the assessment phase often concludes with some initial hypothesizing about the main problems and the family strengths. These hypotheses may well be further developed or discarded but they represent an attempt to nurture some understanding for both the family and social worker of the complex interactions involved in the current issues.

The process of hypothesizing is not about making any definite choices, rather it is about starting to consider and test out those issues that might be relevant. An hypothesis will usually involve: some ideas about the family life cycle and possible changes/transitions; ideas about the relationships within the family; and also some ideas about the function of the problems, in this case Angela's depression. Burnham's work suggests that 'all families experience some difficulties when negotiating a transitional stage' (1986: 33). The family life cycle model (Carter and McGoldrick, 1999) may also reveal other problems and issues faced by the family. For instance, this family may be at the stage of launching children which may include: renegotiating the relationship between Angela and Winston; moving from parent to child relationships to adult to adult; new people, such as the children's partners, entering the family; and perhaps dealing with caring responsibilities and the possible loss of Winston's and Angela's parents. Carr describes this stage as the

> transition of young adult children out of the parental home … parents faced with the task of adjusting to living as a couple again, to dealing with disabilities and deaths in their families of origin and of adjustment to the expansion of the family if their children marry and procreate … mid-life re-evaluation. (2006: 20)

The family life cycle model is also potentially informative for thinking about the three children's perspectives, with the prospect of leaving home and the shifts in responsibility that this may involve, as well as the establishment of themselves as distinct from and independent of their family of origin (Nichols, 2010).

Again, if these hypotheses do not seem to fit well they should be reconsidered and other ideas tested out. Vetere and Dallos (2003), in line with systems theory, suggest that looking at the wider context and interaction of different systems is one way of developing your thinking. The idea that systems tend to regulate themselves and are usually actively trying to maintain equilibrium through a process of feedback which will either reinforce or discourage thoughts, feelings and behaviours also offers opportunities for understanding. This may provide some insights around the anxieties involved in change, even if this appears to be very beneficial change, and the complex interactions that may be involved in family systems maintaining themselves. As a way of getting you to think about these processes, consider the following exercise.

Exercise 8.1 Draw your own genogram

A genogram is a diagrammatical representation of a family, often including three generations. It is used both to gather information about the family and also to help engage the family and facilitate a discussion about the nature of the relationships within that family. McGoldrick et al. (2008) provide detailed instructions and discussion about the use of genograms. There is some variation in the instructions for genograms but usually a woman is represented by a circle and a man by a square. An X in the symbol indicates a person has died. Connecting lines portray the family structure with separation indicated by a single slash and divorce by a double slash. Additional lines may be added to represent the nature of the relationships, such as a zigzagged line for a conflictual relationship and additional lines to indicate close relationships. A line around family members shows who lives together. Additional details such as names, ages and other important information can be added. To illustrate this and to help you draw your own genogram a basic example from the case study is included below.

Intervention

Thinking of families as systems also promotes the use of very specific techniques which may be of particular benefit during the assessment and intervention phases. The use of circular questions, for instance, is based on assumption that exploring and discussing the differing perspectives involved may enable understanding and change. Circular questions usually involve asking members of a family to talk about what they think might be the thoughts, feelings and relationships of the other members of the family system.This type of approach can become quite sophisticated – for example, Burnham (1986) has classified circular questions into six different categories: sequential, action, classification, diachronic (changes over time), hypothetical and mind-reading, but all are based on the theoretical understanding that the subjective views of everyone in the system are important and will have an impact on everyone else. In the case study this way of intervening could involve asking Angela what she thinks may be going on for Winston and what his relationship is like with the other family members and then repeating this process with each of the family members. The focus may

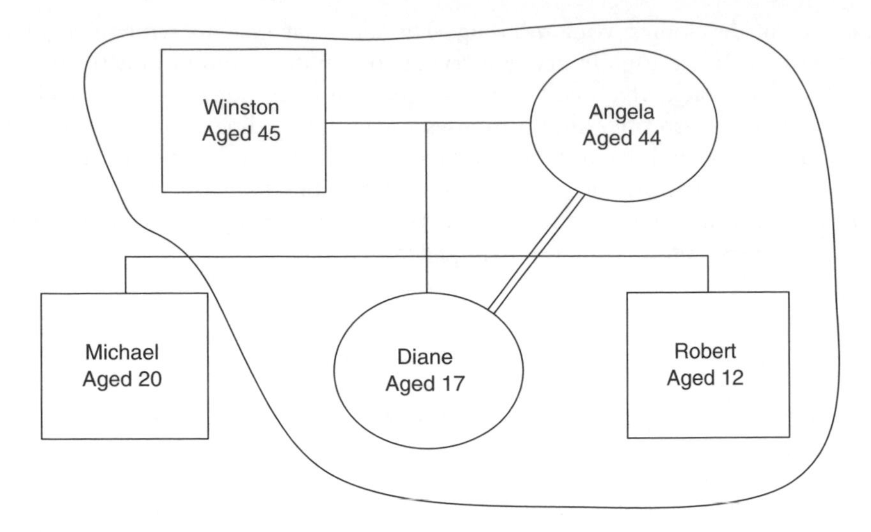

Figure 8.1 Genogram example

not necessarily be on the issue of Angela's depression but this could also be the subject of circular questioning around how things may have changed over time. This might be achieved by asking everyone what they think Angela may be thinking and feeling when she is depressed.

Ending or recontracting

The final stage of disengaging or recontracting with the family should involve a discussion and evaluation of the process and the impact this way of working has had on the family. The relevance of thinking of families as systems is supported by the research evidence on how effective this approach can be. In an overview of the evidence base, Stratton) concluded that:

> Systemic Family Therapy provides effective help for people with an extraordinarily wide range of difficulties. The range covers childhood conditions such as conduct and mood disorders, eating disorders, and drug misuse; and in adults, couple difficulties and severe psychiatric conditions such as schizophrenia. Throughout the life span, it is shown to be effective in treatment and management of depression and chronic physical illness, and the problems that can arise as families change their constitution or their way of life. (2005: 1)

Carr (2000a) also provided an overview of the evidence and supported the use of this approach for child-focused problems such as: child abuse and neglect; conduct problems; emotional problems; and psychosomatic problems. In addition he found evidence for its effectiveness with adult-focused problems including: relationship problems; anxiety; depression; alcohol abuse; chronic pain management; and for families caring for older people with dementia (Carr, 2000b).

Family work

Another important aspect of working with individuals with mental health problems and their families, friends and carers, which may overlap with systemic family therapy, is 'family work'. This approach goes beyond just providing general support and information to carers and aims to improve the capacity of the family to respond to and manage their needs. Family work involves the consideration of how everyone is responding to and coping with the issues; the participation of all relevant people in the assessment, planning, intervention and evaluation process; and the provision of psycho-education. Psycho-education includes elements such as problem solving and communication training as well as education about mental health problems, treatments and services (Bauml et al., 2006). It could be argued that this approach has traditionally been a central part of the mental health social work role and it has also been more formally structured for working with psychosis as 'family work'. Family work has been distinguished from family therapy thus: 'within some systemic family approaches an individual's symptoms are seen as manifestations of a dysfunction within the family system (Corey, 1996). A family work perspective is fundamentally different from this systemic approach in that the family is not viewed as being in need of treatment'(Smith et al., 2007: 31). The distinction from systemic approaches may be less clear in practice but the repeated assertion in recent family work literature that the family should not be blamed or be viewed as needing treatment may be explained by considering the historical development of family work.

Historical development

Askey et al. trace the development of family work to a series of research studies in the late 1960s and early 1970s that examined whether the family context could influence the course of psychosis: 'It was found that service users living with relatives who displayed high levels of criticism, hostility or over-involvement relapsed more than service users whose families were less expressive of their emotions' (2007: 357). These family behaviours were described by the term 'high expressed emotion' (Brown et al., 1972) and contrasted with low expressed emotion families who tended have more positive ways of coping (Kuipers et al., 2002). The approach of working directly with the family to develop more understanding of psychosis, positive ways of communicating and responding to difficulties then developed. The theoretical foundation for this way of working is usually associated with the stress-vulnerability model which was considered in greater depth in Chapter 3. Askey et al. (2007) also identify a second generation of research in the 1990s that focused more on staff responses to people with psychosis. In the literature and guidance on family work it is clear that the workers involved should adopt a non-judgemental approach and avoid any sense of blaming the family (Kuipers et al., 2002) and there has been debate during the development of this approach about the sensitivity that is involved when identifying the role of the family in the course of mental health problems.

Components of family work

Smith et al. (2007) highlight the components that are common to most family work although they also argue that there is a need for flexibility in the way that practitioners engage with families rather than attempt to impose a 'one size fits all' intervention. Here is a summary of their ideas.

> Features that are present in all family work models include:
>
> - promoting a collaborative working relationship
> - using written documentation that is shared with the family
> - an assessment process that elicits the family's strengths and ways of coping, which may offer opportunity for reminiscence and exploration of belief systems
> - a forum for information exchange and education, which should be a three-way process (between the service user, carers and family workers) relating to significant events, diagnosis, medication, available mental health services and coping strategies
> - optimal treatment for psychosis, including early signs monitoring, relapse prevention planning and the use of/or potential for using anti-psychotic medication
> - stress management by promoting clear communication to elicit problems, strengths and needs within the context of identifying and pooling resources to find solutions
> - a problem-solving structure to provide a framework for working towards individuals' goals (2007: 32)

Now try to answer the following questions. As a practising mental health social worker, consider how much of your work involves working in this way with families? Could, or should, this approach be used more in your practice?

Research and policy

There is currently a strong evidence base that not only suggests this approach may be more effective than routine care, in terms of relapse, hospitalization and other outcomes, but also that in order to achieve these results the intervention has to go beyond short-term education programmes alone (Barrowclough, 2003). Leff has also argued that 'there is now unequivocal evidence that working with families to ameliorate the emotional atmosphere in the home significantly reduces the risk of relapse for people with schizophrenia' (2000: 82). He cautions as well that it is not a substitute for anti-psychotic medication and that it is not yet clear what the key aspects of family work are except that education alone is not enough. A further debate he raises is about the best way of providing family work. There are advantages, in terms of staff time and possible peer support, in working with a number of families together, but this may not be appropriate for all families.

This approach has been recommended in policy, for example in Northern Ireland the Department of Health, Social Services and Public Safety has stated that

> It is recognised that service providers should work in partnership with families and carers of service users, as they play an extremely important role in helping the recovery process and preventing relapse in certain conditions. The contemporary model of Family Work aims to educate families and carers about the presenting condition, its management and treatment and its impact on family functioning. This work aims to empower families in enhancing/developing coping strategies, family well-being, maintaining and extending social networks, managing/coping with a crisis and, where appropriate, recognising early signs of relapse. (2010a: 19)

The National Institute for Health and Clinical Excellence in its guidelines for schizophrenia has also recommended family work and specified that it should:

- include the person with schizophrenia if practical
- be carried out for between 3 months and 1 year
- include at least 10 planned sessions
- take account of the whole family's preference for either single-family intervention or multi-family group intervention
- take account of the relationship between the main carer and the person with schizophrenia
- have a specific supportive, educational or treatment function and include negotiated problem solving or crisis management work (2009b: 23).

Application to the case study

Fadden and Smith provide an overview of what the process of intervention may involve in working with families where a mental health problem is present:

1. meeting with the family to discuss the benefits of the approach
2. agreeing with the family that they are willing to try the approach
3. assessment of individual family members
4. assessment of family communications and problem solving
5. formulation by the family worker of family resources, problems and goals; this is done in collaboration with the family
6. meeting with a family to discuss/plan how to process and establishment of family meetings without the family worker
7. sharing of information about the disorder and its impact
8. communication skills training: active listening; expressing positive feelings; making positive requests; expressing unpleasant feelings
9. problem solving
10. booster sessions
11. disengagement from family if appropriate (2009: 27).

Family work does seem to be predominantly used in working with people who have psychoses, especially in the first episode, but as Falloon (2003) highlights, it has also been used with a wider range of mental health problems including depression (although the evidence base is less well developed here). In the case study, if this approach was used with Angela and her family it would involve all the components suggested by Smith et al. (2007) and a process similar to the one proposed by Fadden and Smith (2009). The education and treatment aspects would obviously focus on Angela's depression and its impact upon her family. Now consider the following exercise.

Exercise 8.2

Explore the quality of information, support and intervention available for families in your organization and how routinely these are used with individuals and families.

Interface with child care services

The third aspect of working with families that will be considered in this chapter is the overlap between adult mental health and child care services, including implications for social workers at this interface (Davidson et al., 2010). This section will highlight the extent of parental mental health problems and interventions, followed by a consideration of the important document *Think Child, Think Parent, Think Family* (SCIE, 2009). There are particular interfaces between mental health and child care services that you should be aware of. Parker et al. (2009), drawing on national surveys of mental health problems, suggest that, at any one time, 9–10 per cent of women, aged 16–65, and 5–6 per cent men, aged 16–65, are parents with mental health problems. The majority of these parents will have mental health problems such as depression or anxiety with only a very small proportion having some form of psychosis. Parrott et al. have estimated that

> Over one third of all UK adults with mental health problems are parents ... Two million children are estimated to live in households where at least one parent has a mental health problem but less than one quarter of these adults is in work ... potential stressors leading to parental mental health problems include a lack of money; breakdowns in valued relationships, bereavement, loss of control at work and long working hours. (2008: 1)

Kearney et al. (2003) interviewed a sample of child care social workers who estimated that between 50 and 90 per cent of parents they were working with had mental health and/or substance misuse problems. The Social Exclusion Unit has highlighted that some parents may be at higher risk of developing mental health problems. It reported that:

> Levels of depression are highest among the mothers of young children, lone parents and those who are economically inactive. 28 per cent of lone parents have common mental health problems. Post-natal depression is estimated to affect one

> in ten new mothers and usually starts within six weeks of the birth. Research suggests that a mother's prolonged post-natal depression may have a negative effect on the child's cognitive development and social relationships. (2004: 75)

It also reported that, despite these apparently elevated levels of health and social care need, these families are one of the four groups most likely to be excluded from service provision. Despite these concerns, it is important to acknowledge that most parents with mental health problems do parent their children effectively (Evans and Fowler, 2008; Parrott et al., 2008). Parental mental health problems do not always impact negatively on children's health, development and well-being and a range of factors (including access to treatment and support, the type of mental health problems and the social and economic circumstance of the family) may influence the nature and extent of any impact (Social Exclusion Unit, 2004). Parental mental health problems can affect the health, development and safety of children in a wide range of complex ways and the increased needs of the children may create further stressors for parenting and parental mental health (Falkov, 1998). A number of factors could be at play – genetics, pre-natal development and parental mental health that determine the ability to parent and form a positive, secure attachment after birth. There may also be indirect processes include socio-economic deprivation, exposure to related issues such as substance misuse, relationship conflict and domestic violence, and additional caring responsibilities (Cleaver et al., 1999; Social Exclusion Unit, 2004; Manning and Gregoire, 2006). Sartorius (2007) has also emphasized that stigma may be significant in the way parents and their children view themselves and others, and in turn this will affect how they feel about seeking help and how services may respond. Parents may be extremely anxious about the possible implications of engaging with mental health services in general, but also with a social worker in particular, and these anxieties need to be acknowledged and addressed across the individual, service and societal levels.

The negative impacts of these factors will often combine and interact; and these have been identified in research and in enquiry reports. The overview report *Child Protection: Messages from Research* (Department of Health, 1995) found that there were high levels of parental mental health problems, alcohol and drug misuse, and domestic violence in families of children who become involved in the child protection system. Concerns about the impact of parental mental health problems on children have been reinforced by the repeated finding that parental mental health problems have been a feature of cases in which children have sustained serious injury or been killed. Falkov's (1998) study of serious case reviews found that in a third of cases the parent/s had mental health problems. Sinclair and Bullock (2002) also found that in 18 out of 40 serious case reviews (45 per cent) at least one parent had mental health problems. More recent overviews of Serious Case Reviews in England continue to report very high levels of past or present domestic violence and/or parental mental health problems and/or substance misuse, and that these issues often co-exist (Brandon et al., 2008; 2009).

Responding effectively to these complex needs requires high levels of communication and co-operation between mental health and child care workers but this has, historically, been a problematic interface to manage. Darlington et al. (2005a) separated the issues that may cause these difficulties into two main groups. The first group relates to general issues with collaboration including difficulties in communication, knowledge, role clarity, resources, and siloed agency structures and policies. The second group covers the specific challenges involved in inter-agency working with people with mental health problems and children who may be at risk. This group includes the fluctuating and complex nature of mental health problems and the difficulties involved in trying to balance the, at times, conflicting needs of parents and children. Stanley et al. (2003) also highlighted difficulties with inter-professional problems with confidentiality. Weir and Douglas (1999) emphasize that the workers involved need to feel sufficiently confident and assertive about expressing their concerns across the interface and Lupton et al. (2001) suggest this may also be a factor within multi-disciplinary teams. There may also be wider structural difficulties, such as limited resources and fragmented services, which will contribute to problems with interface working (Darlington and Feeney, 2008; Slack and Webber, 2008).

The SCIE in its *Think Child, Think Parent, Think Family* (2009) guide has made a number of recommendations about how work at this complex interface may be improved. We argue that these overlap with some of the systemic and family work ideas discussed in this chapter. The document recommends that practitioners should focus on developing strengths, recovery and social inclusion rather than symptoms and deficits. It is also suggests that the family should be viewed as a unit and the interactions and relationships within it considered by all the workers involved. Reinforcing the family work approach, the SCIE (2009) recommends that education should be provided about mental health problems, their possible impact on parenting and also the importance of the parent–child relationship. This very positive therapeutic approach needs to be accompanied by appropriate knowledge of the potential risks to parents and children. Intervention should take place as early as possible to protect parents and children. The guide acknowledges that these changes need to be supported by an organizational commitment to this way of working. There is a very strong pragmatic argument suggesting that these positive ways of engaging and working in partnership with families are also the most effective way of assessing and managing risk as well as of supporting the people involved (Davidson and Campbell, 2007).

The importance and complexity of the interface between mental health and child care can be further demonstrated by, once again, considering the case study. Angela and Winston have three children aged 20, 17 and 12. The *Think Child, Think Parent, Think Family* guide has identified that there may be issues starting with the process of involvement from screening through assessment, care planning, intervention and review. At the initial screening and assessment stages the details of the other members of Angela's family should be identified. This may seem to be a very basic point but often such essential information is missing from referral details (for example whether arrangements are in place for the children's care). It may be that there are no concerns that the children are at risk of harm but the family could benefit from some support from children's services while Angela is unwell. She may be reluctant to consider this because of the perceived stigma of using social services and/or concerns that this suggests she is not being a good enough parent. Hopefully, with respectful and sensitive practice, Angela would be given the opportunity to work through these anxieties and allow support to be provided. It may also be that the assessment process identifies the need for support for the whole family when this is not available due to resource limitations. In this case a discussion should take about how best to highlight this unmet need, or to advocate and campaign for the resources required. A more concerning development would be if there were there was evidence of a possible risk of harm to the children. An extreme situation of risk might be if Angela expressed some thoughts that life is not worth living and that, in order to protect her children from such a painful world, she should kill them and then herself. In these circumstances it is necessary, even if Angela has concerns about it and does not give her consent for it, to involve children's services and discuss if any further measures are needed to ensure the safety of the children. The intervention needed could range, depending on the level of risk, from discussing the concerns with Winston and checking them out again with Angela, to considering compulsory admission and very careful discharge planning and follow-up (see Chapter 2).

Conclusion

This chapter has focused on the need to consider the person in the context of their family. The family context is vital to understanding the person in more depth, to exploring opportunities to develop the person and their family's ability to work with and improve their mental health, and to ensuring that everyone is as safe as possible. Systemic ideas are relevant for mental health social work intervention at all levels. They might provide ideas for better grasping what is going on for the individual and for identifying opportunities for change. Family work also emphasizes the need to understand how families respond to mental health problems and to equip them with the knowledge and skills they require. Finally in this chapter the child care dimension of mental health social work has been discussed. This is central to the messages from *Think Child, Think Parent, Think Family* (SCIE, 2009) which, if fully implemented, should address some of the past difficulties between mental health and children's services. In any case, you should consistently and routinely ask about children, identifying any support needs or concerns and, vitally, ensuring these are communicated and addressed.

Recommended reading

Carr, A. (2006) *Family Therapy: Concepts, Process and Practice* (second edition). Chichester: John Wiley and Sons.

Smith, G., Gregory, K. and Higgs, A. (2007) *An Integrated Approach to Family Work for Psychosis: A Manual for Family Workers.* London: Jessica Kingsley.

Social Care Institute of Excellence (2009) *Think Child, Think Parent, Think Family: A Guide to Parental Mental Health and Child Welfare.* London: SCIE.

Recommended websites

The Association for Family Therapy and Systemic Practice in the UK – a good site for information, standards and other resources about family therapy. www.aft.org.uk

The Early Intervention in Psychosis IRIS Network in the UK and the website of the Early Psychosis Prevention and Intervention Centre (EPPIC) in Melbourne both provide useful information on early intervention in psychosis and the role of family work. www.iris-initiative.org.uk and www.eppic.org.au

Parental Mental Health and Child Welfare Network – a source of expertise on mental health in families affected by parental mental health problems, through training, good practice guidance, research and publications. www.pmhcwn.org.uk

9

Working with Communities

National occupational standards

This chapter will help you meet the following National Occupational Standards for Social Work.

Key Role 2: Plan, carry out, review and evaluate social work practice, with individuals, families, carers, groups, communities and other professionals. Unit 7: Support the development of networks to meet assessed needs and planned outcomes. Unit 8: Work with groups to promote individual growth, development and independence.

It will also help meet the following National Occupational Standards for Mental Health.

- Develop and agree priorities and objectives for meeting the mental health needs of a population (SFHMH 51).
- Negotiate and agree with stakeholders the opportunities they are willing to offer to people with mental health needs (SFHMH 72).
- Work with groups and communities to develop policies, strategies and services to improve mental health and address mental health needs (SFHMH 59).

Case study

You are employed in a large voluntary organization that is very involved in working with disadvantaged communities in an inner city area. Of particular concern to these communities has been the rise in self-harming and suicidal behaviour amongst young men. You have been asked by your manager to find ways of dealing with and preventing these risky behaviours. The young men and community groups have been very distrustful of traditional forms of social work interventions, so you have to find ways of addressing these concerns and needs.

Learning outcomes

1. To critically analyse perspectives on community mental health and community work interventions.
2. To develop your understanding of a range of community based interventions with individuals and communities.
3. To apply these ideas to the case material.

Introduction: approaches to working in the community

In Chapter 1 we explained how mental health and organizational policies had developed in the last two decades. This chapter will critically examine the types of community-based approaches used in contemporary mental health services, some of which have been designed following a period of deinstitutionalization during the last two decades in the UK. We have chosen two approaches, each with its own strengths and limitations, to illustrate how you can deliver innovative services to clients their families and communities. The first we describe as the 'community mental health' approach, based on a conventional model of assessment, planning, intervention and evaluation (Payne, 1995). This is the predominant model that has been modified and used in mental health services, often involving a range of professional disciplines (see Chapter 10). CMHTs are often the vehicle used in the delivery of such services but, as we will see below, it is sometimes hard to define what is meant by a CMHT, and evidence for the efficacy of different types of these teams has been mixed. The second is a 'community work' approach where the practitioner uses community work skills in meeting need and encouraging communities of people who have mental health problems to make decisions for themselves.

We will use the case material to illustrate how a mental health social worker can choose either a community mental health, or community work, approach to working with vulnerable young men who have mental health needs. Policy makers, professionals and the wider public have become increasingly concerned about the complex social, health and educational problems faced by some young men; such views are often couched in discourses on risk and vulnerability. Levels of suicide and self-harm among young men have been rising in most developed societies (Biddle et al., 2006; Joe and Niedermeier, 2008). A number of factors may lie behind such behaviours; these may also explain professional and policy responses. It has been argued, for example, that increasing rates of suicide and self-harm coincide with greater numbers of children and young people being diagnosed with psychiatric disorders (Green et al., 2005). Polydrug use is common in some groups of young men, with high associations between cannabis use and other drugs (Kapusta et al., 2006). This, in turn, may lead to an increase in comorbid substance use and mental health problems (Fergusson et al., 2003). It has been argued that young men who had a substance use disorder by age 16 were at higher risk of incarceration or involvement in the criminal justice system (Richardson and Budd, 2003). Young men often encounter a range of other forms of social problems associated with poor educational outcomes and exclusion from the labour market (Hammer, 2003; McAlister et al., 2009). The social and cultural changes that have occurred in the last half of the twentieth century have also resulted in uncertainty about perceptions of gender and masculinity amongst young men (Benyon, 2002; Frosh et al., 2003), often expressed in risky, violent behaviours (Nayak, 2006). Unfortunately many are often reluctant to use health, social care and educational services for a variety of reasons, including feelings of embarrassment and stigma and a distrust of professionals (Armstrong et al., 2000; Biddle et al., 2006).

A community mental health approach

The multiplicity of problems faced by some young people challenges the way professionals and their organizations plan and deliver services. One of the difficulties in terms of the screening and assessment process arises in prioritizing need and risk. Adolescence is usually a time of physical, emotional and social change for young men and it can be difficult to judge what is normal and abnormal in some of the behaviours described above. This partly explains why there are debates about which aspects of young men's thoughts and behaviours become sufficiently worrying to be described, clinically, and diagnosed as a mental disorder. Nonetheless it is likely that only a small percentage of young men will be diagnosed in this way, although high levels of need continue to exist in many communities. As a professionally trained mental health social worker employed by this large voluntary sector organization you will have a significant role to play in identifying and meeting such need. Your organization is involved in a wide range of activities at individual, family and community levels, and sometimes referrals are made to you about young men who are at particular risk and vulnerability in the community.

It may be assumed that the role of the community mental health social worker is made easier by organizational changes that have occurred in the last few decades in the UK, a point we discussed in Chapter 1. In the 1980s the Barclay Report (in Horner, 2003: 92–4) recommended patch-based, generic teams that were thought to be more responsive to individual, family and community needs. The report led to debates about the purpose and function of social work but any optimism that this new space for social work could be developed was rarely achieved, particularly because these occurred at a time of financial retrenchment in funding for social services in the UK. A notable feature of policy development in more recent years has been the drive to support and manage people with mental health problems in community-based settings, and to avoid, where possible, institutional care. On the other hand poorly delivered community services tend to be fractured, lack flexibility and miss opportunities for engagement when high levels of need and risk become apparent but are missed (Reith, 1998).

Although the rhetoric of community care is manifest in policy statements and professional discourses, it is important for practitioners to be aware of the contested ideas on this subject (Kemshall, 2002). The CPA was designed to enable planners to identify and prioritize areas of need and risk that would attract resources to the community. Such initiatives were underpinned by other policies and legal statutes (DH, 1989; 1995a; 1995b; 2007a) that sought to support mental health users and carers with more flexible approaches. An idea was that interventions designed to support service users and their families could be effective in building essential social networks, accessing sources and ensuring that risks could be identified and managed. It has been argued that well-skilled mental health social workers can enhance bridging and bonding forms of social capital in this field, although more research in this area is required to establish the evidence base (Webber, 2005). This task, however, is made more difficult when there is a paucity of community-based resources available to clients, their families and mental health social workers (Leveridge, 2007).

A useful starting point for you to think about your own community care practice is to consider the generic model of care management described by Payne (1995, 2009). This model, a modified version of the case management approach used by services in the USA, became mainstreamed in adult services provision in the UK and was quickly adopted by social work planners and educators. The figure below, for example, sets out this process (Scottish Government, 2005). As you can see there are important relationships between the different parts of a process that begins with screening and then assessment before the planning, intervention and evaluation take place. Payne helpfully uses his updated model to indicate how important decisions should be made, not just about service users, but also about carers (see Chapter 6).

The general principles of this model are regularly transferred to community-based, mental health settings, often managed and delivered by CMHTs, and

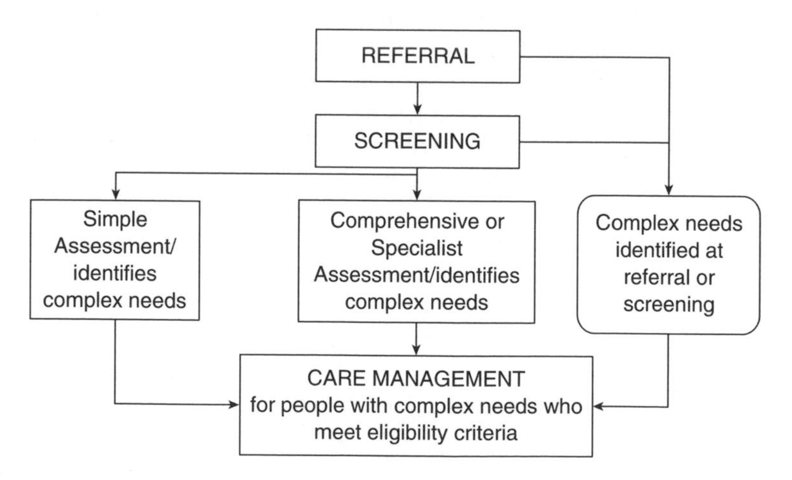

Figure 9.1 Care management model

underpinned by policies in the four jurisdictions of the UK, for example the CPA in England (Agnew, 2005). There is a wide range of types of community-based mental health teams and considerable debates about their efficacy. We will now briefly summarize the three types which we will discuss in more detail in Chapter 10 on multi-disciplinary working. Just to remind you again, these are: standard CMHTs; Assertive Outreach Teams; and Crisis Teams.

Community mental health teams

Standard CMHTs developed in response to legislative and policy changes associated with processes of deinstitutionalization from the 1950s to the 1980s (see Chapter 1). The pace for moving patients from hospital to community has, however, been variable, depending on regional and local decision-making processes. For example, most Victorian psychiatric hospitals in England were closed during a rapid period of change in the 1980s and 1990s whereas all of these facilities remain in use in Northern Ireland (Campbell, 1999). Regardless of the types of buildings and facilities, numbers of hospital beds have been substantially reduced in all regions of the UK, although numbers of admissions remain high. CMHTs were first established in the USA in the 1960s and became mainstreamed in the UK a few decades later, although as we mention in Chapter 10, there has been a great deal of variability in the make-up of these teams; some will be constituted on a multi-disciplinary basis, others more fragmented. Organizational impediments in Britain, particularly the division of responsibilities between local and health authorities, have sometimes hindered the development of coherent community-based services.

Despite these inter-professional and organizational difficulties, CMHTs are a fundamental part of statutory mental health services, with community mental health social workers playing important roles within these teams (DH, 1999b). Notwithstanding the variations in CMHTs across the UK, there are commonalities; they deliver services on a patch-based, geographical system; are constituted from key mental health professional groupings; and are often clinically led, although not usually managed by, a psychiatrist. They tend to work closely with GPs and primary health teams, and other professional referral agents, but working hours are usually restricted to normal office hours (nine to five). CMHTs also tend to provide generic mental health services across a wide range of interventions because they deal with a breadth of mental disorders and social problems (DH, 2002a).

Assertive outreach teams

As we mentioned in Chapter 1, one of the consequences of the rapid period of deinstitutionalization in the UK has been moving people with serious and enduring mental health problems out of hospitals and into community-based living. Policy makers and professionals had recognized that CMHTs may not be equipped to deal with the complex psychological and social needs of these clients especially if they were reluctant to engage with services but presented high levels of risk. For these reasons assertive outreach teams were increasingly used to concentrate resources and expertise in these areas, with a particular intention to prevent relapses and repeated admissions to hospital (DH, 2001b). Critics of this approach to community health argued that risk management as much as therapeutic benefit was the main driver behind the development of assertive outreach teams.

Crisis teams

The third type of team that is regularly found in community mental health services is crisis teams, again pioneered elsewhere in the world in the 1970s before their arrival in the UK. These are designed to provide a complementary approach to other types of teams, as the title suggests, using crisis-based, rather than planned methods (DH, 2001b). Best practice in using this approach implies core professional skills in engaging with clients in dynamic and changing circumstances and working closely with professional colleagues and other services to achieve, where possible, resolutions of crises, the prevention of relapse and possible hospitalization. As we will point out in Chapter 10, there are criticisms of these types of teams, particularly when other complementary parts of the mental health system do not function well; this can lead to a 'sticking plaster' effect with doubtful outcomes for clients and their families. At this point take some time to identify which type of community-based mental health team you work in (or which is favoured by your agency or locality) and consider the following questions.

Exercise 9.1

1 Can you compare your CMHT with any of those described above (you might feel you work in a different type of team altogether and that is fine)?
2 What are (a) its strengths and (b) its weaknesses?
3 What do you think is the evidence base for its effectiveness?

We will now consider the case material in these contexts. Many mental health social workers in the UK are employed by local authorities and will work closely with other disciplines, but others may be working in growing numbers of voluntary and community-sector organizations. Although, in this case, you are not employed in a statutory agency you can play a vital role in the assessment of risk and need, in conjunction with your local CMHT. Because you are not viewed as a statutory social worker, you can use your position within the agency to gain the trust of some groups of people with mental health problems who may be reluctant to access statutory services. At the same time you have a professional responsibility to engage with statutory services when you are assessing need and managing risk.

You have received the following referral. The mother of an 18-year-old man, John, approaches your agency. She is concerned that he is acting strangely, has stopped socializing with his friends and seems to be becoming more introverted. A youth club leader told her that John disclosed to one of his colleagues that he had been thinking about giving it all up and that he had thoughts of suicide. The ability to establish a good relationship with John and his mother will provide the foundations for the work you will be carrying out in the community. In particular there is a need to be careful not to be overly risk averse, but still mindful of the concerns that have been expressed about John's situation. Bailey (2009) helpfully reflects upon the balancing act that many experienced professionals perform in mental health services and rightly highlights how an empowering, non-judgemental approach at the early stages of engaging with clients can create a climate of trust. It is important that you explain your role to John using non-technical language, in particular emphasizing, using verbal and non-verbal cues, a willingness to be there, to 'stay with' him and not to over-react to views and ideas that he might express. This openness also entails the need to be frank and honest about the controlling aspects of the mental health social work role and the statutory requirement of duty of care and risk management.

The early stages of the assessment process require you to interview John alongside the parallel task of information gathering from other key informants (where possible with his permission). For example, you should speak to the leader of the youth club about his concerns and the events leading to John's self-disclosures. It materializes from this contact that John has had intermittent contact with the local CMHT, in particular a Community Psychiatric Nurse (CPN) who was asked by John's GP to call him after he disclosed suicidal ideation at an appointment. Because John is an adult, the process of assessment may be considered using CPA policies and procedures, although indiscriminate use of these may lead to his further alienation from helping services. John is just 18 years old, so the CAMHS (Department of Health, Social Services Inspectorate, Department for Education, 1995) guidance on a four-tiered approach to interventions would also be helpful in the assessment process. In additon you would need to speak directly to the CPN and GP as part of the assessment process.

After a number of meetings with John you manage to elicit some of the reasons for his low mood and suicidal ideation. A combination of events, including poor 'A' level results, unemployment and a series of broken relationships with friends, has undermined John's capacity to cope with life. With his agreement, and in liaison with the local CMHT, an agreed plan is put in place, with you as his mental health social worker taking a lead role. John should be involved at each stage of the planning process (Parker and Bradley, 2007: Chapter 3) and the key features of the plan are as follows:

- John will attend weekly meetings with you.
- John will attend fortnightly meetings with his CPN.
- John will attend a young men's group.
- You will enable John to apply for training and employment opportunities.

The key features of the plan involve three parallel processes. You will meet John on a weekly basis to help him talk through his concerns about the past and hopes for the future. He has agreed to re-engage with his CPN who will meet him fortnightly to assess his mental state and liaise with the multi-disciplinary team. Finally you will develop a holistic, psycho-social approach to helping him meet some of his aspirations in terms of engagement with his peers, and access to the labour market.

Over a six-month period the interventions begin to enable John to deal with his worries. He appears to be benefiting from the listening skills that you use (see Chapter 7) in the weekly meetings. In addition you have been able to use your knowledge of local services to access a community-based group for young men who are vulnerable and at risk of suicide. The community and youth workers in this project are specialist in their knowledge and skills in this area (Harland and Morgan, 2003). John is now feeling more confident about talking about his experiences with other young men in the group. As a result of these interventions, his CPN has noticed a change in his mood and has shared this with the CMHT. Meanwhile you pursue the issue of unemployment identified in the plan. You have arranged for John to speak to an employment advisor in the local Social Security Office and they are confident that they can offer either a training programme or a skills-based placement with a computer firm that would match his A-level subjects.

The planning and intervention processes appear to be working well, although it is vital not to become complacent, given what we know about the vulnerability of young men in these circumstances. You organize a review meeting six months later, which John attends along with the community worker who runs the group and John's CPN. At this review is agreed that he is now feeling more confident and that his ideas of suicide are less frequent. The plan is modified to enable him to take up a new training offer that he has received, and he agrees to meet with you once a month. You will keep in touch with the CPN where necessary in the future, but their involvement is no longer needed.

In conclusion, this account of a mental health social worker's involvement with John highlights some of the key roles that the experienced mental health social worker plays in using community-based strategies. This entails good interpersonal skills and a recognition of the often competing dimensions of care and control, as well a sound knowledge about community-based services.

Using the community work approach

Now that you have considered the community mental health model which is often used to help individuals, we want to explain how the alternative, although sometimes complementary, community work approach is also very helpful for mental health social workers. We have argued above that what we describe as 'traditional' approaches to community mental health services are crucial in the assessment and management of need and risk, but it is our assertion that community work skills are often not used enough in other contexts by mental health social workers; this is can be a missed opportunity to enhance the lives of clients and their families.

What is it, then, about community work perspectives that is important for experienced mental health practitioners? We know that social workers have blown hot and cold in their interest in using these approaches, often as a result of fluctuating policy imperatives in this field. What was fashionable in the 1970s receded in the 1980s, only to return in a revamped form in the 2000s (Popple, 2000; 2006). An early indication of the value of this approach for social workers was the suggestion by Twelvetrees (1982) that a community work style could have advantages for social workers but he also argued that success was only possible if adjustments were made to attitudes about relationships of power between professionals and communities. In addition social workers had to be prepared to acknowledge the complexities and uncertainties associated with this hybrid role. All current UK governments have encouraged providers to engage with communities in planning and delivering services, although concerns remain about policies that substitute relatively well-funded projects for services that are provided by the voluntary and community sectors but not fully supported by the state. Notwithstanding these concerns, there is a convincing argument for mental health social workers to use community work skills in their practice.

Although there are many definitions of 'community' and debates about what constitutes 'community work', there is some degree of consensus on the core meaning of these concepts (Ledwith, 2005; Popple, 2005). However there are also some concerns about how community development programmes can be systematically evaluated. Mayo (2009) suggests that there are opportunities across a range of these traditions either to accept traditional and technicist views on practice, or to adapt a more radical, transformational view on work with clients and communities; these variations are reflected in the literature on the subject. Community work approaches are valuable when addressing the needs of disadvantaged communities and groups and when challenging neo-liberal assumptions about the causes and solutions to inequalities (Popple, 2006). In one study of community development approaches with BME mental health service users, workers used a range of empowering interventions by supporting self-help groups and promoting social inclusion and race equality (Seebohm, 2010). The arguments for community work and community development are often strongly made in support of anti-poverty strategies and these should have some resonance with mental health social workers because of the marginalized lives that many people with mental health problems face (a point we make in Chapter 4). Being labelled 'mentally ill' often leads to a range of social disadvantages, not least exclusion from the labour market and with it poverty, alongside other factors associated with stigma (Repper and Perkins, 2009). Strier (2008) outlines five community anti-poverty strategies that social workers may use, depending upon which model of community practice is preferred:

1 *Neighbourhood and community organizing*: This is a common approach that targets particular communities and their social and physical environments,

to enable communities to confront and deal with these issues. They are often supported by local or central government.

2 *Developing functional communities*: This approach is usually associated with particular issues, and the intention is to build an activist-led capacity to confront authorities.
3 *Community development*: This approach, often by central and local government as well as other funders, is designed to enable communities to make use of resources and investments, by adopting a bottom-up methodology to build capacity and leadership.
4 *Social planning:* This involves strategic and operational plans to supply services and ensure that there is interdepartmental, interagency design and delivery, sometimes with little involvement by communities.
5 *Advocacy model:* This is where activists engage in a range of strategies (as advocates, lobbyists, mediators, trainers, spokespersons) to effect change at policy and governmental levels. In the process of this activity empowerment at different levels occurs.

Now take a moment to consider the following exercise.

Exercise 9.2

Consider Strier's five strategies. Are there similar approaches to community work and development in your area and how do you think these fit with the social work role when working with clients with mental health problems?

Community work: meeting the mental health needs of young men

We hope that you will be able to identify at least some opportunities for the community work approach with your clients. We will now consider how a community work approach can be effective in dealing with the issues that arise from the case study. We start from the premise that our understanding of the mental health needs of vulnerable young men must be informed, not just by individualized, clinical judgements about thoughts and behaviours, but also by the way that these problems are socially constructed or caused (Rogers and Pilgrim, 2009). Mental health social work practice should be underpinned by a critical awareness of power and social structure: 'Social workers can utilize the empowerment-base approach in assessments by exploring the power, powerlessness, strengths and resources at the individual, interpersonal and socio-political levels' (Teater, 2010: 67). Such contexts are important when we seek to explain the causes and solutions to the problems faced by young men with mental health needs (Hatfield, 2004). One way of operationalizing community work is to describe and analyse the micro levels of skills, knowledge and values that inform community work practice (but without losing the important awareness of politics, policy and structure). Mayo (2009: 133) provides a useful list of transferable skills that social workers should consider in the context of this form of intervention in and with the community. Some of these will now be utilized to illustrate mental health social work practice using this skills-base approach to community work.

Engagement and partnership working

You may be in a good position to engage with vulnerable young men because you are employed by an agency that values its involvement with local communities. A crucial part of your role will be to gain the trust of community workers who have access to young men using a variety of methods that are not often used by statutory services, including street work, youth centres and links with a range of provider agencies. It is likely that they will appreciate the specialist knowledge you might bring to their work with these young men, as long as this expertise is used sensitively and in context. For example, what they require is a form of consultancy that you can offer in exceptional situations when young men are at risk to themselves or others because of their mental health problems; it is important to recognize, however, that many situations of risk are manageable by skilled practitioners, whether they have been social work or community work trained.

Assessment

Although you may be asked to carry out individual assessments in the community work setting (this approach was describe earlier in the chapter), you might prove to be just as effective by becoming involved in an area-based needs assessment. As Mayo points out this often involves the use of participatory action research strategies that engage with communities in empowering ways. You have established through your networks that, across your geographical area of work, small pockets of young men appear to be detached from their peers and are involved in drug and alcohol misuse that often leads to their involvement with the police and alienation from the wider community. Their behaviours are reported to be risky, both in terms of self-harm and aggression towards others. A good start would be to access young men who are keen to become peer researchers, who could be provided with supervision to carry out a street-based needs assessment of these problems. It materializes in street interviews that the young men feel stigmatized and have little access to suitable educational and employment opportunities. Building upon this rapport with them and using your skills of report writing and advocacy, it is possible to effect change at different levels in the system. For example, it is necessary to summarize the key points of the community assessment and to make these findings available to health and social care planners and providers in your local authority area. After several meetings with local authority managers, a number of interventions are planned.

Groupwork

Some of the young men who were interviewed feel secure enough to agree to participate in a group process that allows their thoughts and feelings to be aired. Although therapeutic approaches to groupwork are used widely in mental health services, in community work settings their function is more likely to offer space to enable participation and empower those whose voices are not often heard. Although it can sometimes be difficult to achieve substantive and long lasting structural changes in this field, the process of engaging with and enabling disadvantaged groups is a positive aspect of this sort of work (Ferguson and Woodward, 2009: 138). Alongside the peer researcher you could co-lead a group with the young men over a time-limited period. The group is deliberately non-directive and seeks to encourage group members to talk about their experiences, hopes and aspirations. What emerges, slowly at first and then in more detail, are stories about failed educational experiences, barriers to accessing employment opportunities and perceptions of hostility and persecution by the police and general public. The young men grow in confidence enough to disclose their anger about being excluded from the wider community, describing how they construct their norms and roles built around perceptions of masculinity and their use alcohol and drugs to deal with anxiety and stress and social interactions. They identify a number of areas that they feel could help them better manage their lives. They also want to have opportunities to attend community-based facilities that they have been excluded from and need advice about how to access training and employment opportunities.

Negotiating and resourcing

Fortunately you are in a good position, given the role that you occupy in your agency, to negotiate with some key gatekeepers for resources in your local community. You contact a number of youth workers and explain the work that has been carried out with the young men. Good negotiation skills help in the discussion with agencies to explore how a specialist approach might work best with these particularly vulnerable individuals, especially one that has been designed to deal with the problems that were highlighted during the groupwork process. It is hoped that this more specialist engagement with the young men may enable them to deal with the experiences of self-destructive and alienating behaviour; this will also enable them to communicate better with their peers and the wider community. In order to build their social and economic capacity, they are individually assessed for employment and educational projects that are being developed by the local further education college. This also entails a review of their welfare rights, for example in terms of their access to jobseekers' benefits.

Monitoring and evaluation

After three months it is important to review and evaluate the work that has been carried out with the young men. As the discussion implies, there is a complex range of skills and processes involved in using community work approaches in this field. The monitoring and evaluation processes should summarize and assess the level and nature of interventions across these domains, using the core skills you have built up as an experienced mental health social worker. In summary your work with the young men involved carrying out a community assessment in partnership with peer street workers. This enabled you to address some of the needs that emerged from the assessment to co-lead a group that encouraged the young men to discuss aspects of their vulnerability and aspirations. The final stage of community work led to individual assessments about their educational and employment needs and negotiating with educational and other agencies to access resources.

Conclusion

We started this chapter by explaining that community-based interventions in mental health services can be varied and illustrated this point by using case study material about vulnerable young men to demonstrate community mental health and community work approaches. As in other chapters we have emphasized the importance of gaining a critical awareness of the policy and organizational contexts that shape mental health social work practice. In the first part of the chapter a more individualized, person-centred intervention was discussed – a recognizable approach used by many CMHTs. The second part of the chapter examined the different, although it could be argued complementary, approach of adopting a community work perspective to explore interventions with a group of young men at risk. In both contexts, the significance of a flexible skills base, the ability to engage and communicate and an awareness of the structural and organizational impediments to mental health social work practice was highlighted.

Recommended reading

At a glance 18: Personalisation briefing: Implications for community mental health services (www.scie.org.uk/publications/ataglance/ataglance18.asp). A practice-based overview of how principles of personalisation should be applied to community settings.

INFED www.infed.org/community/b-comwrk.htm#aspects. This provides a good overview of the historical development of community work, including competing perspectives and approaches to practice.

Mantel, G. and Backwith, D. (2010) 'Poverty and social work', *British Journal of Social Work*, 40 (8): 2380–97. A critical discussion of past and present debates about the relationships between poverty and social work, with some focus on community work approaches.

10

Multi-Disciplinary Working

National occupational standards

This chapter will help you meet the following National Occupational Standards for Social Work.

Key Role 2: Plan, carry out, review and evaluate social work practice, with individuals, families, carers, groups, communities and other professionals. Unit 6: Prepare, produce, implement and evaluate plans with individuals, families, carers, groups, communities and professional colleagues.

Key Role 5: Manage and be accountable, with supervision and support, for your own social work practice within your organization. Unit 17: Work within multi-disciplinary and multi-organizational teams, networks and systems.

It will also help meet the following National Occupational Standards for Mental Health.

- Lead the development of inter-agency services for addressing mental health needs (SFHMH 48).
- Lead the implementation of inter-agency services for addressing mental health needs (SFHMH 85).
- Enable workers and agencies to work collaboratively (SFHMH 79).

Case study

Derrick is 25-year-old Afro-Caribbean man who has been homeless for two years and is currently living in hostel accommodation. You are a member of a forensic CMHT and Derrick has been referred to you by the hostel manager. He explains that Derrick has had a number of different diagnoses since the age of 16 including schizophrenia and bipolar disorder. More recently a multi-disciplinary assessment has indicated that he may have a borderline personality disorder. His behaviour has become more erratic in recent years, involving a number of criminal convictions leading to fines and a suspended jail sentence. You have been asked by your team leader to assess Derrick's needs.

Learning outcomes

1 To gain an understanding of organizational, multi-disciplinary and multi-agency dynamics drawn from the policy and research literature on mental health and social care services in UK.
2 To develop an understanding of key skills that can be used to negotiate professional and organizational boundaries.
3 To consider the value issues raised by the interface between mental health, offending behaviour and the diagnosis of a personality disorder.

Introduction

Mental health social workers play important roles within a range of multi-disciplinary mental health teams across the UK. The following chapter builds upon the introductory discussion about the types of community teams in the UK. We begin by describing and reviewing the literature on multi-disciplinary team working and then summarize the structures, as well as the strengths and weaknesses of three types of multi-disciplinary teams that you will be familiar with as a mental health social worker – the conventional CMHT, the Assertive Outreach Team (AOT) and the Crisis Team (CTs). The second part of the chapter will focus on the case material, explaining how a mental health social worker employed in a forensic CMHT should assess and intervene alongside multi disciplinary colleagues.

Analysing multi-disciplinary working

Most mental health social workers either participate directly in multi-disciplinary teams or are involved in partnership with other professionals. In this first section we will be exploring the often contested ideas associated with multi-disciplinary working. Although there are many perceived advantages to such working, not least the expectation that there will be good outcomes for service users and carers, in practice the interface that social workers have with other professionals can be fraught with ambiguity and conflict, as well as offering rewards when systems work well (Smith, 2009). These include boundary disputes, perceptions about status, competing responsibilities and conflicts about the knowledge base. Smith argues that the sources of conflicts can, in part, be explained by issues of *structure* (the position and role of social workers in systems and bureaucracies); issues of *policy* (how policy shapes social workers' practices with other professionals); issues of *organization* (how individual authorities and organizations arrange multi-professional working); issues *of procedure* (the legal and policy requirements that guide practice); *professional difficulties* (a failure to recognize the legitimacy of other professional views); and *personal idiosyncracies* (non-co-operation caused by interpersonal differences). If these impediments can be dealt with, and that is often a difficult task, then benefits should accrue, in terms of increased efficiency, more responsive, holistic services and creative practices that should improve services for clients and carers. He makes the point that social workers can be particularly effective in multi-disciplinary settings given their particular skills in service co-ordination, the value base and the relational qualities that are used in social work practice. Now take a moment to think about Smith's summary of the difficulties and opportunities that social workers experience in working with other disciplines, and reflect upon your own practice. Which areas have been problematic for you as a mental health social worker and which have been rewarding?

In addition to these problems that arise in multi-disciplinary practice, there are continuing debates about what the term means. Morris (2008: 2) helpfully uses the following three-part classification to distinguish the detail and levels of multi-agency working that most social workers will experience.

Multi-agency working as a process of arriving at some shared strategic goals but with single agency activity within the overarching plans (Galvanil, Jordan)

Multi-agency working as a process of involving collective goals for service provision but with independent execution of the various tasks and activities by each professional at the point of service delivery (Edwards et al., Ward)

Multi-agency working as a shared process of both planning and direct delivery of services with co-location of staff and services (Hughes and Prior)

Mental health social work involves a wide range of different types and levels of contact with other professionals, but in this chapter we will be focusing on the third type of activity described by Morris where social workers are employed to work alongside other professionals on the same site.

Multi-disciplinary team working in community mental health services

We will now examine the three types of community mental health teams where most multi-disciplinary working takes place in the UK: conventional CMHTs; AOTs and CTs. The emergence of these teams followed the process of deinstitutionalization which began in the UK in the mid 1950s. Burns (2004) argues that some community-based initiatives were associated with the introduction of the 1959 *Mental Health Act,* and similar legislation in Scotland and Northern Ireland. This led to the increased use of day hospitals, therapeutic communities, and some measure of resettlement and out-patient care. It was not, however, until professionals started to meet together regularly, to discuss and agree on what they could do to meet the person's needs, that CMHTs, as we think of them now, emerged.

Community mental health teams

The CMHT has been defined in terms of the composition of the team, how it operates, who the service is for and the types of interventions it carries out (DH, 2002c). However, there is a good deal of variation in the composition of CMHTs, depending on the resources available to the organization, levels of local need and the relationship to other forms of mental health services. A CMHT usually comprises nurses, social workers, occupational therapists, psychiatrists, psychologists and, increasingly, support workers. The Department of Health (2002c) suggests that a typical CMHT, covering a population of between one and six thousand, with a caseload of up to 300–350, would consist of three to four CPNs, two to three social workers, one to one-and-a-half Occupational Therapists, one to one-and-a-half clinical psychologists, one consultant psychiatrist, one to one-and-a-half senior house officers and one to three mental health support workers. These government guidelines suggest that there would be a limited workload of 35 cases per team member. It is also acknowledged that adequate IT and administrative support is essential for a fully functioning CMHT. These teams are designed to offer a wide range of services and interventions, including advice and information, psychological and psychiatric interventions, social support and liaison with other agencies (DH, 2002c). CMHTs typically operate from nine to five, Monday to Friday, with some flexibility to arrange to see people outside those hours if need be, but usually not to provide crisis cover. The majority of referrals tend to originate from primary care professionals, with some teams only accepting referrals from GPs. Others, however, are directly accessible by any organization and self-referrals. These teams are often structured to work both with people with time-limited mental health problems and those with severe and enduring mental health problems. The balance between these overlapping groups is one of the key operational issues for CMHTs (Burns, 2004: 54). Achieving this balance can be problematic and, at times, clients with severe and enduring problems can be neglected due to the immediate nature of the shorter-term work carried out by CMHTs. Another related criticism of the model is that CMHTs can become unfocused, inefficient and overwhelmed, which may then lead to professionals feeling demoralized and de-skilled (Paxton, 1995). This is a point we return to later in the chapter.

Assertive outreach teams

It has been argued that the process of deinstitutionalization has led to many people, who would previously have received long-term institutional care, now being offered community services. But some of those clients will have a combination of characteristics which traditional services will find difficult to respond to effectively (Sainsbury Centre, 1998). This small population are sometimes referred to as the 'revolving door group', 'the new long-stay' or the 'difficult-to-engage' group. The key characteristics of this group include difficulties with engagement, risk to self and/or others and high use of in-patient services. People referred to as AOTs usually have complex needs including:

- 'A history of violence or persistent offending
- Significant risk of persistent self-harm or neglect
- Poor response to previous treatment
- Dual diagnosis of substance misuse and serious mental illness
- Having been detained under mental health law on at least one occasion in the past 2 yrs
- Unstable accommodation or homelessness' (DH, 2001b: 26).

The original model, then called 'Training in Community Living', was developed at the Mendota Mental Health Institute, Madison, Wisconsin and described by Stein and Test (1978). Its focus was to ensure that service users could develop the skills necessary to maintain community living. Stein and Test provided a comprehensive account of how the model worked, and it is interesting to consider how little the approach has changed since the 1970s. When a person presented to services for admission to hospital they were interviewed by a member of the community treatment staff and, where possible, returned to a community setting to begin working with the team. There was an explicit emphasis on avoiding hospital admission, but when this occurred it was used only when a person was assessed as being at immediate risk of committing suicide or homicide, or when a hospital environment was necessary to manage very high doses of medication. Even if someone was admitted the aim was to minimize their length of stay so that work in the community could begin as soon as possible. The focus, once the person was in their community setting, was on *in vivo* learning. In other words, the intervention focused on the development of community living skills in the setting in which these skills were needed and were going to be used. This approach, however, also acknowledged the problems of trying to transfer learning across settings, particularly the difficulty of teaching skills for community living following time in a ward environment.

The 'treatment' part of the intervention consisted mainly of community activities, but also the use of medication where appropriate. The emphasis was on workers doing activities with their clients rather than for them, thus providing support and encouragement rather than direct help. The range of activities included the basic tasks of managing their home, through negotiating interactions in shops, to facilitating access to different forms of employment. Another aspect of the 'treatment' was the recognition of the importance of social and recreational activities so that staff helped to build up the client's confidence and informal support network to the point where they could manage more independent living. This aspect of the 'treatment' was a good example of the greater flexibility this model offered, not only in terms of evening and weekend working, but also in terms of what people viewed as therapeutic mental health practice. In general, staff attempted to maintain what would now be considered a strengths-based approach, involving a focus on the client's abilities and resources and promoting a positive approach rather than concentrating on symptom management. The original model was managed by a professionally mixed hospital staff team who had been specifically retrained for this approach. This included a psychiatrist, psychologist, social worker, and occupational therapist, as well as nurses and support workers, or aides, as they were known at that time. The team were encouraged to spend the majority of their time with clients in community settings supporting them to develop the skills they needed for greater independence. Hours of operation were from 7 a.m. to 11 p.m., seven days a week, with one member of staff on call overnight providing 24-hour cover.

There are several key differences between the UK description of the model and the original. The first is that the UK approach tends to focus on the individual responsibility of each worker, suggesting a key worker system, whereas the Madison model emphasizes a team approach and shared responsibility. There appears as well to be some difference in the emphasis placed on paid employment for clients, although this may reflect the differences in opportunities between the early 1970s in Madison and the 2010s in the UK. Finally, the UK type acknowledges the importance of considering how assertive outreach fits into the wider system of mental health care, whereas in Madison in the early 1970s there were virtually no generic community mental health services to integrate with.

The Department of Health (2001b) guidelines emphasized the specialism of the team, with a clear responsibility for the full range of services necessary to meet their clients' needs, including care-co-ordination, which would promote continuity of care. These suggested that the majority of these services should be provided in community settings and for as long as they were needed. They also recommended that individual caseloads should not exceed 12 and there should be a doctor who was an integral member of the team and had medical responsibility for their caseload. In the guidance there was also explicit reference to providing effective inter-agency working and processes of risk assessment and management, perhaps reflecting the political and social concerns of the time. The evidence for the effectiveness of assertive outreach in the UK (Killaspy et al., 2006; Killaspy et al., 2009) has been less compelling than the early studies in the USA, possibly because the standard services it is compared to are much better than was the case in the USA, and increasingly these specialist teams are being merged back into CMHTs.

Crisis teams

CTs were pioneered in the 1970s in Madison, Sydney, and more recently in the UK in North Birmingham, and can be defined as 'an alternative to in-patient hospital care for service users with serious mental illness, offering flexible, home-based care, 24 hours a day, seven days a week' (Sainsbury Centre for Mental Health, 2001: 2). Crisis resolution/home treatment can be offered in a range of settings and provides alternatives to in-patient care (DH, 2001b: 11–12). McGlynn and Smyth (1998: 13) break down the involvement of CTs into four stages that will be recognizable to most mental health social workers:

1 *Assessment*: rapid response; home assessment; multi-disciplinary assessment; focus on the 'here and now'; involvement of relevant others, carers and family; problem-solving approach; risk assessment
2 *Planning*: team approach; focused crisis plan with short-term goals; based on negotiation with client; decisions about the number of visits and level of input; based on available options; focus on discharge planning at an early stage
3 *Intervention*: establishing engagement and therapeutic alliances; allocate 'named worker' in the team; commence medication; family work; frequent monitoring and continual assessment; explanation as to why crisis has happened; practical intervention, for example benefits, day care; giving a contact number of team in case crisis occurs during treatment
4 *Resolution*: linkage with ongoing care; maintaining contact until services are well in place; offering learning opportunities about why the crisis happened; relapse prevention strategies; coping strategies; joint visits with key worker prior to discharge; developing longer- term community care plans; involving family/carer; liaising with relevant others, and requesting feedback from client.

Although CTs in many parts of the UK provide an essential service when emergencies in the community take place, they are sometimes isolated from general mental health services (Rosen, 1988), leading to what has been described as 'a sticking plaster for all the faults in existing services'(Sainsbury Centre, 2001: 6).

CTs may prevent hospitalization (Johnson et al., 2005a; 2005b; Glover et al., 2006; Barker et al., 2011), but it has been argued (Joy et al., 2006) that leaving service users and their families in the community may lead to potential risk and harm in the following ways:

1 Interventions may be difficult to monitor.
2 They may be time consuming and stressful to implement – thus leading to staff burnout.
3 Fragmented services may result in poor long-term follow up.
4 They may be expensive.

In a more positive vein, a recent review of research on service users' views of crisis services (Winness et al., 2010) concluded that a commitment to community-based services partnership, and user-empowerment were the foundation of successful CT interventions. You should now consider the following exercise.

Exercise 10.1

Spend some time summarizing the origins, purpose, and advantages and disadvantages of these different teams

Evaluating CMHTs: two examples

We now want to examine, in more depth, some of the issues faced by mental health social workers in managing professional roles and relationships, using two well-known studies of CMHTs. Most mental health social workers will have had variable experiences of working with other mental health professionals; these can be conflictual and frustrating, but also at times rewarding, reflecting Smith's (2009) views on this subject discussed earlier in this chapter. An early, widely quoted study was revealing in this respect. Onyett et al. (1995) used a mixed methods approach to examine the work of CMHTs in England (of 517 teams identified, 302 returned questionnaires). A high proportion of the teams were located in a specialist community base centre and were involved in a wide variety of activities, including therapeutic interventions and help with social problems. They provided specialist services for people with severe and enduring mental health problems as well as those making a first contact with services. At this time (1995) they were less involved in providing services for carers, and there was little evidence of cultural competence in working with BME communities. The interesting findings for the purposes of this chapter focused on the various working of the different professionals. Although some teams met regularly and used a single referral route, indicating a degree of coherence to multi-disciplinary working, a high proportion of other teams were more fragmented in terms of the regularity of meetings and systems of referral. Some used professional managers and care management processes were often carried out by the teams themselves. Interestingly, strong lines of professional, rather than general managerial, responsibilities were evident in many responses to the survey. As we will point out below, the introduction of general management after this study took place has altered these professional relationships; today community mental health social workers are much more likely to be supervised by a non-social work professional. CPNs and social workers were generally present in most teams; psychiatrists were also members, but sometimes not on a full-time basis. Other professionals such as psychologists and occupational therapists were also often included in CMHTs. Onyett et al. (1995) highlight one potential difficulty in these arrangements, namely that quite a lot of multi-professional engagement was carried out on a part-time basis.

The second part of Onyett et al.'s study surveyed practitioners' views of their teams. Medics reported the highest levels of satisfaction, with social workers and community support workers reporting the lowest. There were considerable levels of burnout and sickness, again with social workers reporting higher levels of stress than some other colleagues. This issue of stress and burnout amongst mental health social workers has since been confirmed in more up-to-date research (Huxley et al., 2005). Onyett et al. speculate about some of the reasons for these levels of stress and burnout across professional groupings in CMHTs. They suggest that a clear and valued role, and a positive sense of belonging within the team, could be protective against stress. Three areas of work were viewed to be particularly rewarding: team/multi-disciplinary working; being effective clinically; and clinical work generally. Conversely the three main impediments to positive experiences of work were: a lack of resources/workload; bureaucracy; and management. In the final section of the study the authors examine the experiences of individual disciplines, and it is important to summarize the findings on mental health social work responses. Interestingly these social workers reported that they did not have particularly large caseloads, nor did they work with a large proportion of people with severe and enduring mental health problems. Over half reported being emotionally exhausted, and as having a comparatively low sense of personal accomplishment and job satisfaction compared to other professionals. Onyett et al. speculate that these relatively high levels of stress and dissatisfaction may be associated with a lack of clarity of role, but suggest that the then imminent introduction of the CPA and joint authority working may provide a more positive, enhanced role for social workers for the future.

In the years since Onyett et al.'s seminal study, the landscape of multi-disciplinary working in community-based services has changed, but many fundamental characteristics of team working remain. We are now going to focus on a more recent study that examined this area. Freeman and Peck (2006) examined the work of generalist and specialist mental health professionals across five localities in England. They used a number of methods, including focus groups with service users and carers, in-depth interviews with members of these two types of teams and a survey of staff views about their experiences. By this stage in the policy cycle, earlier systems of mental health care, as described by Onyett et al. (1995) above, had become more mainstream, but there was increasing pressure on services caused by funding and organizational change. As a result they found some boundary problems, particularly between CMHTs and CTs leading, ultimately, to perverse outcomes such as compulsory hospital admissions. In addition there were ongoing problems with many CMHTs whose workloads were becoming so elevated, partly because of problematic interfaces with AOTs and CTs, that they were unable to provide the generic services they were designed to. There were, however, some good examples of the system working well where extra resources and proficient management approaches were introduced and maintained. When specialist integrated teams (AOT and CT) worked well, then service users and carers were more likely to find them of benefit. The messages from such research are also echoed in other reviews of the literature (Mental Health Commission, 2006). Now consider the following exercise.

Exercise 10.2

We believe that some of the findings from these two important studies will resonate with some of your working experiences. If you do work in a community-based team (whether generic or specialist) take a moment to consider whether any of the findings make sense in terms of your practice.

Application of theory to the case material

So far we have considered a range of models for multi-disciplinary working and the different types of community-based multi-disciplinary teams that exist in the UK. Importantly, these discussions revealed considerable practice variations and debates about meaning and the fidelity, or otherwise, to models. If you work in one of these teams, then this sense of variability between and across organizations is something you will easily recognize. Despite these problems of form and function, multi-disciplinary approaches to mental health care and treatment, if well delivered, promise many benefits. In this section we will explore some of this potential in our discussion of the case material.

There are a number of contextual issues that will help you consider Derrick's situation before a multi-disciplinary assessment and intervention should take place. In considering the complexities of the case we want you to draw upon some of the learning from earlier parts of the book, particularly Chapters 3 and 4, and also from Chapter 11. Mental health services for people from BME communities in the UK have been consistently criticized on a number of grounds, including the use of higher levels of coercion and of medication-only regimes, alongside the tendency by white professionals to use Eurocentric assumptions in making clinical judgements about diagnosis and risk (Keating, 2002). Ferns (2005) appeals for professionals to become more culturally competent in dealing with black service users, by addressing the following areas of practice: organizations should always seek to humanize their interaction with service users; teams of professionals should always build services that are inclusive and that address inequalities; services to ethnic minority populations should be more creative, reflecting cultural nuances; services should also be accessible, with much better systems of information; and many service users and carers value practical assistance as much as therapeutic interventions.

Unfortunately Derrick has now been diagnosed with a borderline personality disorder, a controversial diagnostic category that, historically, has been viewed as difficult to treat. In their systematic review of the research literature on the subject Warren et al. (2003) found there were weaknesses in most of the methodologies used to justify treatment and care. Of particular note was the lack of an agreed definition about the condition. There is some limited evidence that, for people with borderline personality disorders, therapeutic community-based approaches in secure settings may be effective and cognitive behavioural and dialectical behavioural interventions have demonstrated some positive outcomes. It may also be the case that psychodynamic day hospital-based programmes can be effective in treating self-harming people with borderline personalities. On the other hand there is only limited evidence of the efficacy of drug-based and physical treatments for these conditions.

Although there are a variety of approaches to dealing with personality disorders and, as we have mentioned, many not well evidence-based, Bateman and Tyrer (2004) argue that team-based structures of service delivery are probably more beneficial than individual professional interventions. Specialist community mental health teams may be more appropriate and provide holistic approaches to assessment and intervention. Now take some time to consider Bateman and Tyler's (2004: 427) summary of the types of tasks that multi-disciplinary team carry out in this field:

- development of a management plan agreed with the patient
- referral to specialist services if necessary
- risk assessment
- co-ordination of a crisis plan
- identification of a keyworker
- access to acute in-patient care
- family and social support
- prescription of medication.

As a part of the forensic multi-disciplinary team the community mental health social worker has a range of valuable contributions to make in these processes, but only in areas where the skills and knowledge base are secure (for example, the prescription of medication is outside the social worker's remit, although you should be prepared to advocate for Derrick if you believe that the use of medication is being counter-productive). Fortunately you are a member of a specialist team that recognizes your experiences and skills level, because of your previous role as a probation officer. You have been asked to consider three of these areas: assessment/risk assessment; family and community support; and the development of a management plan. A number of boundary disputes inevitably arise, but these can be managed through open discussion at team meetings and supervision.

Assessment and risk assessment

You have been allocated a key work responsibility for Derrick and therefore take a central role in the first stage of the assessment process. The point we made earlier about cultural competence and humanizing the experience for clients is crucial at the initial stage of contact. Derrick has been living a rootless life and has drifted away from his family and community, and his behaviours have not been well understood by professionals and helping agencies. This has led to his involvement with the police, resulting in convictions for petty crimes. A confounding issue here is the way in which mental health professionals have not been able, to date, to establish a diagnosis. You manage, for the first time, to carry out a detailed social history with Derrick, revealing that he had troubles during his teenage years when he was forced to live with grandparents after his parents separated. He lost interest in school and became involved in small-scale crimes with some his peers, as well as experimenting with a range of drugs. He had also been subjected to a number of violent racist attacks that had left him hospitalized. Derrick has always felt that professionals generally, and mental health professionals in particular, didn't really understand his needs and problems. He often rejected any advice that they had given him. It is important that, where possible, service users and carers should be involved in the planning and delivery of services in these circumstances.

An essential feature of forensic mental health social work is risk assessment, bearing in mind the need to avoid the excessively risk-averse practices that we described in Chapters 1 and 2. The team has a well validated risk assessment tool that is easily administered. When used with Derrick it has resulted in a score that indicates a mild to moderate likelihood of some form of intra- or interpersonal risk, but certainly not of the serious kind. In your clinical judgement, he appears much more likely to put himself at risk, either through neglect or by becoming vulnerable to abuse by others. Nonetheless this is still a risk that has to be managed, using a partnership approach with Derrick. At this early stage there is, with his permission, a good opportunity to engage in purposeful multi-disciplinary working. It may be that his needs are so complex that he will require the specialist input of colleagues from your organization's AOT. In the meantime, one of your team members, a forensic psychologist, has agreed to carry out a fuller assessment of Derrick's problem behaviours with a view to developing a cognitive behavioural programme, and in preparation for this, you contact the hostel manager to help you fill out, in more detail, what the nature of the incidents were that led to the difficulties with the police. Derrick appears to trust you enough to agree to this information being shared.

Family and social support

In the meantime you begin to explore with him some of the issues that appear to be troubling him, in particular his apparent isolation from his family and community. It has been argued that mental health professionals are not sufficiently knowledgeable about existing community-based BME resources in their local areas (Wilson et al., 2004). As we discussed in the sections above, a number of studies found that mental health social workers play a valuable networking and care planning role in multi-disciplinary teams, and the community development approaches (see Chapter 9) can be particularly effective in accessing resources and supports. This is, therefore, a good opportunity to introduce

Derrick to a local Afro-Caribbean mental health drop-in centre which uses peer and professional advocates to support young men in his situation. They also have access to support housing and employment opportunities; again, as a mental health social worker you are well positioned to strengthen these social networks in discussions with him during your weekly meetings. Unfortunately Derrick has lost contact with his family, but it may be possible to explore with him the reasons for this estrangement and whether it would be possible to re-engage with some of his family support system.

Develop and deliver an agreed management plan

As you move into the planning and intervention stages, a management plan is formulated with Derrick, multi-disciplinary colleagues and external agencies. Such planning is fundamental to the delivery of mental health services, especially where there are situations of risk and vulnerability caused by personality disorders. The plan should be regularly reviewed and all those involved made aware of their responsibilities. The initial assessment by the team is indicating that, using a tiered model (DHSSPS, 2010b: 25), Derrick is judged to have a level two risk where the following services could be recommended:

- community-based PD-specific treatments;
- a therapeutic community;
- community case management with PD practitioners;
- generic mental health services;
- access to mainstream community mental health services;
- access to community addiction services.

The multi-disciplinary team has now met once a week over a month to plan services for Derrick, and he is invited to two of these meetings to ensure that he is aware of the views of the team and encourage his commitment. He has agreed to the following.

You will remain with Derrick as his key worker and a contract is drawn up to meet with him on a weekly basis. In a discussion with the hostel manager, he is agreeable to stay on in the hostel on a temporary basis, and the manager will report any situations of risk that arise. Your clinical psychology colleague has now carried out a fuller assessment indicating that there have been quite deep-seated problems in Derrick's history of problematic behaviour that seem to involve relationships with family, and the limited social networks he has managed to maintain may explain his self-destructive behaviours. For this reason, it is agreed that he will be considered for a specialist, psychodynamically orientated therapeutic organization which has been contracted to offer places in a new residential unit designed to respond to the policy drivers highlighted earlier in the chapter. Most significantly, this referral to the therapeutic community, which eventually proves to be successful, does not mean that you are absolved from a key working role as part of the multi-disciplinary team.

We have already discussed the reasons why practice in this field should involve a consistent, well-managed approach which ensures that service users and carers receive good quality services and that risk can be quickly assessed and minimized. For those reasons you maintain contact with Derrick and the therapeutic community organization.

Review and evaluation

Derrick has now been living in the therapeutic community for three months and it is a good time to review his progress and any difficulties he is encountering. You have a busy caseload, but you have followed agency protocol in fulfilling your role as key worker for him. This entails regular visits to the therapeutic community where you meet with Derrick and the manager of the unit. They have reported that he had some initial difficulties in settling in and engaged in some 'acting-out' behaviours that appeared to be designed to test the capacity of staff and other residents to contain his emotional outbursts, although there was little risk associated with these and the staff were confident and competent in understanding and dealing with them. In the following months good progress is reported about the way that Derrick has been more comfortable in therapeutic group sessions with other residents and staff and has disclosed some issues of physical abuse that occurred in his adolescent years. These initial improvements are reported to a review meeting in the CMHT and a medium-term planning process is started. It is crucial that Derrick's progress in the therapeutic community is not disrupted, but some plans should be made, with him, about his possible future re-engagement with important social networks, including community-based groups and resources, and, possibly, some members of his family. Meanwhile you continue to provide an essential linking role between the work of the therapeutic community and the specialist forensic expertise of your team, once again demonstrating the significance of the mental health worker and the holistic, community-based approaches that are so valuable to CMHTs.

Conclusion

The mental health social worker is an essential member of the CMHT in the UK but, as we have argued in this chapter, the way we describe and analyse such CMHTs is open to some discussion and dispute. The first part of the chapter explored general principles and theories about CMHTs before discussing key research studies on the experiences of a variety of multi-disciplinary mental health teams. Despite the commonly reported difficulties that service users and carers, as well as professionals, report in making CMHTs more fit for purpose, when these work well they can be efficient in enabling clients to live more fulfilled lives and more ably managing risk in the community. The final sections of the chapter used the case material to explain the role of the mental health social worker in a specialist community mental health team, suggesting ways in which research findings and government policies can be interpreted and operationalized.

Recommended reading

British Psychological Association (2006) *Understanding Personality Disorder: A Report by the British Psychological Society*. Leicester: BPS. This is a detailed review of systems of classification and evidence-based practice in this area.

Department of Health (2003) *Mental Health Policy Implementation Guide: Community Mental Health Teams*. London: HMSO. A good, brief guide on the structure and purpose of CMHTs.

Mental Health Commission (Ireland) (2006) 'Multidisciplinary Team Working: from Theory to Practice, A discussion paper'. Dublin, MHC. A useful summary of literature and examples of good multi-disciplinary practice in community mental health services.

11

The Role of the Approved Mental Health Professional

National occupational standards

This chapter will help you meet the following National Occupational Standards for Social Work.

Key Role 2: Plan, carry out, review and evaluate social work practice, with individuals, families, carers, groups, communities and other professionals. Unit 4: Respond to crisis situations.

Key Role 5: Manage and be accountable, with supervision and support, for your own social work practice within your organization. Unit 16: Manage, present and share records and reports.

It will also help meet the following National Occupational Standards for Mental Health.

- Assess the need for intervention and present assessments of individuals needs and related risks (SFHMH 17).
- Assess, diagnose and formulate an individual's mental health disorder (FMH 1).
- Help an individual prepare for transition from secure institutional to community living (FMH 16).

Case study

Tom is a 52-year-old man who lives alone in a housing association flat. He was diagnosed with paranoid schizophrenia in his mid-twenties and has been in contact with mental health services since then. He has had many admissions to hospital over the years, mostly involuntary. Tom's mother lives nearby and is supportive of him. He also has some contact with his ex-wife (they divorced when he first became unwell), and their two children, now aged 28 and 26. Tom usually attends a nearby voluntary day centre and has ongoing difficulties managing to look after his basic needs. You are working in a Recovery Team that provides support to people with ongoing mental health problems and complex needs and

(Continued)

(Continued)

have been approved to carry out assessments under mental health legislation. You visit Tom every two weeks and over recent visits you have noticed that he has seemed more withdrawn, is smoking more and expressing some delusional, religious ideas. You have also been contacted by Tom's pharmacist, who knows him very well, to say that he has not collected his medication for the past two weeks. On your visit today Tom said that he could no longer attend the day centre, visit his mother or go to the local shops as there were evil forces working at these places which intended to harm him. He also stated that he thought that you may be working for these forces and so said that you should stop visiting him.

Learning outcomes

1 To understand the range of duties carried out by the Approved Mental Health Professional (AMHP).
2 To develop skills relevant to assessments for admission, report writing and presenting evidence to an MHRT.
3 To be aware of professional and ethical dilemmas raised by compulsory intervention, the use of coercion, rights/risks, reciprocity.

Introduction

In Chapter 2 we reviewed the purpose and use of mental health laws across the UK. You will now be aware that there is some variation in the types of statutory roles that mental health social workers play in these jurisdictions, depending on where they practise. In this chapter we will now focus on the particular role of the AMHP in England and Wales, and issues of risk assessment that need to be considered as part of this role. A key difference between the AMHP and the MHO in Scotland, and the ASW in Northern Ireland, is that the role is not only restricted to the profession of social work. In addition there are important contrasts between the reasonably self-contained and manageable systems of administration and law that exist in Scotland and Northern Ireland, when compared to the more complex organizational and legal structures across England and Wales. The chapter will begin with an overview of the background and development of the role and its introduction to England and Wales in 2008 and discuss a number of key policy and practice areas in the context of the case material.

The role of the AMHP

Reflections on the past

In Chapter 2 the development of the role of the ASW was discussed and explained. A key expectation about this exclusive social work role was that practitioners would provide a wider, systemic perspective that would complement the clinical judgements made by medics when assessments were being made about compulsory admissions to hospital. In the 1980s there were much clearer differences between multi-disciplinary professionals in terms of training, role and focus. The separate structures of health and social services in Scotland, England and Wales (unlike Northern Ireland) also helped emphasize this sense of difference and independence; ASWs were employed by local authorities and clinicians by health authorities. Interestingly in Northern Ireland, with its integrated system of health and social welfare, the Bamford Review is proposing a continuance of the ASW role, despite the fact that professional boundaries have generally been broken down into more integrated mental health services.

The arguments for the AMHP role

It was the Richardson Committee (Department of Health, 1999b), when reviewing the 1983 Act, that first suggested extending the role of applicant to other professions for two main reasons. First, mental health services had developed since the 1980s and new forms of practice had changed the nature of the social work function within multi-disciplinary teams. In particular the government were keen to integrate systems of health and social services delivery and management. The Committee also argued that a modification of the role would complement other proposed changes to mental health law, in particular ending the role of NR as applicant and having a judicial body involved after the assessment period. This second argument offered by the Committee was less clear and convincing. Perhaps it was envisaged that ending the role of NR as applicant would increase the number of assessments needed and that revised judicial processes would offer the independence that the ASW role had originally been intended to provide. A third, and more pragmatic, reason for changes to the role, not expressed by the Committee, was the shortage of ASWs in England at that time (Huxley et al., 2005). In the period since the Richardson Report there has been considerable debate about the extension of the role of applicant to other mental health professions, despite resistance by some social work organizations. For example, the British Association of Social Workers has argued that other professions do not provide the same level of independence and so the protection of the service user's rights could be diminished (Rapaport, 2006). These are arguments that appear to have been listened to in Scotland and Northern Ireland where social workers solely retain this role.

The legal responsibilities of the AMHP

Brown et al. (2008) and Barber et al. (2009: 10–11) have described the functions of an AMHP as being involved in:

- deciding whether to make an application for compulsory admission to hospital for assessment or for treatment under Part 2 of the Act (s13);
- deciding whether to make an application for guardianship under s7 of the Act (s13);
- informing or consulting with the nearest relative (NR) about an application (s11);
- conveying a patient to hospital (or a place of residence) on the basis of an application as above (s6);
- responding to a referral from a NR for an MHA assessment, and, if an application is not made, giving the reasons for this in writing to the NR (s13);
- providing a social circumstances report for the hospital for any patient detained on the basis of an application made by the NR (s14);
- confirming that a CTO should be made and agreeing to any conditions (s17A);
- agreeing to the extension of a CTO (s20A);
- agreeing to the revocation of a CTO (s17F);
- applying to the county court for the displacement of an existing nearest relative and/or the appointment of an acting nearest relative (s29);
- having the right to enter and inspect premises where a mentally disordered patient is living (s115);
- applying for a warrant to enter premises under section 135 to search for and remove a patient to a place of safety (s135);
- having the power to take a patient into custody and take them to the place they ought to be when they have gone absent without leave (AWOL) (s138);
- interviewing a patient arrested by the police on s136;
- making a decision on whether a patient subject to s136 should be moved from one place of safety to another.

The knowledge base

The AMHP is a relatively new phenomenon, so there is limited research evidence and other forms of knowledge about the role. Early reports suggest that other professionals, especially nurses and some occupational therapists, are training to carry out this role but initially in relatively small numbers (Hunter, 2009; Parker, 2009; The Care Quality Commission, 2010). AMHPs are required to have specialist legal knowledge of the specific statutory roles, grounds and duties, as discussed in Chapter 2, but this specialist knowledge needs to be supported by a much broader understanding of mental health policy, practice and research issues and practice-based awareness of local area and services. There are three areas of the knowledge base that generate considerable discussion and debate when considering the AMHP role. We will now outline these.

Risk assessment and management

A key aspect of the AMHP role is the assessment to determine whether the risk criterion for compulsory intervention is being met. The risk criterion for detention for assessment is specified in s2.2(b) of the Mental Health Act 1983, namely that the person 'ought to be so detained in the interests of his own health or safety or with a view to the protection of other persons'. The risk criterion for detention for treatment is that 'it is necessary for the health or safety of the patient or for the protection of other persons that he should receive such treatment and it cannot be provided unless he is detained under this section' (s3.2(c)). For a Community Treatment Order it is that 'it is necessary for his health or safety or for the protection of other persons that he should receive such treatment' (s17A.5(b)). Chapter 4 of the Mental Health Code of Practice (Department of Health, 2008) provides clear guidance on the range of factors that should be considered in the process of this assessment.

Mental health professionals are increasingly being expected to balance issues of care and control – this is a theme we have returned to throughout the book. Importantly they are required to manage quite complex situations of risk, but this may not always involve the use of legal and other forms of coercion and the Mental Health Act Code of Practice specifies that all alternative means of providing care and treatment should be considered. Ryan and Morgan (2004; ix) argue 'that (paradoxically) the best route to safety may be the one that seeks to empower users, not control them, which seeks to help them create a better and fulfilling life'. Laurance (2003; 189) also asserts that 'Services that involve and maintain contact with people with mental health problems offer the best protection for the public. Ethics and pragmatism thus fall satisfyingly together'. The aims of increasing voluntary engagement, user satisfaction with services and public safety are interdependent rather than contradictory or opposing goals (a point we make in Chapter 5). Laurance makes the point that engaging service users is crucial in this field:

> The most effective way to improve the safety of the public and the care of those who are mentally ill is to devise services that genuinely engage users and meet their desire for greater control so that they are encouraged to seek treatment and lead stable, risk-free lives. If, instead, politicians pander to public prejudice and adopt a heavy-handed, coercive approach, they will drive people away from services and increase the risk of further tragedies. (2003: xxi)

In December 2006, the National Confidential Inquiry into Suicide and Homicide by People with Mental Illness published its second five-year report covering the period March 1999 to December 2004. It was provocatively entitled *Avoidable Deaths* (National Confidential Inquiry into Suicide and Homicide, 2006), referring to the relatively small proportion of the deaths in this area identified as those which were potentially preventable by clinicians. The report identified key factors which may have been relevant in these cases and it is these issues are important to consider in the context of attempting to reduce risk: 'In 1,017 cases (19%), the respondent believed that the suicide could have been prevented ... Cases of suicide by patients with severe mental illness (3,966) were seen as more preventable (727 cases, 20%); suicides by people with drug dependence (206 cases) were seen as the least preventable (22 cases, 14%)' (2006: 92). The report acknowledged that the calculation of preventable suicides was crude, depending as it did on the sometimes idiosyncratic views of clinicians. Nonetheless,

> Clinicians identified 41 (21%) cases in contact with services within 12 months of the homicide where the homicide could have been prevented. These included 23 (56%) patients with schizophrenia, 6 (15%) with more than 5 previous admissions and 25 (61%) who had been previously detained under the Mental Health Act. Clinicians were able to identify factors that would have made the homicide less likely. The factors most frequently mentioned were better patient compliance, closer contact with the patient's family, closer patient supervision, improved staff communication and better staff training. (2006: 138)

A second issue of obvious concern to mental health professionals is the variable rates of suicide, and possible relationships with mental ill-health, across the UK. The Third Annual Report of the National Suicide Prevention Strategy for England (National Institute for Mental Health in England, 2006) reported the lowest suicide rate (at 8.56 per 100,000) since records began. This included the first sustained downward trend in the numbers of young men committing suicide for 25 years. In England and Wales from 1993 to 2003 suicides declined by 9 per cent (although more recent developments in the economy may reverse this). Over the same period in Northern Ireland, however, there was a 27 per cent increase, which included a doubling of suicides by men aged 25–34 (Main, 2006). Suicide seems to be a particularly severe problem in North and West Belfast, an area of extremely high levels of deprivation: in 2002 the suicide rate was 19 per 100,000 compared to 10 for the whole of Northern Ireland (Health Action Zone North and West Belfast, 2005). Again, it is difficult to determine whether any of these deaths could have been prevented if better services had been available, but the Suicide Prevention Strategy for Northern Ireland (DHSSPS, 2006) is attempting to address these complex issues.

In terms of homicide, the Audit Commission reported in 1997 that over the previous 20 years, which covered the transition to community care described in Chapter 1, the number of homicides committed by people with mental health problems did not increase, while those committed by others more than doubled. The Confidential Inquiry into Suicide and Homicide by People with a Mental Illness (1999) emphasized that most homicides are committed by young men who are unmarried and/or unemployed and that substance misuse is common. Shaw et al. (2005) demonstrated that the overall rising rate of homicides could be correlated with the social exclusion and inequalities affecting young men. Between 1997 and 2005, however, the National Confidential Inquiry into Suicide and Homicide by People with Mental Illness (2010) reported an increase in the numbers of homicides committed by people with mental health problems (from 22 cases in 1997 to 48 cases in 2005), but detailed analysis of this trend suggested the most likely explanation related to substance misuse and that the increase may not be continuing.

Personality disorder

Another issue that provokes some debate and much controversy in practice, is whether mental health services should be used to care for people who have a primary diagnosis of personality disorder (we discussed this in more detail in Chapter 10 on multi-disciplinary working). Personality disorder is a controversial diagnostic label which describes a range of problematic thought processes and behaviours often associated with considerable childhood trauma and adversity which may not be routinely addressed by mental health professionals, despite the fact of high numbers of clients experiencing such distress: 'Research suggests that about ten percent of people have problems that would meet the diagnostic criteria for personality disorder. Estimates are much higher among psychiatric patients, although they vary considerably: some studies have suggested prevalence rates among psychiatric outpatients that are in excess of 80 percent (Alwin et al., 2006:. 1).

At present in Northern Ireland, a primary diagnosis of personality disorder is specifically excluded as grounds for detention in hospital unless it is accompanied by another form of mental health problem. Under the proposed new capacity-based framework it would be included if the person's decision-making capacity was sufficiently impaired. In England and Wales it is included if there is appropriate medical treatment available, although the definition of medical treatment is very broad (see Chapter 35 of the Mental Health Act Code of Practice). The first Act of the Scottish Parliament, the Mental Health (Public Safety and Appeals) (Scotland) Act 1999, widened the definition of mental disorder to explicitly include personality disorder and this is also included in the definition of mental disorder in the 2003 Act. A Home Office report, in 2003, reviewed the evidence on treatments for personality disorder and found that, although there were weaknesses in the methodology of most of the research, 'a large number of studies have been carried out which suggest that various treatments may have a positive impact among personality disordered offenders on a range of outcome measures' (Home Office, 2003: 5). It is also important to remember that the current legislation in all jurisdictions does not in any way exclude people from being offered voluntary treatment, but it appears that sometimes in practice people with personality disorders do have considerable difficulties accessing appropriate care and treatment (Bateman and Tyrer, 2004).

Substance misuse

The arguments about the need to include or exclude people with personality disorders often run parallel with discussions about substance misuse. There are perhaps three points that are important to reinforce in this respect. Firstly the prevalence of substance misuse among people with other mental health problems (sometimes referred to as dual diagnosis) has been found to be high. The Pan-London Study of assertive outreach and CMHTs reported a 29 per cent six-month prevalence of some form of substance misuse or dependency (Priebe et al., 2003). Secondly, in the same study 30 per cent and 34 per cent of assertive outreach and CMHT staff respectively rated their training in substance misuse as very inadequate, an issue which may negatively affect the effectiveness of services (Billings et al., 2003). Finally, in considering both personality disorder and substance misuse, there is a general point about mental health services prioritizing services for people who need them most, even if there is considerable difficulty in accessing, engaging and working with these groups. For example, it has been noted that 'A number of studies point to a historical reluctance among mental health professionals to work with client groups who are perceived as not improving or frequently relapsing' (Graham, 2004: 463). Although it may be reasonable to argue that community mental health services may not be the best approach for people whose difficulties are primarily related to personality and/or addiction, it is still necessary to consider which services are best and/or how the approach could be adapted to work effectively with these issues.

Applying theory to the case study

So far we have briefly summarized the origins of the AMHP and core functions; this area of mental health social work is extremely varied and challenging. It will often involve working in crisis and pressured situations and there may also often be unexpected and unusual aspects to individual cases. On the other hand, there are a number of generic tasks and processes that will be common to the majority of assessments. The AMHP will need to:

- gather information;
- interview the service user;
- consult the named person/nearest relative/nominated person/carers;
- discuss with colleagues;
- assess risk;
- assess capacity;
- consider the alternatives to admission;
- consider the legal grounds and rights;
- devise a plan;
- ensure that plan is safely implemented.

The situation also requires a high level of skills, especially around engagement, assessment, communication, assertiveness and multi-disciplinary/inter-agency working. It is perhaps the area of mental health social work practice that also generates the most difficult and complex ethical issues (see Chapter 10). These areas of knowledge, skills and ethical issues will be explored by considering the process of how an AMHP responds to the case study. So let us begin by considering the following exercise.

Exercise 11.1

Identify any guidelines within your organization for the completion and reporting of an AMHP assessment.

Preparation

In the case study you are already working with Tom and have been visiting him every two weeks. This means that you have considerable background information about his circumstances and mental health problems, but you should still attempt to gather and review all relevant information in preparation for your assessment. It may be possible to identify at this stage whether the person has an advance statement or decision in place and how to access it. Advanced statements may be devised when a person is well and has the capacity to make important decisions. These enable service users to express their positive and negative preferences for future mental health care and treatment when their capacity may be impaired. Advanced statements should, if at all possible, be respected by mental health professionals but are not legally binding. An advance decision, in contrast, is legally binding but its scope is more narrow as it is an advance refusal of specified forms of treatment (Henderson et al., 2008). If it is not known whether either of these is in place, the person should be asked about this as part of the assessment process being carried out by the AMHP (see Chapter 17 of the Mental Health Act Code of Practice). The preparation stage also requires you to consider how, when and where the assessment will be conducted. These decisions will be influenced by a range of factors including: the availability of those conducting the clinical assessment; whether there may be issues around locating the service user and/or gaining entry; and whether there are initial indicators that raise concerns about risks during in the process of assessment.

Most mental health social workers in their everyday practice recognize the various levels of potential conflict and coercion that they encounter; the AMHP should be particularly conscious of the inherent power they possess in forcing a person to do something that they do not want to do. This in itself raises the potential risk of violence involved in the role. You should also be mindful that Tom has expressed some delusional ideas, that he believes that there may be evil forces and that you may be working for them. There is a range of ways of managing these risks. It may be, if you know the person well and there is no history or other indicators of aggression and violence, that you will decide to go ahead with the assessment without further measures. You may perhaps also consider asking a colleague to accompany you, but there is a need for caution here as well; often processes will be delayed because of difficulties in liaising with other professionals, so your colleague would need to provide their commitment to what might end up being a lengthy assessment. If you have sufficient concerns then the police should be asked to attend (see paragraph 4.46 of the Mental Health Act Code of Practice). Depending on the level of your concern, this could be for police officers to accompany you throughout the assessment process and to accompany the person to hospital. In this case, there are some concerns about how Tom may respond to the assessment, especially given his delusional ideas about evil forces, and so it may be appropriate to ask the police to be available initially outside or near the address.

Assessment

Even though Tom knows you well, part of your introduction on this visit should be to explain that you are there to determine whether you feel he needs to be admitted to hospital and, if there are sufficient concerns about him, that you have the legal powers available to go ahead with this even if he refuses. There is a danger here that when a person is made aware of your role and the powers available to you, they may agree to a voluntary admission because of this and so be de facto detained but not have the safeguards provided by the law available to them (Mental Health Act Commission, 2009). It may also be that a person, even if they are reluctant to go into hospital, may wish to avoid the possible stigma and discrimination associated with detention and the potential implications for emigrating, insurance and employment. In practice, in some cases, there may be some negotiation around whether formal powers are used but this is a complex ethical area and if someone has been refusing admission and then agrees in response to an explanation of the law, then the reasons for this agreement should be explored (Campbell and Davidson, 2009).

There are a number of key components to your assessment and these may be included within a standard format depending on where you work. The central aspect of the assessment is the interview with the service user. This may be complex, especially if the person is very distressed, delusional and/or unwilling to engage at all. If possible though, this interview should involve exploring the background social circumstances, the issues leading up to the assessment, the person's view of what is happening, and what they think might help. Within this it is essential to assess the risks of harm to self, others and of self-neglect, and the person's strengths and other protective factors. There are many different models and guides available for assessing risk. The DHSSPS (2009b: 14–15) suggests that, in general, risk assessment should contain the following tasks.

- collecting and communicating information on risk behaviour(s);
- identifying the causes and consequences of risk behaviour(s);
- considering individual static and dynamic factors;

- identifying external risk factors (e.g. service issues);
- formulating a risk statement based upon risk factors and protective factors;
- developing risk reduction and management plans; and
- monitoring, feeding back, evaluating and modifying plans.

Another aspect of your assessment should be determining whether the person has the mental capacity to make the decisions that are being considered. The assessment of capacity is necessary in Scotland where significantly impaired decision-making ability (SIDMA) is one of the criteria for compulsion. In Northern Ireland it is proposed that capacity would be the single gateway criterion under the new legal framework. In England and Wales, however, this is not one of the criteria. Nonetheless it should still be considered as an important aspect of assessing need which helps in your understanding of the person's situation and what may be required to support them in making the required decisions.

The next key task in the assessment process is to identify the service user's NR, determine whether suitable and, if so, inform them (if application is for assessment, s11(3)) or consult them (if the application is for treatment, s11(4)(b)). This is one of the statutory duties of the role, and there is developing case law which suggests that AMHPs may not have made sufficient efforts to do this in the past (Davidson, 2009). However, the NR's perspective may also provide vital information about what has been happening. You should also consider contacting others who may be also contribute to the assessment. In Tom's case, this could include communication with the day centre, other members of his family and members of the multi-disciplinary team. As we mentioned in Chapter 2, the least restrictive alternative should always be considered by the AMHP, so alternatives to admission should also be explored. This is not only good practice, it is required by both mental health and human rights law. If you are considering depriving someone of their Article 5 right to liberty then you have to explicitly demonstrate, including in your report, that you have considered all possible alternatives. In Tom's case this could involve considering whether the Crisis Team could become engaged and offer short-term intensive support in his home; in any case they will probably be part of the assessment process as the gatekeeper to in-patient beds. Other options could include an increase in support from the day centre, his mother, other family and yourself, although it seems unlikely that Tom will agree to more input from the people he has been avoiding. The final aspect of the assessment process is to discuss with your clinical colleagues whether you feel the grounds for a compulsory intervention are being met.

AMHPs and the use of CTOs

As we discussed above, a key statutory function of the AMHP is to assess risk, and, if necessary, become involved in compulsorily admitting service users to hospital. We believe that mental health social workers should be able to provide particularly skilled interventions in this area because of the holistic approaches they take towards assessment and intervention (see Chapters 2 and 3). However difficult this role is, and the problematic ethical dilemmas associated with it, mental health social workers are well positioned to consider issues of empowerment and risk management in the community. One other key function of the AMHP in England and Wales involves the use of CTOs. We have already described and analysed some of the advantages and disadvantages of using CTOs in Chapter 2; notably the evidence base is particularly weak. Nonetheless, it may be that if Tom were to be compulsorily admitted to hospital then a CTO might be considered later on, if it was judged that this would provide the least restrictive outcome. Barber et al. (2009: 42–7) describe the processes involved in using CTOs in England and Wales, which are quite similar to those used in Scotland and proposed for Northern Ireland. Key to the AMHP is working closely with Tom, his Responsible Clinician (RC), carers and community-based services. Critically a CTO cannot take place unless the AMHP agrees that all the criteria are being met, including that appropriate medical treatment is available for Tom (s17A(5)(e)). Typically the AMHP will liaise with the RC across a number of mandatory and discretionary conditions, medical and social. Although there is some legal ambiguity in this field, it is argued by Barber et al. (2009) that practitioners should be mindful of deprivation of liberty issues. CTOs can be revoked, or discharged, but again, there must be agreement between the RC and AMHP.

Review

Although the role of the AMHP is particularly focused on the statutory functions described above, we argue that the mental health social workers who are often AMHPs can both humanize what are often coercive processes and prevent the need for compulsory powers to be used. It has been demonstrated that if people feel that they are being listened to and respected during these processes, even if the outcome is compulsion, they are less likely to feel coerced (Lidz et al., 1995). As part of your role with Tom, a concerted effort should be made to continue and build on his engagement with community services, following the revocation of his CTO. This recent admission and use of compulsion should also be seen as an opportunity to attempt to prevent the need for a future use of legal powers. There is a range of possible ways by which this could be attempted from informal discussion to more structured, written work and plans. This process may also identify other important aspects of what Tom is hoping for in the future, perhaps about what he is doing during the day and relationships with his family that he would like to develop.

An initial issue may be to explore with Tom about what his recent experiences were like for him. The experience of compulsory laws involves a potentially traumatic process, and so Tom should have the opportunity to talk about these issues and whether, in retrospect, there were aspects of the process he now feels were necessary. There may be a chance to look in detail at what the early signs of relapse were for Tom and these may form a pattern, or relapse signature, that you could both, and perhaps Tom's family as well could be alert to in the future. Joint crisis plans have been demonstrated to reduce the need for compulsory admissions (Henderson et al., 2004) and using this type of more structured plan would be a further opportunity to talk both about the recent admission and how Tom would prefer support to be provided in the future. Mental health social work often involves working with people who are reluctant to fully engage with you and/or the care, treatment and services that might address their mental health problems. If someone's capacity to make these decisions is not impaired and they do not present any risk to themselves or others then clearly this decision should be fully respected and perhaps just some information should be provided about services. At the other end of the spectrum there will be times, as with Tom, when formal legal powers are needed. In between no coercion and formal compulsion is a wide range of approaches and strategies that can be used by mental health social workers when there are concerns about risk and capacity but formal powers are not necessary and/or possible. Szmukler and Appelbaum (2008) have suggested a spectrum or hierarchy of treatment pressures which consists of persuasion, interpersonal leverage, inducements (such as housing), threats (for example of hospital admission) and compulsory treatment. There are ethical complexities with all of these forms of pressure but they are routinely used in mental health social work (Davidson and Campbell, 2007) and it is extremely important that you carefully consider why, how and with whom these approaches are used and whether or not, in each case, they are indeed necessary.

Conclusion

In this chapter the role of the AMHP has been explored. The historical development of the role was discussed and the range of AMHP duties outlined. The relevant knowledge for the role was also considered and it was argued that this consists of a much wider base than just the detail of the laws and codes of practice. It is also necessary to have greater general knowledge of mental health issues and of the local area in which you are working. Some of the complexities and ongoing debates about the law were also covered, including the difficulties with risk assessment and whether personality disorder and substance misuse should be within the scope of mental health law. The second half of the chapter worked through the case study of Tom to explore the role of the AMHP in practice and highlighted some of the ethical tensions and positive opportunities this challenging work creates.

Recommended Reading

Brown, R. (2009) *The Approved Mental Health Professional's Guide to Mental Health Law* (second edition). Exeter: Learning Matters.

Littlechild, B. and Hawley, C. (2010) 'Risk Assessments for Mental Health Service Users: Ethical, Valid and Reliable?', *Journal of Social Work*, 10(2): 211–29.

Webber, M. (2008) *Evidence-Based Policy and Practice in Mental Health Social Work*. Exeter: Learning Matters.

Recommended Websites

Department of Health Mental Capacity Act 2005: training materials at www.dh.gov.uk/en/Publicationsandstatistics/Publications/PublicationsPolicyAndGuidance/DH_074491

Mental health law online at www.mentalhealthlaw.co.uk/

Social Care Institute of Excellence Mental Capacity Act Resource at www.scie.org.uk/publications/mca/index.asp

Conclusion: Looking to the Future

Introduction

We hope that we have succeeded in our aim to helping you understand the complexities of the mental health social work role and encouraging you to continue to update your knowledge and skills base in this important area of practice. All qualified social workers in the UK, as part of their professional registration, are requested to demonstrate ongoing training, learning and development. We believe that this approach will further strengthen the professional status of social work in mental health services. Our intention in the book was to stimulate you to think critically about the role and recognize that, although there are rarely times when professional judgement can be absolutely certain, it is possible to examine competing arguments and value the importance of research to support your views about practice. In this concluding section we will summarize the broad perspectives presented in the book before looking to the future to assess the challenges and opportunities for mental health social workers.

Reflections on the book

Let us now take a bit of time to consider the learning outcomes of the book. We started by presenting what we believe is the core knowledge base for mental health social work. As we mentioned in the Preface, our view is that there is a distinct and significant role for social workers in mental health services above and beyond the generic skills, knowledge and values that are shared with other professionals in this field. For this reason we did not provide a comprehensive account of 'the medical model' with its many, detailed formulae for diagnosis and prognosis; that task has been covered in many other texts (Brown et al., 2009), nor have we provided complete coverage of the account of the role of the AMHP (Brown, 2009). The book has instead focused on other, contested areas of knowledge that are fundamental to our understanding of the mental health role. It has included discussions about the construction of mental health policy and organizational arrangements for the delivery of services in the UK. It also included reviews of theories on models of mental disorder and discrimination that are fundamental to recognizing the many difficulties that people with mental health problems face in terms of individual, family and community contexts. Throughout we have been mindful to highlight the growing awareness of positive experiences that clients report and which can be built upon in partnership with professionals; the empowering approaches, including the recovery approach, are notable in this respect.

We hope that the preceding chapters assisted you in reflecting upon the application of ideas to practice, using a range of case studies. We deliberately chose practice contexts that would be relevant and recognizable to many mental health social workers, working with a wide variety of client groups in different settings. We believe that engaging with these case studies, and the depth of the knowledge and evidence base that was used along the way, will enable you to consider how these ideas can be applied to the world of work you are involved in. This will also enable you to reflect upon this learning as part of your PQ studies. At the start of the book we acknowledged the necessity of a reasonably standardized approach to such learning through the use of National Occupational Standards and social care council requirements, but we hope that you have taken on board our appeal to avoid a mechanistic attitude to learning. Although the notion of 'reflection' in social work education and training is often an over-used idea, when incorporated into styles of learning it can lead to productive outcomes, leading to what we would describe as the thoughtful practitioner who recognizes the often piecemeal, contested nature of knowledge in the field of mental health policy and practice. If you continue in this mode, then you can advance your skills and awareness of theories which can be adjusted to deal with the many issues that face both you and your clients. This is a virtuous professional space to occupy.

Looking to the future

Throughout the book we have emphasized the complex and contested nature of our knowledge of mental health and interventions that seek to improve the lives of clients. You will not be surprised, therefore, to read that we believe this necessary uncertainty is, paradoxically, a predictable aspect of the mental health social work role as we look to the future; why should this be any different from the experiences of the past, described in the early chapters of the book? We now wish to highlight what we feel are a number of important areas of knowledge and practice that will shape the way mental health social workers carry out their function and roles as we look towards the next few decades. In the spirit of the way we have conceived this book, we argue that these are necessarily interrelated themes that are hard to disentangle.

Partnerships and social movements

When we discussed the way the profession developed within the UK's welfare state it was suggested that social workers have, in the view of many clients, occupied a specific position within welfare bureaucracies. It is only in the last decade that the power of mental health professionals has been somewhat diffused within the system, partly as a result of public criticisms about the management of risk, but also because of the actions of bottom-up social movements demanding change. There seems little doubt that this is a major area of change which mental health social workers will have to engage with in the future. It also seems reasonable to assume that in 50 years' time social workers will view our current practice as oppressive and paternalistic, just as we now reflect upon the well intentioned, but segregated and often damaging institutional care of the past. There has been some progress in shifting the balance of power in mental health services more towards its appropriate place with service users, but practice is still often characterized by a focus on symptoms and deficits with insufficient efforts to work in partnership to promote independence and recovery. Mental health social workers have a key role with multi-disciplinary teams to ensure that the wider family and societal context of the service user is assessed and considered and, based on that, that the full range of interventions across levels is advocated for and provided. There are a number of key drivers that may facilitate further positive change here. Service users and carers continue to lobby and campaign, at all levels, for better services. There also appears to be some potential in the developments in personalization for service users to have greater control and choice about the services they feel are most beneficial, although it is difficult not to suspect that some of the motivation behind these developments is to reduce funding. As was seen with the deinstitutionalization process, unholy alliances between positive policy directions and governments who are determined to cut public spending can produce radical change but often with other negative outcomes. A key issue, therefore, will be how effectively service users, carers and mental health professionals engage with politicians and the wider public to ensure they understand the issues and the services that are needed, and so provide the necessary funding. Mental health social workers should view this political engagement as a key aspect of their role, vital as it is in ensuring that service users and carers have access to the full range of mental health services.

Risk and dangerousness

Concerns about risk, and especially of violence to others, have had a disproportionate influence on mental health services and practitioners over the past 20 years. It may be that this is part of a wider societal concern about risk issues and is heavily reinforced by media portrayals of mental health, but mental health professionals have responded to these pressures by also developing a disproportionate concern with risk. Risk assessment and management are, and will continue to be, central aspects of mental health social work practice, but there is an urgent need for a more open and clear assertion that it is not possible for us to accurately predict all suicides and homicides and that, tragically, these will continue. All efforts should be made to increase the usefulness and accuracy of risk assessment but we need to be honest about the limitations of our current knowledge and practice.

Anti-stigma campaigns and initiatives at all levels also have an important role in informing the debate about mental health and risk. There has been considerable progress in public attitudes towards people with mental health problems and the general policy shift towards mental health promotion and the prevention of mental health problems should ensure that public awareness of mental health issues continues to increase. As has been repeatedly argued in this book, the most effective way to minimize risk is to provide effective, accessible services that have the resources to engage positively with people in a societal context that doesn't segregate, isolate and discriminate against people with mental health problems.

Organizations and other professionals

Similarly we expect substantial changes in the way that organizations are shaped and managed to deal with the issues faced by mental health systems in the UK. It would appear that there will be no return to the apparent certainty and centralized approach to service delivery that characterized the high point of the welfare state. The shift rightwards in the politics of welfare that has occurred in all jurisdictions across the UK presents various challenges to most professionals employed by the state, but even here there are opportunities to achieve change and mental health social workers should be well placed to embrace these. An area which does seem to offer great opportunities is the developments across government to address mental health, especially in terms of social housing, criminal justice, education and employment. The economic or pragmatic case for appropriately responding across all aspects of government is very strong and repeatedly reinforced by estimates of the direct and indirect costs of not doing so. Mental health social workers also have opportunities to influence their multi-disciplinary colleagues, by working together on ways to further develop existing community resources. Community mental health services need to engage with the communities they are working in. There is also a great range of opportunities for mental health social workers to further develop their therapeutic skills. This is dependent on the resources being available to fund the additional training and time they will need, but specialist therapeutic training will make them more effective practitioners and so the case should be made, repeatedly if need be.

The legal context

For a variety of reasons, mental health social workers, across the UK, will continue to carry out a range of substantive, mandated functions as we look toward the future. We have argued in this book that we must be very careful about how the profession uses such powers and resists, if it can, the tendency for the state to increase the use of coercion, particularly in community-based settings. In particular the use of CTOs is not well understood generally by mental health practitioners and the evidence base for this is frail. We know even less about how mental health social workers are carrying out these functions. In addition the complex nature of capacity laws raises many ethical issues that we believe should be debated by mental health social workers. The respect for autonomy within capacity laws and the development of supported decision making to avoid the need for substitute decision making are significant and potentially very influential developments. The argument for a separate mental health law that enables compulsory treatment, even if the person has the capacity to refuse it does seem anomalous and is perhaps an aspect of mental health practice that will be viewed as both negative and extraordinary in the future. The proposed capacity-based law in Northern Ireland may contribute to informing these debates.

International opportunities

In this, the final area for discussion, we want to emphasize the importance of thinking internationally when we consider the mental health social work role. When we reflect about the many issues that we have raised in the book, and the variety of sources used, we confess that not enough was said about other, international experiences of the mental health social work role. We have tried to make sense of the gradual divergences that have occurred following political devolution within the UK and the impact these have had on mental health social workers, particularly in the area of legal responsibilities. But it is a particularly British (we take a risk here in including Northern Ireland in this identifier) view that is presented and one that is often assumed by policy makers and professionals to be comparable with other systems in the developed and developing world.

This is not necessarily the case and it is vital that the specific historical, cultural and societal context/s in the UK should be considered in the process of developing mental health social work policy and practice in other parts of the world. In some countries, such as Australia, the mental health social work role seems to be increasingly merged into a generic mental health worker or case manager role. There are also countries where the distinctive role of mental health social work has been retained and, in some cases, attracts a higher status than in the UK (such as Licensed Social Workers in the USA). We should in addition consider alternative approaches which reach beyond the traditional casework approaches favoured in the UK. Thus social pedagogical methods applied in northern Europe may be of interest to professionals as well as clients (Lorenz, 2008).

Conclusion

Mental health social workers have played a central role in facilitating the deinstitutionalization process, in the development of community services, and in encouraging an understanding and acceptance of the importance of social factors to people's mental health. They have also engaged with the complex, and at times troubling, use of compulsion and coercion in mental health services and advocated for the human rights of people with mental health problems to be fully respected. There has been considerable progress here and you are in an excellent position to contribute to further positive developments in mental health services and wider society. In order to do this it is necessary to: look after your own mental health; routinely critically reflect on your practice; ensure that you are not colluding with services that may be oppressing people; and that you are continuing to argue for services that are clearly focused on supporting people with mental health problems to make their own decisions, access the resources they need to maximize their mental health, and so be able to pursue their hopes and dreams. We hope the ideas that we have used in this book will encourage you to engage with these complex but essential issues for practice.

Appendix 1

Abridged Summary of the National Occupational Standards for Social Work Key Roles

Key Role 1: Prepare for, and work with, individuals, families, carers, groups and communities to assess their needs and circumstances

Unit 1 Prepare for social work contact and involvement
Unit 2 Work with individuals, families, carers, groups and communities to help them make informed decisions
Unit 3 Assess needs and options to recommend a course of action

Key Role 2: Plan, carry out, review and evaluate social work practice, with individuals, families, carers, groups, communities and other professionals

Unit 4 Respond to crisis situations
Unit 5 Interact with individuals, families, carers, groups and communities to achieve change and development and to improve life opportunities
Unit 6 Prepare, produce, implement and evaluate plans with individuals, families, carers, groups, communities and professional colleagues

Source: Topss UK Partnership (2002) National Occupational Standards for Social Work (available at: www.skillsforcare.org)

Unit 7 Support the development of networks to meet assessed needs and planned outcomes
Unit 8 Work with groups to promote individual growth, development and independence
Unit 9 Address behaviour which presents a risk to individuals, families, carers, groups and communities

Key Role 3: Support individuals to represent their needs, views and circumstances

Unit 10 Advocate with, and on behalf of, individuals, families, carers, groups and communities
Unit 11 Prepare for, and participate in, decision-making forums

Key Role 4: Manage risk to individuals, families, carers, groups, communities, self and colleagues

Unit 12 Assess and manage risk to individuals, families, carers, groups and communities
Unit 13 Assess, minimize and manage risk to self and colleagues

Key Role 5: Manage and be accountable, with supervision and support, for your own social work practice within your organization

Unit 14 Manage and be accountable for your own work
Unit 15 Contribute to the management of resources and services
Unit 16 Manage, present and share records and reports
Unit 17 Work within multi-disciplinary and multi-organizational teams, networks and systems

Key Role 6: Demonstrate your professional competence in social work practice

Unit 18 Research, analyse, evaluate, and use your current knowledge of best social work practice
Unit 19 Work within agreed standards of social work practice and ensure your own professional development
Unit 20 Manage complex ethical issues, dilemmas and conflicts
Unit 21 Contribute to the promotion of best social work practice

Appendix 2

The National Occupational Standards for Mental Health (NOSMH) competencies used in the book

Enable people with mental health needs to access and benefit from services (SFHMH 2)

Work with service providers to support people with mental health needs in ways which promote their rights (SFHMH 3)

Empower families, carers and others to support individuals with mental health needs (SFHMH 9)

Manage hostility and risks with non-cooperative individuals, families and carers (SFHFHM12)

Assess the need for intervention and present assessments of individuals' needs and related risks (SFHMH 17)

Respond to potential crisis and relapse for an individual in the communitySF-HFMH 18)

Work with individuals with mental health needs to negotiate and agree plans for addressing those needs (SFHMH 20)

Respond to crisis situations (SFHMH 21)

Maintain active continuing contact with individuals and work with them to monitor their mental health needs (SFHMH 22)

Plan and review the effectiveness of therapeutic interventions with individuals with mental health needs (SFHMH 23)

Enable individuals and families to identify factors affecting, and options for optimising, their mental health and social well-being (SFHMH 39)

Enable people with mental health needs to participate in social, economic and cultural activities and networks (SFHMH42)

Challenge injustice and inequalities in access to mainstream provision for people with mental health needs (SFHMH 43)

Enable people with mental health needs to develop coping strategies (SFHMH 45)

Lead the development of inter-agency services for addressing mental health needs (SFHMH 48)

Identify trends and changes in the mental health and mental health needs of a population and the effectiveness of different means of meeting their needs (SFHMH 50)

Develop and agree priorities and objectives for meeting the mental health needs of a population (SFHMH 51)

Work with groups and communities to develop policies, strategies and services to improve mental health and address mental health needs (SFHMH 59)

Determine the concerns and priorities of individuals and families in relation to their mental health and mental health needs (SFHMH 62)

Assess how environments and practices can be maintained and improved to promote mental health (SFHMH 66)

Encourage stakeholders to see the value of improving environments and practices to promote mental health (SFHMH 67)

Monitor and review changes in environments and practices to promote mental health (SFHMH 70)

Negotiate and agree with stakeholders the opportunities they are willing to offer to people with mental health needs (SFHMH 72)

Enable workers and agencies to work collaboratively (SFHMH 79)

Lead the implementation of inter-agency services for addressing mental health needs (SFHMH 85)

Assess the need for, and plan awareness raising of mental health issues (SFHMH 87)

Project manage action targeted at addressing mental health issues (SFHMH 89)

Enable people to recover from distressing mental health experiences (SFHMH 94)

Assess, diagnose and formulate an individual's mental health disorder (SFHFMH 1)

Help an individual prepare for transition from secure institutional to community living (SFHFMH 16)

Source: Skills for Health (2010) National Occupational Standards: Mental Health Suite, version number 1. Available at: https://tools.skillsforhealth.org.uk

References

Adair, C.E., McDougall, G.M., Mitton, C.R., Joyce, A.S., Wild, T.C., Gordon, A., Costigan, N., Kowalsky, L., Pasmeny, G. and Beckie, A. (2005) 'Continuity of care and health outcomes among persons with severe mental illness', *Psychiatric Services*, 56 (9): 1061–9.

Adams, R. (2007) 'Reflective, critical and transformational practice', in W. Tovey (ed.), *The Post-Qualifying Handbook for Social Workers*. London: Jessica Kingsley.

Age Concern (2007) *Improving Services and Support for Older People with Mental Health Problems*. London: Age Concern.

Agnew, L. (2005) 'The care programme approach', in T. Ryan and J. Pritchard (eds), *Good Practice in Adult Mental Health*. London: Jessica Kingsley.

Allotte, P., Clark, M. and Slade, M. (2006) *Taking DREEM Forward: Background and Summary of Experience with REE/DREEM so far and Recommendations* – 20th June 2006. Available at www.imhrec.ie/wp-content/uploads/2009/03/Taking-DREEM-Forward-Final2-P.Allott.doc (last accessed 20 October 2011).

Alwin, N., Blackburn, R., Davidson, K., Hilton, M., Logan, C. and Shine, J. (2006) *Understanding Personality Disorder: A Report by the British Psychological Society*. Leicester: British Psychological Society.

American Psychiatric Association (1994) *Diagnostic and Statistical Manual of Mental Disorders IV*, fourth edition. Arlington: American Psychiatric Association Publishing.

Andresen, R., Oades, L. and Caputi, P. (2003) 'The experience of recovery from schizophrenia: towards an empirically validated stage model', *Australian and New Zealand Journal of Psychiatry*, 37 (5): 586–94.

Anthony, W.A. (1993) 'Recovery from mental illness: the guiding vision of the mental health service system in the 1990s', *Psychosocial Rehabilitation Journal*, 16 (4): 11–23.

Appelbaum, P.S. (1994) *Almost a Revolution: Mental Health Law and the Limits of Change*. New York: Oxford University Press.

Arber, S. and Ginn, J. (1990) 'The meaning of informal care: gender and the contribution of elderly people', *Aging and Society*, 10 (4): 429–54.

Archambeault, J. (2009a) *Reflective Reader: Social Work and Mental Health*. Exeter: Learning Matters.

Archambeault, J. (2009b) *Social Work and Mental Health*. Exeter: Learning Matters.

Armstrong, C., Hill, M. and Secker, S. (2000) 'Young people's perception of mental health', *Children and Society*, 14 (1): 60–72.

Arnstein, S. (1969) 'A ladder of citizen participation in the USA', *Journal of the American Institute of Planners*, 35 (4): 216–24.

Askey, R., Gamble, C. and Gray, R. (2007) 'Family work in first-onset psychosis: a literature review', *Journal of Psychiatric and Mental Health Nursing*, 14(4): 356–65.

Audit Scotland (2009) *Overview of Mental Health Services*. Edinburgh: Audit Scotland.

Australian Government (2003) *Australian Health Ministers National Mental Health Plan 2003 – 2008*. Canberra: Australian Government.

Bailey, D. (2009) 'Mental health', in R. Adams, L. Dominelli and M. Payne (eds), *Critical Practice in Social Work*. Basingstoke: Palgrave Macmillan.

Bale, R., Cathy, J., Watt, H., Greenwood, N. and Burns, T. (2006) 'Measures of the therapeutic relationship in severe psychotic illness: A comparison of two scales', *International Journal of Social Psychiatry*, 52 (3): 256–66.

Barber, P., Brown, R. and Martin, D. (2009) *Mental Health Law in England and Wales*. Exeter: Learning Matters.

Barker, V., Taylor, M., Taylor, I., Stewart, K. and Le Fevre, P. (2011) 'Impact of crisis resolution and home treatment services on user experience and admission to psychiatric hospital', *The Psychiatrist,* 35: 106–10

Barnes, M., Bowl, R. and Fisher, M. (1990) *Sectioned: Social Services and the 1983 Mental Health Act*. London: Routledge.

Barrowclough, C. (2003) 'Issues in the dissemination of family intervention for psychosis', *World Psychiatry,* 2(1): 31–2.

Bartlett, P. and Sandland, R. (2003) *Mental Health Law: Policy and Practice*, second edition. Oxford: Oxford University Press.

Bartlett, P. and Wright, D. (1999) *Outside the Walls of the Asylum: The History of Care in the Community 1730–2000*. London: Athlone Press.

Bateman, A.W. and Tyrer, P. (2004) 'Services for personality disorder: Organisation for inclusion', *Advances in Psychiatric Treatment*, 10 (6): 425–33.

Bateson, G. (1972) *Steps to an Ecology of Mind*. New York: Ballantine.

Bauml, J., Frobose, T., Kraemer, S., Rentrop, M. and Pitschel-Walz, G. (2006) 'Psychoeducation: a basic psychotherapeutic intervention for patients with schizophrenia and their families', *Schizophrenia Bulletin*, 32(suppl 1): S1–S9.

Beck, A.T. (1976) *Cognitive Therapy and the Emotional Disorders*. New York: Penguin Books.

Beckett, C. and Maynard, A. (2005) *Values and Ethics in Social Work: An Introduction*. London: Sage.

Becvar, D.S. and Becvar, R.J. (2006) *Family Therapy: A Systematic Integration*, sixth edition. Boston: Pearson.

Beecher, B. (2009) 'The medical model, mental health practitioners, and individuals with schizophrenia and their families', *Journal of Social Work Practice*, 23 (1): 9–20.

Bentall, R.P. (2003) *Madness Explained: Psychosis and Human Nature*. London: Penguin Books.

Bentall, R.P. (2009) *Doctoring the Mind: Is Our Current Treatment of Mental Illness Really Any Good?* London: Allen Lane.

Benyon J. (2002) *Masculinities and Culture*. Buckingham: Open University Press.

Beresford, P. (2005) 'Social approaches to madness and distress', in J. Tew (ed.), *Social Perspectives in Mental Health: Developing Social Models to Understand and Work with Mental Distress*. London: Jessica Kingsley.

Beresford, P. (2007) The changing roles and tasks of social work from service users' perspectives: a literature informed discussion paper. London: Shaping our Lives (available online at http://www.shapingourlives.org.uk).

Biddle, L., Donovan, J.L., Gunnell, D. and Sharp, D. (2006) 'Young adults' perceptions of GPs as a help source for mental distress: a qualitative study', *British Journal of General* Practice, 56(533): 924–31.

Billings, J., Johnson, S., Bebbington, P., Greaves, A., Priebe, S., Muijen, M., Ryrie, I., Watts, J., White, I. and Wright, C. (2003) 'Assertive outreach teams in London: Staff experiences and perceptions. Pan-London assertive outreach study, part 2', *British Journal of Psychiatry*, 183(2): 139–47.

Bindman, J., Maingay, S. and Szmukler, G. (2003) 'The Human Rights Act and mental health legislation', *British Journal of Psychiatry*, 182 (2): 91–4.

Black, J. (1992) *User Involvement in Mental Health Services. An Annotated Bibliography 1985–1992*. Birmingham: University of Birmingham.

Blofeld, J. (2003) *Independent Inquiry into the Death of David Bennett*. Cambridge: Norfolk, Suffolk and Cambridgeshire Strategic Health Authority.

Borg, M. and Kristiansen, K. (2004) 'Recovery-oriented professionals: Helping relationships in mental health services', *Journal of Mental Health*, 13 (5): 493–505.

Borthwick, A., Holman, C., Kennard, D., McFetridge, M., Messruther, K. and Wilkes, J. (2001) 'The relevance of moral treatment to contemporary mental health care', *Journal of Mental Health*, 10 (4): 427–39.

Bowers, L., Clark, N. and Callaghan, P. (2003) 'Multidisciplinary reflections on assessment for compulsory admission: the views of approved social workers, general practitioners, ambulance crews, police, community psychiatric nurses and psychiatrists', *British Journal of Social Work*, 33 (7): 961–8.

Bowl, R. (2009) 'PQ social work practice in mental health', in P. Higham (ed.), *Post-Qualifying Social Work Practice*. London: Sage.

Bowlby, J. (1951) *Maternal Care and Mental Health: World Health Organisation Monograph*. New York: Schocken.

Boyle, M. (2002) 'It's all done with smoke and mirrors. Or, how to create the illusion of a schizophrenic brain disease', *Clinical Psychology*, 12 (April): 9–16.

Bracken, P. and Thomas, P. (2001) 'Postpsychiatry: a new direction for mental health', *British Medical Journal*, 322 (7288): 724–7.

Bradley, C., Marshall, M. and Gath, D. (1995) 'Why do so few patients appeal under section 2 of the Mental Health Act?', *British Medical Journal*, 310 (6976): 346–7.

Brandon, D. (1991a) *Innovation Without Change? Consumer Power in Psychiatric Services*. Basingstoke: Macmillan.

Brandon, D. (1991b) 'User power', Chapter 1 in P.J. Barker. and S. Baldwin (eds), *Ethical Issues in Mental Health*. London: Chapman and Hall.

Brandon, M., Bailey, S., Belderson, P., Gardner, R., Sidebotham, P., Dodsworth, J., Warren, C. and Black, J. (2009) *Understanding Serious Case Reviews and their Impact: A Biennial Analysis of Serious Case Reviews 2005–07*, Research Report DCSF-RR129, University of East Anglia.

Brandon, M., Belderson, P., Warren, C., Howe, D., Gardner, R., Dodsworth, J. and Black, J. (2008) *Analysing Child Deaths and Serious Injury through Abuse and Neglect: What Can We Learn? A Biennial Analysis of Serious Case Reviews 2003–2005*, Research Report DCSF-RR023, University of East Anglia.

Brayley, J. (2009) *Supported Decision Making in Australia*. Available at www.opa.sa.gov.au/documents/08_News_&_Articles/Supported%20Decision%20Making.pdf (last accessed 16 October 2011).

British Psychological Society (2000) *Recent Advances in Understanding Mental Illness and Psychotic Experiences*. Leicester: British Psychological Society.

British Psychological Society and Social Care Institute of Excellence (2010) *Audit Tool for Mental Capacity Assessments*. Leicester: British Psychological Society.

Bronfenbrenner, U. (1979) *The Ecology of Human Development*. Cambridge, MA: Harvard University Press.

Brophy, L., Campbell, J. and Healy, B. (2003) 'Dilemmas in the case manager's role: implementing involuntary treatment in the community', *Psychiatry, Psychology and the Law*, 10 (1): 154–63.

Brown, G.W. and Harris, T. (1978) *Social Origins of Depression: A Study of Psychiatric Disorder in Women*. London: Routledge.

Brown, G. W., Birley, J. L. and Wing, J. K. (1972) 'Influence of family life on the course of schizophrenic disorders: a replication', *British Journal of Psychiatry*, 121: 241–58.

Brown, K. and Keen, S. (2004) 'Post-qualifying awards in social work (part 1): necessary evil or panacea?' *Social Work Education*, 23 (1): 77–92.
Brown, K., McCloskey, C., Galpin, D., Keen, S. and Immins, T. (2008) 'Evaluating the impact of post-qualifying social work education', *Social Work Education*, 27 (8): 853–67.
Brown, R. (2009) *The Approved Mental Health Professional's Guide to Mental Health Law*. Exeter: Learning Matters.
Brown, R., Adshead, G. and Pollard, A. (2009) *The Approved Mental Health Professional's Guide to Psychiatry and Medication*. Exeter: Learning Matters.
Brown, R., Barber, P. and Martin, D. (2008) *Mental Health Law in England and Wales: A Guide for Approved Mental Health Professionals*. Exeter: Learning Matters.
Brown, R., Barber, P. and Martin, D. (2009) *The Mental Capacity Act 2005: A Guide for Practice*. Exeter: Learning Matters.
Brown, W. and Kandirikirira, N. (2006) *Recovering Mental Health in Scotland: Report on Narrative Investigation of Mental Health Recovery*. Glasgow: Scottish Recovery Network.
Buchanan, A. (2004) 'Mental capacity, legal competence and consent to treatment', *Journal of the Royal Society of Medicine*, 97 (9): 415–20.
Burnham, D. (2006) *Only Get Better? A Guide to Social Services Performance Measurement Processes for Front Line Staff*. Lyme Regis: Russell House Publishing.
Burnham, J.B. (1986) *Family Therapy*. London: Routledge.
Burns, T. (2004) *Community Mental Health Teams: A Guide to Current Practices*. Oxford: Oxford University Press.
Burr, J. (2002) 'Cultural stereotypes of women from South Asian communities: mental health care professionals' explanations for patterns of suicide and depression', *Social Science and Medicine*, 55 (5): 835–45.
Burton, M. (2004) 'Grounding constructions of carers: exploring the experiences of carers through a grounded approach', *British Journal of Social Work*, 28 (3): 493–506.
Busfield, J. (1986) *Managing Madness: Changing Ideas and Practice*. London: Unwin Hyman.
Cairns, R., Maddock, C., Buchanan, A., David, A.S., Hayward, P., Richardson, G., Szmukler, G. and Hotopf, M. (2005) 'Reliability of mental capacity assessments in psychiatric in-patients', *British Journal of Psychiatry*, 187 (4): 372–8.
Campbell, J. (1999) 'Mental health policy, care in the community and political conflict: the case of the integrated service in Northern Ireland', in P. Bartlett and D. Wright (eds), *Outside The Walls of the Asylum*. London: Athlone Press.
Campbell, J. (2007) 'Social Work, Political Violence and Historical Change', *Social Work and Society*, Volume 5, available online at www.socwork.net/2007/festschrift/arsw/campbell
Campbell, J. (2010) 'Deciding to detain: the use of compulsory mental health law by UK social workers', *British Journal of Social Work*, 40 (1): 328–34.
Campbell, J. and Davidson, G. (2009) 'Coercion in the community: a situated approach to the examination of ethical challenges for mental health social workers', *Ethics and Social Welfare*, 3(3): 249–63.
Campbell, J. and McLaughlin, J. (2000) 'The "joined up" management of adult health and social care services in Northern Ireland: lessons for the rest of the UK?' *Managing Community Care*, 8 (5): 6–13.
Campbell, J., Brophy, L., Healy, B. and O'Brien, A.M. (2006) 'International perspectives on the use of community treatment orders: implications for mental health social workers', *British Journal of Social Work*, 36 (7): 1101–18.

Campbell, P. (1996) 'The history of the user movement in the United Kingdom', Chapter 24 in T. Heller, J. Reynolds, R. Gomm, R. Muston and S. Pattison (eds), *Mental Health Matters: A Reader*. Basingstoke: Macmillan/Open University Press.

Campbell, P. (2005) 'From little acorns: the mental health service user movement', Chapter 6 in A. Bell and P. Lindley (eds), *Beyond the Water Towers: The Unfinished Revolution in Mental Health Services 1985–2005*. London: The Sainsbury Centre for Mental Health.

Canvin, K., Bartlett, A. and Pinfold, V. (2002) 'A "bittersweet pill to swallow": learning from mental health service users' responses to compulsory community care in England', *Health and Social Care in the Community*, 10 (5): 361–69.

Care Quality Commission (2010) *Monitoring the use of the Mental Health Act in 2009/10: The Care Quality Commission's first report on the exercise of its functions in keeping under review the operation of the Mental Health Act 1983*. Newcastle upon Tyne: Care Quality Commission.

Care Services Improvement Partnership (CSIP), Royal College of Psychiatrists and Social Care Institute for Excellence (2007) *A Common Purpose: Recovery in Future Mental Health Services*. London: Social Care Institute for Excellence.

Carers UK (2007) *Real Change, Not Short Change: Time to Deliver for Carers*. London: Carers UK.

Carpenter, M. (2009) 'A third wave, not a third way? New Labour, human rights and mental health in historical context', *Social Policy and Society*, 8 (2): 215–30.

Carr, A. (2000a) 'Evidence-based practice in family therapy and systemic consultation I', *Journal of Family Therapy*, 22 (1): 29–60.

Carr, A. (2000b) 'Evidence-based practice in family therapy and systemic consultation II', *Journal of Family Therapy*, 22 (3): 273–95.

Carr, A. (2006) *Family Therapy: Concepts, Process and Practice*, second edition. Chichester: John Wiley and Sons.

Carr, S. (2010) *Personalisation: A Rough Guide*, revised edition. London: Social Care Institute for Excellence.

Carter, E. and McGoldrick, M. (eds) (1999) *The Expanded Family Life Cycle*, third edition. Boston: Allyn and Bacon.

Chartres, D. and Brayley, J. (2010) *Office of the Public Advocate South Australia: Submission to the Productivity Commission Inquiry into Disability Care and Support*. Collinswood: Office of the Public Advocate.

Churchill, R., Owen, G., Hotopf, M. and Singh, S. (2007) *International Experiences of Using Community Treatment Orders*. London: Department of Health and Institute of Psychiatry, King's College London.

Clarke, J. (2004) *Changing Welfare Changing States: New Directions in Social Policy*. London: Sage.

Cleaver H., Unell, I., Aldgate, J. (1999) *Children's Needs – Parenting Capacity: The Impact of Parental Mental Illness, Problem Alcohol and Drug Use and Domestic Violence on Children's Development*. London: The Stationery Office.

Collins, J. and Collins. M. (1981) *Achieving Change in Social Work*. London: Heinemann.

Commonwealth of Australia (2009) *Suicide and Mental Illness in the Media*. Barton: ACT, Commonwealth of Australia.

Confidential Inquiry into Suicide and Homicide by People with a Mental Illness (1999) *Safer Services*. London: Department of Health.

Cooper, B. and Rixon, A. (2001) 'Integrating post-qualification study into the workplace: the candidates' experience', *Social Work Education*, 20 (6): 701–16.

Copeland, M. E. (1997) *Wellness Recovery Action Plan*. West Dummerston, VT: Peach Press.

Corrigan, P.W. and Watson, A.C. (2002) 'The paradox of self-stigma and mental illness', *Clinical Psychology*, 9 (1): 35–53.

Cree, V.E. and Wallace, S. (2009) 'Risk and protection', in R. Adams, L. Dominelli and M. Payne (eds), *Practising Social Work in a Complex World*. Basingstoke: Palgrave Macmillan.

Crisp, A.H., Gelder, M.G., Rix, S., Meltzer, H. and Rowlands, O.J. (2000) 'Stigmatisation of people with mental illnesses', *British Journal of Psychiatry*, 177 (1): 4–7.

Crisp, B.R., Anderson, M.R., Orme, J. and Green Lister, P. (2003) *Knowledge Review 1: Learning and Teaching Assessment Skills in Social Work Education*. London: SCIE.

Dallos, R. and Draper, R. (2005) *An Introduction to Family Therapy: Systemic Theory and Practice,* second edition. Maidenhead : McGraw Hill/OU Press.

Darlington, Y. and Feeney, J.A. (2008) 'Collaboration between mental health and child protection services: Professionals' perceptions of best practice', *Children and Youth Services Review*, 30: 187–198.

Darlington, Y., Feeney, J.A. and Rixon, K. (2005a) 'Practice challenges at the intersection of child protection and mental health', *Child and Family Social Work,* 10: 239–47.

Davidson, G. and Campbell, J. (2007) 'An examination of the use of coercion by assertive outreach and community mental health teams in Northern Ireland', *British Journal of Social Work*, 37 (3): 537–55.

Davidson, G. and Campbell, J. (2009) 'An audit of assessment and reporting by approved social workers (ASWs)', *British Journal of Social Work*, 40 (5): 1609–27.

Davidson, G., Devaney, J. and Spratt, T. (2010) 'The impact of adversity in childhood on outcomes in adulthood: research lessons and limitations', *Journal of Social Work*, 10 (4): 369–90.

Davidson, G., Shannon, C., Mulholland, C. and Campbell, J. (2009) 'A longitudinal study of the effects of childhood trauma on symptoms and functioning of people with severe mental health problems', *Journal of Trauma and Dissociation*, 10(1): 57–66.

Davidson, L. (2009) 'Nearest Relative Consultation and the Avoidant Approved Mental Health Professional', *Journal of Mental Health Law*, Spring : 70–80.

Davidson, L., O'Connell, M., Tondora, J., Styron, T. and Kangas, K. (2006) 'The ten top concerns about recovery encountered in mental health system transformation', *Psychiatric Services*, 57 (5): 640–45.

Davis, A. (2008) 'What service users expect from social work', International Conference on Social Work Education, Profession and Practice.

Davis, A., Davis, A. and Glynn, T. (2008) 'Making sense of social work practice in multi-agency mental health services', in K. Morris (ed) *Social Work and Multi-agency Working: Making a Difference*. Bristol: Policy Press.

Dawson, J. and Szmukler, G. (2006) 'Fusion of mental health and incapacity legislation', *British Journal of Psychiatry*, 188 (6): 504–9.

de Botton, A. (2004) *Status Anxiety*. London: Hamish Hamilton.

de Chenu, L. (2007) 'Mental health social work', in W. Tovey (ed.), *The Post-Qualifying Handbook for Social Workers*. London: Jessica Kingsley.

Denny, D. (1998) *Social Policy and Social Work*. Oxford: Oxford University Press.

Department of Health (1995a) *The Care Programme Approach for People with a Mental Illness Referred to the Specialist Psychiatric Services*. London: HMSO.

Department of Health (1995b) *The Carers' (Recognition and Services) Act (1995)*. London: HMSO.

Department of Health. (1995c) *Child Protection: Messages from Research*. London: HMSO.

Department of Health (1996) *Carers (Recognition and Services) Act 1995*. London: DH.

Department of Health (1998) *Modernising Mental Health Services: Safe, Sound and Supportive*. London: DH.

Department of Health (1999a) *Caring About Carers: A National Strategy for Carers*. London: DH.

Department of Health (1999b) *National Service Framework for Mental Health: Modern Standards and Service Models*. London: DH.

Department of Health (2001a) *Treatment Choice in Psychological Therapies and Counselling: Evidence Based Clinical Practice Guidelines*. London: DH.

Department of Health (2001b) *Mental Health Policy Implementation Guide*. London: DH.

Department of Health (2002a) *Developing Services for Carers and Families of People with Mental Illnesses*. London: DH.

Department of Health (2002b) *National Suicide Prevention Strategy for England*. London: DH.

Department of Health (2002c) *Community Mental Health Teams – Mental Health Policy Implementation Guide*. London: DH.

Department of Health (2007a) *Mental Health: New Ways of Working for Everyone*. London: DH.

Department of Health (2007b) *Independence, Choice and Risk: A Guide to Best Practice in Supported Decision Making*. London: DH.

Department of Health (2007c) *Best Practices for Managing Risk: Principles and Evidence for Best Practice in the Assessment and Management of Risk to Self and Others in Mental Health Services*. London: DH.

Department of Health (2008) *Attitudes to Mental Illness*. London: DH.

Department of Health (2009) *New Horizons: Towards a Shared Vision for Mental Health*. London: DH.

Department of Health (2010) *Personalisation Through Person-Centred Planning*. London: DH.

Department of Health and Human Services (2003) *Achieving the Promise: Transforming Mental Health Care in America. President's New Freedom Commission on Mental Health*, Pub no. SMA–03–3832. Rockville, MD: Department of Health and Human Services.

Department of Health and Social Services (1990) *People First: Community Care for People in Northern Ireland in the 1990s*. Belfast: Department of Health and Social Services.

Department of Health, Social Services Inspectorate, Department for Education (1995) *Handbook on Child & Adolescent Mental Health*. London: Department of Health.

Department of Health, Social Services and Public Safety (2006) *Protect Life – A Shared Vision: The Northern Ireland Suicide Prevention Strategy and Action Plan 2006–2011*. Belfast: Department of Health, Social Services and Public Safety.

Department of Health, Social Services and Public Safety (2009a) *Delivering the Bamford Vision: The Response of Northern Ireland Executive to the Bamford Review of Mental Health and Learning Disability. Action Plan 2009–2011*. Belfast: Department of Health, Social Services and Public Safety.

Department of Health, Social Services and Public Safety (2009b) *Promoting Quality Care Good Practice Guidance on the Assessment and Management of Risk in Mental Health and Learning Disability Services*. Belfast: Department of Health, Social Services and Public Safety.

Department of Health, Social Services and Public Safety (2010a) *A Strategy for the Development of Psychological Therapies Services*. Belfast: Department of Health, Social Services and Public Safety.

Department of Health, Social Services and Public Safety (2010b) *Personality Disorder: A Diagnosis for Inclusion*. Belfast: Department of Health, Social Services and Public Safety.

Dieterich, M., Irving, C.B., Park, B. and Marshall, M. (2010) *Intensive case management for severe mental illness, Cochrane Database of Systematic Reviews 2010, Issue 10*. Art. No.: CD007906. DOI: 10.1002/14651858.

Dillenburger, K., Fargas, M. and Akhonzada, R. (2008) 'Long-term effects of political violence: narrative inquiry across a 20-year period', *Qualitative Health Research*, 18 (10): 1312–22.

Dinniss, S., Roberts, G., Hubbard, C., Hounsell, J. and Webb, R. (2007) 'User-led assessment of a recovery service using DREEM', *Psychiatric Bulletin*, 31 (4): 124–7.

Doel, M., Flynn, E. and Nelson, P. (2008) 'Experiences of post-qualifying study in social work', *Social Work Education*, 27 (5): 549–71.

Douglas, H. (2007) 'Preparation for contact: an aid to effective social work intervention', *Social Work Education*, 27(4): 380–9.

Dowling, S., Manthorpe, J., Cowley, S., King, S., Raymond, V., Perez, W. and Weinstein, P. (2006) *Person-centred Planning in Social Care*. York: Joseph Rowntree Foundation.

Dryden, W. (ed.) (2007) *Dryden's Handbook of Individual Therapy*, fifth edition. London: Sage.

Duffy, J. (2008) *Looking Out from the Middle: User Involvement in Health and Social Care in Northern Ireland*. Belfast: Social Care Institute for Excellence.

Duffy, M., Gillespie, K. and Clark, D.M. (2007) 'Post-traumatic stress disorder in the context of terrorism and other civil conflict in Northern Ireland: randomised controlled trial', *British Medical Journal*, 334 (7604): 1147–50.

Egan, G. (2009) *The Skilled Helper: A Problem Management and Opportunity Development Approach to Helping*, International edition. Belmont, Canada: Wadsworth Publishing Company.

Engel, G.L. (1980) 'The clinical application of the biopsychosocial model', *American Journal of Psychiatry*, 137 (5): 535–44.

Erikson, E.H. (1968) *Identity: Youth and Crisis*. New York: Norton.

Evans J. and Fowler R. (2008) *Family Minded: Supporting Children in Families Affected by Mental Illness*. Ilford: Barnardo's.

Evans, S., Huxley, P., Gately, C., Webber, M., Mears, A., Pajak, S., Medina, J., Kendall, T. and Katona, C. (2006) 'Mental health, burnout and job satisfaction among mental health social workers in England and Wales', *British Journal of Psychiatry*, 188 (1): 75–80.

Fadden, G. and Smith, J. (2009) 'Family work in early psychosis', in F. Lobban and C. Barrowclough (eds), *A Casebook of Family Interventions for Psychosis*. Chichester: John Wiley and Sons.

Fakhoury, W.K.H. and Wright, D. (2004) 'A national survey of approved social workers in the UK: information, communication and training needs', *British Journal of Social Work*, 34 (5): 663–75.

Falkov, A. (ed.) (1998) *Crossing Bridges: Training Resources for Working with Mentally Ill Parents and Their Children: Reader for Managers, Practitioners and Trainers*. Brighton: Pavilion.

Falloon, I.R.H. (2003) 'Family interventions for mental disorders: efficacy and effectiveness', *World Psychiatry*, 2(1): 22–8.

Fardella, J.A. (2008) 'The recovery model: discourse ethics and the retrieval of the self', *Journal of Medical Humanities*, 29 (2): 111–26.

Faulkner, A. (2009) 'User involvement in 21st century mental health services', Chapter 2, pp. 14-26 in C. Brooker and J. Repper (eds), *Mental Health: from Policy to Practice*. London: Churchill Livingstone Elsevier.

Felitti, V.J., Anda, R.F., Nordenberg, D., Williamson, D.F., Spitz, A.M., Edwards, V., Koss, M.P. and Marks, J.S. (1998) 'Relationship of adult health status to childhood abuse and household dysfunction to many of the leading causes of death in adults', *American Journal of Preventive Medicine*, 14(4): 245–58.

Ferguson, I. and Woodward, R. (2009) *Radical Social Work in Practice: Making a Difference*. Bristol: The Policy Press.

Fergusson, D.M., Horwood, D.J. and Swain-Campbell, D.R. (2003) 'Cannabis dependence and psychotic symptoms in young people', *Psychological Medicine*, 33 (1): 15–21.

Fernando, S. (2001) *Mental Health Race and Culture*, second edition. Basingstoke: Palgrave.

Fernando, S. and Keating, F. (eds) (2009) *Mental Health in a Multi-Ethnic Society: A Multidisciplinary Handbook*, second edition. Abingdon: Routledge.

Ferns, P. (2005) 'Finding a way forward: a black perspective', in J. Tew (ed.), *Social Perspectives in Mental Health*. London: Jessica Kingsley.

Fitch, C., Hamilton, S., Bassett, P. and Davey, R. (2009) *Debt and Mental Health: What Do We Know? What Should We Do?* London: Royal College of Psychiatrists and Rethink, available online at http://www.rcpsych.ac.uk/debt

Fook, J. (2002) *Social Work: Critical Theory and Practice*. London: Sage.

Foucault, M. (1975) *Madness and Civilisation*. New York: Random House.

Fox, J.W. (1990) 'Social class, mental illness, and social mobility: the social selection-drift hypothesis for serious mental illness', *Journal of Health and Social Behavior*, 31 (4): 344–53.

Freeman, T. and Peck, E. (2006) 'Evaluating partnerships: a case study of integrated specialist mental health services', *Health and Social Care in the Community*, 14 (5): 408–17.

Frosh, S., Phoenix, A. and Pattman, R. (2003) 'The trouble with boys', *The Psychologist*, 16 (2): 84–7.

Furminger, E. and Webber, M. (2009) 'The effect of crisis resolution and home treatment on assessments under the 1983 Mental Health Act: An increased workload for Approved Social Workers?', *British Journal of Social Work*, 39 (5): 901–17.

Galon, P.A. and Wineman, N.M. (2010) 'Coercion and procedural justice in psychiatric care: state of the science and implications for nursing', *Archives of Psychiatric Nursing*, 24 (5): 307–16.

Galpin, D. (2009) 'Who really drives the development of post-qualifying social work education and what are the implications of this?', *Social Work Education*, 28 (1): 65–80.

General Assembly of the United Nations (1948) *The Universal Declaration of Human Rights*. Available at www.un.org/en/documents/udhr/ (last accessed 18 August 2011).

George, C. (2008) 'Recovery' Approach in Mental Health is Idea 'Whose Time has Come'. Available at www.psychminded.co.uk/news/news2008/march08/recovery_in_mental_health002.htm. (last accessed 31 July 2009).

Gibbs, A., Dawson, J., Ansley, C. and Mullen, R. (2005) 'How patients in New Zealand view community treatment orders', *Journal of Mental Health*, 14 (4): 357–68.

Gillespie, M., Smith, J., Meaden, A., Jones, C. and Wane, J. (2004) 'Clients' engagement with assertive outreach services: a comparison of client and staff perceptions of engagement and its impact on later engagement', *Journal of Mental Health*, 13 (5): 439–52.

Gitterman, A. and Germain, C.B. (2008) *The Life Model of Social Work Practice: Advances in Theory and Practice*, third edition. New York: Columbia University Press.

Glover, G., Arts, G. and Babu, K.S. (2006) 'Crisis resolution/home treatment teams and psychiatric admission rates in England', *British Journal of* Psychiatry, 189: 441–5.

Goffman, E. (1961) *Asylums: Essays on the Social Situation of Mental Patients and Other Inmates*. New York: Doubleday Anchor.

Goffman, E. (1963) *Stigma: Notes on the Management of Spoiled Identity*. Englewood Cliffs, NJ: Prentice-Hall.

Goldenberg, I. and Goldenberg, H. (2004) *Family Therapy: An Overview*, second edition. New York: Brooks/Cole Thomson Learning.

Golightly, M. (2008) *Social Work and Mental Health*, third edition. Exeter: Learning Matters.

Gomm, R. (2009) 'Mental health and inequality', in J.Reynolds, R. Muston, T. Heller, J. Leach, M. McCormick, J. Wallcraft and M. Walsh (eds), *Mental Health Still Matters*. Basingstoke: Palgrave Macmillan.

Gostin, L. (1975) *A Human Condition*, Vol. 1. London: National Association for Mental Health.

Gostin, L.O. and Gable, L. (2004) 'The human rights of persons with mental disabilities: a global perspective on the application of human rights principles to mental health', *Maryland Law Review*, 63 (1): 20–121.

Gould, N. (2006) 'An inclusive approach to knowledge for mental health social work and policy', *British Journal of Social Work*, 36 (1):109–25.

Gould, N. (2010) *Mental Health Social Work in Context*. Abingdon: Routledge.

Graham, H. L. (2004) 'Implementing integrated treatment for co-existing substance use and severe mental health problems in assertive outreach teams: training issues', *Drug and Alcohol Review*, 23 (4): 463–70.

Green, H., McGinnity, A., Meltzer, H., Ford, T. and Goodman, R. (2005) *Mental Health of Children and Young People in Great Britain*. London: Department of Health.

Guru, S. (2010) 'Social work and the War on Terror', *British Journal of Social Work*, 40 (1): 272–89.

Hale, B. (2010) *Mental Health Law,* fifth edition. Andover: Sweet and Maxwell.

Hammer, T. (2003) 'The probability for unemployed young people to re-enter education or employment: a comparative study in six northern European countries', *British Journal of Sociology of Education*, 24 (2): 209–23.

Hanley, B. and Staley, K. (2005) *User and Carer Involvement: A Good Practice Guide*. London: Long-term Medical Conditions Alliance.

Harland, K. and Morgan, S. (2003) 'Work with young men in Northern Ireland – an advocacy approach', *Youth & Policy*, 81: 74–85.

Harris, E.C. and Barraclough, B. (1998) 'Excess mortality of mental disorder', *British Journal of Psychiatry*, 173 (1): 11–53.

Harrison, G. and Turner, R. (2011) 'Being a "culturally competent" social worker: making sense of a murky concept in practice', *British Journal of Social Work*, 41 (2): 333–50.

Hatfield, B. (2004) 'Gender and Mental Health', in Ryan, T. and Prichard, J. (eds), *Good Practice in Adult Mental Health*. London: Jessica Kingsley.

Hatfield, B. (2007) 'Powers to detain under mental health legislation in England and the role of the approved social worker: an analysis of patterns and trends under the 1983 Mental Health Act in six local authorities', *British Journal of Social Work*, 38 (8): 1553–71.

Hatfield, B. and Mohamad, H. (1994) 'Women, men and the Mental Health Act 1983', *Research, Policy and Planning*, 12 (3): 6–10.

Hatfield, B., Huxley, P. and Mohamad, H. (1997) 'Social factors and compulsory detention of psychiatric patients in the UK', *International Journal of Law and Psychiatry*, 20 (3): 389–97.

Hatfield, B., Mohamad, H. and Huxley, P. (1992) 'The 1983 Mental Health Act in five local authorities: a study of the practice of approved social workers', *International Journal of Social Psychiatry*, 38 (8): 189–207.

Hayes, B.C. and Prior, P.M. (2003) *Gender and Health Care in the UK: Exploring the Stereotypes*. Basingstoke and New York: Palgrave-Macmillan.

Health Action Zone North and West Belfast (2005) *Suicide Briefing*. Belfast: Health Action Zone North and West Belfast.

Henderson, C., Swanson, J.W., Szmukler, G., Thornicroft, G. and Zinkler, M. (2008) 'A typology of advance statements in mental health care', *Psychiatric Services*, 59: 63–71.

Henderson, C., Flood, C., Leese, M., Thornicroft, G., Sutherby, K. and Szmukler, G. (2004) 'Effect of joint crisis plans on use of compulsory treatment in psychiatry: single blind randomised controlled trial', *British Medical Journal*, 329 (7458):. 136–40.

Henderson, J. (2002) 'Experiences of "care" in mental health', in J. Reynolds, R. Muston, T. Heller, J. Leach, M. McCormick, J. Wallcraft and M. Walsh (eds), *Mental Health Still Matters*. Milton Keynes: Open University Press.

Henderson, R. and Pochin, M. (2001) *A Right Result? Advocacy, Justice and Empowerment*. Bristol: The Policy Press.

Hepworth, D. (2005) 'Asian carers' perceptions of care assessment and support in the community', *British Journal of Social Work*, 35 (3): 337–53.

Hervey, N. (2001) 'Social Work Provision', in R. Ramsey, C. Cerada, S. Mars and G. Szmukler (eds), *Mental Illness: A Handbook for Carers*. London: Jessica Kingsley.

Hewitt, J. (2010) 'Rational suicide: philosophical perspectives on schizophrenia', *Medicine, Health Care and Philosophy*, 13 (1): 25–31.

Hewitt, J. and Coffey, M. (2005) 'Therapeutic working relationships with people with schizophrenia: Literature review', *Journal of Advanced Nursing*, 52 (5): 561–70.

Hietanen, O.M., and Punamaki, R. (2006) 'Attachment and early working alliance in adult psychiatric inpatients', *Journal of Mental Health*, 15(4): 423–35.

Higham, P. (ed.) (2009) *Post-Qualifying Social Work Practice*. London. Sage.
HM Government (2007) *Putting People First*. London: HM Government.
Hope, R. (2004) *The Ten Essential Shared Capabilities – A Framework for the Whole of the Mental Health Workforce*. London: Department of Health.
Horner, N. (2003) *What is Social Work? Context and Perspectives*. Exeter: Learning Matters.
Houghton, S. and Saxon, D. (2007) 'An evaluation of large group CBT psycho-education for anxiety disorders delivered in routine practice', *Patient Education and Counselling*, 68 (1): 107–10.
Hughes, R., Hayward, M. and Finlay, W.M.L. (2009) 'Patients' perceptions of the impact of involuntary inpatient care on self, relationships and recovery', *Journal of Mental Health*, 18 (2): 152–60.
Humphreys, C. and Thiara, R. (2003) 'Domestic violence and mental health: I call it symptoms of abuse', *British Journal of Social Work*, 33 (2): 209–26.
Hunter, M. (2009) 'New approved mental health professionals discuss the role', *Community Care*, available at www.communitycare.co.uk (last accessed 15 June 2009).
Huxley, P., Evans, S., Gately, C., Webber, M., Mears, A., Pajak, S., Kendall, T., Medina, J. and Katona, C. (2005) 'Stress and pressure in mental health social work: the worker speaks', *British Journal of Social Work*, 35 (7): 1063–79.
Huxley, P. and Kerfoot, M. (1994) 'A survey of Approved Social Work in England and Wales', *British Journal of Social Work*, 24 (3): 311–24.
James, O. (2007) *Affluenza: How to be Successful and Stay Sane*. London: Vermilion.
Jerrom, C. (2011) 'Minding your PQs', *Professional Social Work*, July/August, pp. 28–9.
Joe, S. and Niedermeier, D. (2008) 'Preventing suicide: a neglected social work research agenda', *British Journal of Social Work*, 38 (3): 507–30.
Johnson, S., Nolan, F., Pilling, S., Sandor, A., Hoult, J., McKenzie, N., White, I.R., Thompson, M. and Bebbington, P.M. (2005a) 'Randomised controlled trial of acute mental health care by a crisis resolution team: the North Islington study', *British Medical Journal*, 331: 599–62.
Johnson, S., Nolan, F., Hoult, J., White, I.R., Bebbington, P., Sandor, A., McKenzie, N. and Patel, S.N. (2005b) 'Outcomes of crises before and after the introduction of a crisis resolution team', *British Journal of Psychiatry*, 187: 68–75.
Jones, D.W. (2004) 'Families and serious mental illness working with loss and ambivalence', *British Journal of Social Work*, 34 (7): 961–79.
Jones, K. (1998) *Mental Health and Social Policy*, 1845–1959. London: Routledge.
Jones, L. (1960) *Mental Health and Social Policy 1845–1959*. London: Routledge and Kegan Paul.
Jordan, R. and Parkinson, C. (2001) 'Reflective practice in a process for the re-approval of ASWs: an exploration of some inevitable resistance', *Journal of Social Work Practice*, 15 (1): 67–79.
Joy, C. B., Adams, C. E. and Rice, K. (2006) 'Crisis intervention for people with severe mental illnesses', *Cochrane Database of Systematic Reviews,* (4), 001087. Retrieved from http://ovidsp.ovid.com/athens/ovidweb.cgi?T=JS&CSC=Y&NEWS=N&PAGE=fulltext&D=med4&AN=17054133
Kapur, R. and Campbell, J. (2004) *The Troubled Mind of Northern Ireland*. London: Karnac.
Kapusta, N.D., Ramskogler, K., Hertling, I., Schmid, R., Dvorak, A., Walter, H. and Lesch, O.M. (2006) 'Epidemiology of substance use in a representative sample of 18-year-old males', *Alcohol and Alcoholism*, 41 (2): 188–92.

Kearney P., Levin E., Rosen, G. (2003) *Alcohol, Drug and Mental Health Problems: Working with Families*. London: SCIE.

Keating, F. (2002) 'Black-led initiatives in mental health: an overview', *Research, Policy and Planning*, 20 (2): 9–19.

Keeney, B. (1983) *The Aesthetics of Change*. New York: Guilford Press.

Kelly, C.B. (1998) 'An audit of acute psychiatric admission bed occupancy in Northern Ireland', *Ulster Medical Journal*, 67 (1): 44–8.

Kemshall, H. (2002) *Risk, Social Policy and Welfare*. Buckingham: Open University Press.

Killaspy, H., Bebbington, P., Blizard, R., Johnson, S., Nolan, F., Pilling, S., et al. (2006) 'The REACT study: Randomised evaluation of assertive community treatment in north London', *British Medical Journal*, doi: 10.1136/bmj.38773.518322.7C , 815–20.

Killaspy, H., King, M., Wright, C., White, S., McCrone, P., Kallert, T., et al. (2009) 'Study protocol for the development of a European measure of best practice for people with long term mental health problems in institutional care' (DEMoBinc). *BMC Psychiatry*, 9.

King, M.L., King, C.S. and Harding, V. (2010) *Where Do We Go from Here: Chaos or Community?* Boston: Beacon Press.

Kuipers, E., Leff, J. and Lam, D. (2002) *Family Work for Schizophrenia: A Practical Guide*. London: Gaskell Press.

Laing, R.D. (1960) *The Divided Self: An Existential Study in Sanity and Madness*. Harmondsworth: Penguin.

Laurance, J. (2003) *Pure Madness: How Fear Drives the Mental Health System*. Abingdon: Routledge.

Lawn, T. and McDonald, E. (2009) 'Developing a policy to deal with sexual assault on psychiatric in-patient wards', *The Psychiatrist*, 33 (3): 108–11.

Lawton, A. (2007) *SCIE Position paper 6: Supporting self-advocacy*. Available online at www.scie.org.uk/publications/positionpapers/pp06.asp

Lawton-Smith, S. H. (2011) 'Supervised community treatment', *The Psychiatrist*, 35: 197.

Lawton-Smith, S. and Dawson, J. (2008) 'Community treatment orders are not a good thing', *British Journal of Psychiatry*, 193 (2): 96–100.

Layard, R. (2005) *Happiness: Lessons From a New Science*. London: Penguin.

Leavey, G., Galway, K., Rondon, J. and Logan, G. (2009) *A Flourishing Society: Aspirations for Emotional Health and Wellbeing in Northern Ireland*. Belfast: Northern Ireland Association for Mental Health.

Ledwith, M. (2005) *Community Development: A Critical Approach*. Bristol: The Policy Press.

Leece, J. and Leece, D. (2011) 'Personalisation: perceptions of the role of social work in a world of brokers and budgets', *British Journal of Social Work* 41 (2): 204–23.

Lefevre, M. (2010) *Communicating with Children and Young People: Making a Difference*. Bristol: The Policy Press.

Leff, J. (2000) 'Family work for schizophrenia: practical application', *Acta Psychiatric Scandinavica*, 102 (supplement 407): 78–82.

Leveridge, M. (2007) 'Community care and care management', in W.Tovey (ed.), *The Post-qualifying Handbook for Social Workers*. London: Jessica Kingsley.

Lewis, L. (2005) 'User involvement in Scottish mental health policy: locating power and inequality', *Scottish* Affairs, 51 (Spring): 79–106.

Lidz, C.W., Hoge, S.K., Gardner, W., Bennett, N.S., Monahan, J., Mulvey, E.P. and Roth, L.H. (1995) 'Perceived coercion in mental hospital admission: pressures and process', *Archives of General Psychiatry*, 52 (12):1034–39.

Link, B.G., Cullen, F.T., Struening, E., Shrout, P.E. and Dohrewend, B.P. (1989) 'A modified labeling theory approach to mental disorders: an empirical assessment', *American Sociological Review*, 54 (3): 400–23.

Link, B.G. and Phelan, J.C. (2001) 'Conceptualizing stigma', *Annual Review of Sociology*, 27 (1): 363–85.

Lishman, J. (1998) 'Personal and Professional Development' in R. Adams, L. Dominelli and M. Payne (eds), *Social Work: Themes, Issues and Critical Debates*. London: Macmillan.

Lister, R. (2010) *Understanding Theories and Concepts in Social Policy.* Bristol: Policy Press.

Lorenz, W. (2008) 'Paradigms and politics: understanding methods paradigms in an historical context: the case of social pedagogy', *British Journal of Social Work*, 38 (4): 625–44.

Lupton, C., North, N., Khan, P. (2001) *Working Together or Pulling Apart? The NHS and Child Protection Networks*. Bristol: Policy.

Ma, K. (2006) 'Attachment theory in adult psychiatry. Part 1: conceptualisations, measurement and clinical research findings', *Advances in Psychiatric Treatment*, 12 (6): 440–49.

Ma, K. (2007) 'Attachment theory in adult psychiatry. Part 2: importance to the therapeutic relationship', *Advances in Psychiatric Treatment*, 13 (1): 10–16.

Main, L. (2006) 'Into the fire: suicide rates in Northern Ireland', *Mental Health Today*, February: 10–11.

Maingay, S., Thornicroft, G., Huxley, P., Jenkins, R. and Szmukler, G. (2002) 'Mental health and human rights: the MI Principles – turning rhetoric into action', *Journal of Mental Health*, 14 (1): 19–25.

Manktelow, R., Hughes, P., Britton, F., Campbell, J., Hamilton, B. and Wilson, G. (2002) 'The experience and practice of Approved Social Workers in Northern Ireland', *British Journal of Social Work*, 32 (4): 43–61.

Manning, C. and Gregoire, A. (2006) 'Effects of parental mental illness on children', *Psychiatry*, 5(1): 10–12.

Manthorpe, J., Rapaport, J. and Stanley, N. (2009) 'Expertise and experience: people with experiences of using services and carers' views of the Mental Capacity Act 2005', *British Journal of Social Work,* 39 (5): 884–900.

Marmot Review (2010) *Fair Society, Healthy Lives: Strategic Review of Health Inequalities in England Post-2010*. London: The Marmot Review.

Marsh, P., Fisher, M., Mathers, N. and Fish, S. (2005) *Developing the Evidence-base for Social Work and Social Care Practice*. Bristol: Policy Press, Social Care Institute for Excellence.

Masterson, S. and Owen, S. (2006) 'Mental health service users' social and individual empowerment: using theories of power to elucidate far-reaching strategies', *Journal of Mental Health*, 15 (1): 19–34.

Mayo, M. (2009) 'Community work', in R. Adams, L. Dominelli and M. Payne (eds), *Critical Practices in Social Work*. Basingstoke: Palgrave Macmillan.

McAlister, S., Scraton, P. and Haydon, D. (2009) *Childhood in Transition: Experiencing Marginalisation and Conflict in Northern Ireland*. Belfast: Queen's University Belfast, Save the Children, The Prince's Trust.

McCabe, R. and Priebe, S. (2004) 'The therapeutic relationship in the treatment of severe mental illness: a review of methods and findings', *International Journal of Social Psychiatry,* 50 (2): 115–28.

McCormack, J. (2007) *Recovery and Strengths Based Practice: SRN Discussion Paper Series, Report No.6*. Glasgow: Scottish Recovery Network.

McGlynn, P., and Smith, M. (1998) *The Home Treatment Team: Making it Happen*. London: Sainsbury Centre for Mental Health.
McGoldrick, M., Gerson, R. and Petry, S.S. (2008) *Genograms: Assessment and Intervention*, third edition. New York: W.W. Norton and Company.
McKenna, B.G., Simpson, A.I.F. and Coverdale, J.H. (2000) 'What is the role of procedural justice in civil commitment?' *Australian and New Zealand Journal of Psychiatry*, 34 (4): 671–6.
McKeown, P., Weich, S., Kamaldeep, S.B. and Scott, J. (2011) 'Association between provision of mental illness beds and rate of involuntary admissions in the NHS in England 1988–2008: ecological study', *British Medical Journal,* 343: d3736. Available online.
McLaughlin, K. (2005) 'From ridicule to institutionalization: anti-oppression, the state and social work', *Critical Social Policy*, 25 (3): 283–305.
Meaden, A., Nithsdale, V., Rose, C., Smith, J. and Jones, C. (2004) 'Is engagement associated with outcome in assertive outreach?', *Journal of Mental Health,* 13 (4): 415–24.
Mental Health Act Commission (2009) *Coercion and Consent: Monitoring the Mental Health Act 2007–2009, MHAC Thirteenth Biennial Report 2007–2009*. London: The Stationery Office.
Mental Health Commission (1998) *Blueprint for Mental Health Services in New Zealand*. Wellington: Mental Health Commission.
Mental Health Commission (2005) *A Vision for a Recovery Model in Irish Mental Health Services*. Dublin: Mental Health Commission.
Mental Health Commission (2006) *Multidisciplinary Team Working: From Theory to Practice*. Dublin: Mental Health Commission.
Mental Health North East (2009) *Personalisation – Chaos or Empowerment? The Impact of Personalisation, Personal Budgets and Increased Direct Payments on Voluntary Sector Mental Health Organisations in the North East of England*. Sunderland: Mental Health North East.
Meyer, A. (1952) *The Collected Papers of Adolf Meyer*. Baltimore, MD: Johns Hopkins University Press.
Milgram, S. (1974) 'The perils of obedience', *Harper's Magazine*, 247 (1483): 62–77.
Min, M., Farkas, K., Minnes, S. and Singer, L.T. (2007) 'Impact of childhood abuse and neglect on substance abuse and psychological distress in adulthood', *Journal of Traumatic Stress*, 20(5): 833–44.
Mind (2009) *Men and Mental Health: Get It Off Your Chest*. London: Mind.
Mind (2010) *The History of Mental Health and Community Care*, Available online. Accessed 20 August 2011 at www.mind.org.uk/help/research_and_policy/the_history_of_mental_health_and_community_care-key_dates
Mind Out for Mental Health (2007) *Mindshift: A Guide to Open-Minded Media Coverage of Mental Health*. London: Mind Out for Mental Health.
Moncrieff, J. (2003) 'The politics of a new Mental Health Act', *British Journal of Psychiatry,* 183: 8–9.
Moncrieff, J. (20) *The Myth of the Chemical Cure*. Basingstoke: Macmillan.
Moorey, S. (2007) 'Cognitive Therapy', in W. Dryden (ed.), *Dryden's Handbook of Individual Therapy*, fifth edition. London: Sage.
Morely, C. (2003) 'Towards critical social work practice in mental health: a review', *Journal of Progressive Human Services*, 14 (1): 61–84.
Morris, K. (ed.) (2008) *Social Work and Multi-Agency Work*. Bristol: Policy Press.
Myers, F., Woodhouse, A., Whitehead, I., McCollam, A., McBryde, L., Pinfold, V., Thornicroft, G., McBrierty, R. and Wilson, L. (2009) 'Evaluation of "See Me" – the

national Scottish campaign against stigma and discrimination associated with mental ill-health', Edinburgh, Scottish Government. Available online at www.scotland.gov.uk/Resource/Doc/259319/0076902.pdf

National Confidential Inquiry into Suicide and Homicide (2006) *Avoidable Deaths: Five-year Report of the National Confidential Inquiry into Suicide and Homicide by People with Mental Illness*. Manchester: University of Manchester.

National Confidential Inquiry into Suicide and Homicide by People with Mental Illness (2010) *Annual Report England and Wales July 2010*. Manchester: University of Manchester.

National Institute for Mental Health in England (2006) *National Suicide Prevention Strategy for England: Annual Report on Progress 2005*. London: Department of Health.

National Mental Health Development Unit (2010a) *Factfile 5: Equalities in Mental Health*. London: National Mental Health Development Unit.

National Mental Health Development Unit (2010b) *Factfile 6: Stigma and Discrimination in Mental Health*. London: National Mental Health Development Unit.

National Institute for Health and Clinical Excellence (NICE) (2009a) *Depression: The Treatment and Management of Depression in Adults*. London: National Institute for Health and Clinical Excellence.

National Institute for Health and Clinical Excellence (2009b) *Schizophrenia: Core Interventions in the Treatment and Management of Schizophrenia in Adults in Primary and Secondary Care*. London: National Institute for Health and Clinical Excellence.

National Institute for Mental Health in England (2005) *The Social Work Contribution to Mental Health Services: The Future Direction: A Discussion Paper.* Leeds: National Institute for Mental Health in England.

Nayak, A. (2006) 'Displaced masculinities: chavs, youth and class in the postindustrial city', *Sociology* 40 (5): 813–31.

Nichols, M.P. (2010) *Family Therapy: Concepts and Methods*, ninth edition. Boston: Pearson.

Novak, L. and Svab, V. (2009) 'Antipsychotics side effects' influence on stigma of mental illness: focus group study results', *Psychiatria Danubina*, 21 (1): 99–102.

O'Brien, A-M. and Farrell, S.J. (2005) 'Community treatment orders: a profile of a Canadian experience', *Canadian Journal of Psychiatry*, 50(1): 27–30.

O'Hagan, K. (2007) *Competence in Social Work Practice*, second edition. London: Jessica Kingsley.

O'Malley, L. and Croucher, K. (2003) *Supported Housing Services for People with Mental Health Problems: Evidence of GoodPpractice?* York: Centre for Housing Policy, University of York.

O'Reilly, R.L. (2004) 'Why are Community Treatment Orders controversial?' *Canadian Journal of Psychiatry*, 49 (9): 579–84.

Olsen, R.M. (ed.) (1984) *Social Work and Mental Health: The Role of the Approved Social Worker.* London: Tavistock.

Onyett, S. (2003) *Teamworking in Mental Health*. Basingstoke: Palgrave Macmillan.

Onyett, S., Pillinger, T. and Muijen, M. (1995) *Making Community Mental Health Teams Work*. London: Sainsbury Centre for Mental Health.

Oxford Community Treatment Order Evaluation Trial (OCTET) (2010) www.psychiatry.ox.ac.uk/research/researchunits/socpsych/research/OCTET

Owen, G.S, Szmukler, G., Richardson, G., David, A, Hayward, P., Hotopf, M. (2009) 'Mental capacity and psychiatric inpatients: some implications for the new mental health law', *British Journal of Psychiatry*, 195: 257–63.

Parker G, Beresford B, Clarke S, Gridley K, Pitman R, Spiers G, Light K. (2009) *Research Reviews on Prevalence, Detection and Interventions in Parental Mental Health and Child Welfare: Summary Report*. London: Social Care Institute of Excellence.

Parker, J. (2009) 'Approved social worker to approved mental health professional: evaluating the impact of changes within education and training', *Journal of Mental Health Training, Education and Practice*, 5 (2): 19–26.

Parker, J. and Bradley, G. (2007) *Social Work Practice: Assessment, Planning, Intervention and Review*. Exeter: Learning Matters.

Parrott L., Jacobs G. and Roberts, D. (2008) *Research Briefing 23: Stress and Resilience Factors in Parents with Mental Health Problems and Their Children*. London: SCIE.

Paxton, R. (1995) 'Goodbye community mental health teams – at last', *Journal of Mental Health*, 4(4): 331–34.

Payne, M. (1995) *Social Work and Community Care*. Basingstoke: Palgrave Macmillan.

Payne, M. (2005) *Modern Social Work Theory*, third edition. Basingstoke: Palgrave Macmillan.

Payne, M. (2009) 'Adult services and health-related social work', in R. Adams, L. Dominelli and M. Payne (eds), *Social Work: Themes, Issues and Critical Debates*, Basingstoke: Palgrave Macmillan.

Pearsall, A. and Yates, L. (2004) 'Carer perspectives', in T. Ryan and J. Pritchard (eds), *Good Practice in Adult Mental Health*. London: Jessica Kingsley.

Peck, E., Gulliver, P. and Towell, D. (2002) 'Information, consultation or control? User involvement in mental health services in England at the turn of the century', *Journal of Mental Health*, 11 (4): 441–51.

Perkins, R., Farmer, P. and Litchfield, P. (2009) *Realising Ambitions: Better Employment Support for People with a Mental Health Condition*. London: Department for Work and Pensions.

Petrila, J.D. and Christy, A. (2008) 'Florida's outpatient law: a lesson in failed reform?' *Psychiatric Services*, 59 (1): 21-21.

Pilgrim, D. (2002) 'The biopsychosocial model in Anglo-American psychiatry: past, present and future?' *Journal of Mental Health*, 11 (6): 585–94.

Pilgrim, D. (2008) '"Recovery" and current mental health policy', *Chronic Illness*, 4 (4): 295–304.

Pilgrim, D. and Rogers, A. (1993) *A Sociology of Mental Health and Illness*. Buckingham: Open University Press.

Pilling, S., Roth, A.D. and Stratton, P. (2010) *The Competences Required to Deliver Effective Systemic Therapies*. Available at www.ucl.ac.uk/CORE (last accessed 15 December 2010).

Pinkerton, J. and Campbell, J. (2002) 'Social work and social justice in Northern Ireland: towards a new occupational space', *British Journal of Social Work*, 32 (6): 723–37.

Popple, K. (2000) 'Critical commentary: community work (2)', *British Journal of Social Work,* 30 (5): 673–8.

Popple, K. (2005) *Analysing Community Work: Its Theory and Practice*. Milton Keynes: Open University.

Popple, K. (2006) 'Community development in the 21st century: a case of conditional development', *British Journal of Social Work*, 36 (2): 333–40.

Postle, K., Edwards, C., Moon, R., Rumsey, H. and Thomas, T. (2002) 'Continuing professional development after qualification – partnerships, pitfalls and potential', *Social Work Education*, 21 (2): 157–69.

Priebe, S., Fakhoury, W. and Watts, J. (2003) 'Assertive outreach teams in London: patient characteristics and outcomes: Pan-London assertive outreach study, part 3', *British Journal of Psychiatry,* 183 (2): 148–54.

Priebe, S., Watts, J., Chase, M., and Matanov, A. (2005) 'Processes of disengagement and engagement in assertive outreach patients: qualitative study', *British Journal of Psychiatry,* 187 (5): 438–43.

Prior, P.M. (1992) 'The Approved Social Worker: reflections on origins', *British Journal of Social Work*, 22 (2): 105–19.

Prior, P.M. (1999) *Gender and Mental Health*. London: Macmillan.

Prior, P.M. (2001) 'Protective Europe: does it still exist for people with mental disorders?' *Journal of European Social Policy*, 11 (1): 25–38.

Pritchard, C. (2006) *Mental Health Social Work: Evidence-Based Practice.* Abingdon: Routledge.

Quirk, A., Lelliott, O., Audini, B. and Buston, K. (2003) 'Non-clinical and extra legal influences on decisions about compulsory admission to psychiatric hospital', *Journal of Mental Health*, 12 (2): 119–30.

Ramon, S. (ed.) (2008) *Social Work in Political Conflict.* Birmingham: Venture/BASW.

Ramon, S. (2009) 'Adult mental health in a changing international context: the relevance to social work', *British Journal of Social Work*, 39 (8): 1615–22.

Ramon, S., Healy, B. and Renour, N. (2007) 'Recovery from mental illness as an emergent concept and practice in Australia and the UK', *International Journal of Social Psychiatry*, 53 (2): 108–22.

Ramsey, R. (2001) 'Bipolar affective disorder or manic depression', in R. Ramsey, G. Szmukler, C. Gerada and S. Mars (eds), *Mental Illness: A Handbook for Carers.* London: Jessica Kingsley.

Rapaport, J. (2005) 'Policy swings over thirty-five years of mental health social work in England and Wales 1969–2004', *Practice*, 17 (1): 43–56.

Rapaport, J. (2006) 'New roles in mental health: the creation of the approved mental health practitioner', *Journal of Integrated Care*, 14, 5: 37–46.

Rapaport, J. and Manthorpe, J. (2008) 'Family matters: developments concerning the role of the nearest relative and social worker under mental health law in England and Wales', *British Journal of Social Work*, 38 (6): 1115–31.

Rapp, C.A. (1998) *The Strengths Model: Case Management with People Suffering from Severe and Persistent Mental Illness.* New York: Oxford University Press.

Rapp, R.C. (2006) 'Strength-based case management: enhancing treatment for persons with substance abuse problems', in D. Saleeby (ed.), *The Strengths Perspective in Social Work Practice*, fourth edition. Boston: Allyn and Bacon/Longman.

Ray, M., Pugh, R., Roberts, D. and Beech, B. (2008) *Mental Health and Social Work: Research Briefing 26.* London: Social Care Institute for Excellence.

Read, J., Fink, P., Rudegeair, T., Felitti, V. and Whitfield, C. (2008) 'Child maltreatment and psychosis: a return to a genuinely integrated bio-psycho-social model', *Clinical Schizophrenia and Related Psychoses*, 2 (3): 235–54.

Read, J., Mosher, L.R. and Bentall, R.P. (eds) (2004) *Models of Madness: Psychological, Social and Biological Approaches to Schizophrenia*. Hove: Routledge.

Read, J., van Os, J., Morrison, A.P. and Ross, C.A. (2005) 'Childhood trauma, psychosis and schizophrenia: a literature review with theoretical and clinical implications', *Acta Psychiatrica Scandinavica*, 112 (5): 330–50.

Reeves, A. and Dryden, W. (eds) (2008) *Key Issues for Counselling in Action*, second edition. London: Sage.

Reilly, S., Challis, D., Donnelly, M., Hughes, J. and Stewart, K. (2007) 'Care management in mental health services in England and Northern Ireland: do integrated organizations promote integrated practice?' *Journal of Health Services Research and Policy*, 12 (4): 236–41.

Reith, M. (1998) *Community Care Tragedies: A Practical Guide to Mental Health Inquiries*. Birmingham: Venture Press.

Repper, J. and Perkins, R. (2009) 'Challenging discrimination: promoting rights and citizenship', in J. Reynolds, R. Muston, T. Heller, J. Leach, M. McCormick, J. Wallcraft and M. Walsh (eds), *Mental Health Still Matters*. Basingstoke: Palgrave Macmillan.

Reynolds, J., Muston, R., Heller, T., Leach, J., McCormick, M., Wallcraft, J. and Walsh, M. (eds) (2009) *Mental Health Still Matters*, second edition. London: Palgrave Macmillan.

Richards, D. (2007) 'Behaviour therapy', in W. Dryden (ed.) (2007) *Dryden's Handbook of Individual Therapy*, fifth edition. London: Sage.

Richardson, A. and Budd, T. (2003) *Alcohol, Crime and Disorder: A Study of Young Adults*. Home Office Research Study No. 263. London: Home Office.

Ridgeway, P.A. and Press, A. (2004) *Assessing the Recovery Commitment of your Mental Health Services: A User's Guide for the Developing Recovery Enhancing Environments Measure (DREEM) – UK Version* 1 December, being edited for use in the UK by Allott, P. and Higginson, P. and available at www.recoverydevon.co.uk/download/DREEM%20total%20dft4%20no%20tc.pdf (last accessed 20 October 2011).

Rivett, M. and Street, E. (2009) *Family Therapy: 100 Key Points and Techniques*. London: Routledge.

Roberts, G. (2000) 'Narrative and severe mental illness: what place do stories have in an evidence-based world?', *Advances in Psychiatric Treatment*, 6 (6): 432–41.

Roberts, G. and Wolfson, P. (2006) 'New directions in rehabilitation: learning from the recovery movement', in G. Roberts, S. Davenport, F. Holloway and T. Tattan (eds), *Enabling Recovery: The Principles and Practice of Rehabilitation Psychiatry*. London: Gaskell/Royal College of Psychiatrists.

Roberts, G., Davenport, S., Holloway, F. and Tattan, T. (eds) (2006) *Enabling Recovery: The Principles and Practice of Rehabilitation Psychiatry*. London: Gaskell/Royal College of Psychiatrists.

Rogers, A. and Pilgrim, D. (1991) 'Pulling down churches: accounting for the British Mental Health Users' Movement', *Sociology of Health and Illness*, 13 (2): 129–48.

Rogers, A. and Pilgrim, D. (1996) *Mental Health Policy in Britain: A Critical Introduction*. Basingstoke: Macmillan.

Rogers, A. and Pilgrim, J. (2009) *A Sociology of Mental Health and Illness*, fourth edition. Buckingham: Open University Press.

Rogers, T. (2009) 'Innovatory and regulatory practice in contemporary child care social work', in G. Ruch (ed.), *Post-Qualifying Child Care Social Work: Developing Reflective Practice*. London: Sage.

Romans, S., Dawson, J., Mullen, R. and Gibbs, A. (2004) 'How mental health clinicians view community treatment orders: a national New Zealand Survey', *Australian and New Zealand Journal of Psychiatry*, 38 (10): 836–41.

Romme, M. and Escher, S. (2000) *Making Sense of Voices*. London: Mind Publications.

Roscoe, K.D. and Madoc, I. (2009) 'Critical social work practice a narrative approach', *International Journal of Narrative Practice*, 1 (1): 9–18.

Rose, D., Thornicroft, G. and Kassam, A. (2007) '250 labels used to stigmatise people with mental illness', *BMC Health Services Research*, 7: 97. Available online at www.biomedcentral.com/content/pdf/1472-6963-7-97.pdf

Rose, D., Wykes, T., Bindman, J. and Fleischmann, P. (2005) 'Information, consent and perceived coercion: consumers' views on ECT', *British Journal of Psychiatry*, 186 (1): 54–59.

Rosen, A. (1998) 'Crisis management in the community', *Medical Journal of Australia*, Practice Essential Ch. 8: 44–49.

Rosenhan, D.L. (1973) 'On being sane in insane places', *Science*, 179 (4070): 250–58.

Roth, A. and Fonagy, P. (2005) *What Works For Whom? A Critical Review of Psychotherapy Research*. New York: Guilford.

Royal College of Psychiatrists (2011a) *Anxiety, Panic, Phobias*. London: Royal College of Psychiatrists. Available online at www.rcpsych.ac.uk/mentalhealthinfoforall.aspx

Royal College of Psychiatrists (2011b) *Bipolar Disorder*. London: Royal College of Psychiatrists. Available online at www.rcpsych.ac.uk/mentalhealthinfoforall.aspx

Royal College of Psychiatrists (2011c) *Depression*. London: Royal College of Psychiatrists. Available online at www.rcpsych.ac.uk/mentalhealthinfoforall.aspx

Royal College of Psychiatrists (2011d) *Schizophrenia*. London: Royal College of Psychiatrists. Available online at www.rcpsych.ac.uk/mentalhealthinfoforall.aspx

Ryan, P. and Morgan, S. (2004) *Assertive Outreach: A Strengths Approach to Policy and Practice*. London: Churchill Livingstone.

Ryan, T. and Pritchard, J. (eds) (2004) *Good Practice in Adult Mental Health*. London: Jessica Kingsley.

Sainsbury Centre for Mental Health (1998) *Keys to Engagement*. London: Sainsbury Centre for Mental Health.

Sainsbury Centre for Mental Health (2001) *Crisis Resolution*. London: Sainsbury Centre for Mental Health.

Sainsbury Centre for Mental Health (2009) *Briefing 40: Removing Barriers: The Facts About Mental Health and Employment*. London: Sainsbury Centre for Mental Health.

Saleeby, D. (ed.) (2006) *The Strengths Perspective in Social Work Practice*, fourth edition. Boston: Allyn and Bacon/Longman.

Sartorius, N. (2007) 'Stigma and mental health', *The Lancet*, 370 (9590): 810–11

Sayce, L. (2000) *From Psychiatric Patient to Citizen: Overcoming Discrimination and Social Exclusion*. Basingstoke: Macmillan.

Sayce, L. (2003) 'Beyond good intentions: making anti-discrimination strategies work', *Disability and Society*, 18 (5): 625–42.

Scheff, T. (1966) *Being Mentally Ill: A Sociology Theory*. Chicago: Aldine.

Schön, D. (1987) *Educating the Reflective Practitioner*. San Francisco: Jossey-Bass.

Scottish Executive (2006) *Changing Lives: Report of the 21st Century Social Work Review*. Edinburgh: Scottish Executive.

Scottish Executive (2007) *Delivering for Mental Health: The Scottish Recovery Indicator*, Report of Conference, 30 April. Edinburgh: Scottish Executive.

Scottish Government (2002) *National Strategy and Action Plan to Prevent Suicide in Scotland*. Edinburgh: The Scottish Government.

Scottish Government (2005) Circular CCD8/2004: *Guidance on Care Management in Community Care*. Available at www.scotland.gov.uk/Publications/2005/02/20728/53037 (last accessed 20 August 2011).

Scottish Government (2008) *Adults with Incapacity (Scotland) Act 2000: Communication and Assessing Capacity: A guide for social work and health care staff:* Edinburgh: Scottish Government. Available at www.scotland.gov.uk/Publications/2008/02/01151101/0

Scull, A. (1977) *Decarceration: Community Treatment and the Deviant – A Radical View*. Englewood Cliffs, NJ: Prentice Hall.

Seddon, D., Robinson, C., Reeves, C., Tommis, Y., Woods, B. and Russell, I. (2007) 'In their own right: translating the policy of careraAssessment into practice', *British Journal of Social Work*, 37 (8): 1335–52.

Seebohm, P. (2010) 'Community development approaches to working with groups of people with mental health problems: race equality and mental health', *Diversity in Health and Care*, 7 (4): 249–60.

Seebohm Report (1968) *Report by the Committee on Local Authority and Allied Social Service*. London: HMSO.

Shah, P. and Mountain, D. (2007) 'The medical model is dead – long live the medical model', *British Journal of Psychiatry*, 191 (5): 375–7.

Shaw, I. and Lishman, J. (1999) *Evaluation and Social Work Practice*. London: Sage.

Shaw, M., Tunstall, H. and Dorling, D. (2005) 'Increasing inequalities in risk of murder in Britain: trends in the demographic and spatial distribution of murder, 1981–2000', *Health and Place*, 11 (1): 45–54.

Shepherd, G., Boardman, J. and Slade, M. (2008) *Making Recovery a Reality*. London: Sainsbury Centre for Mental Health.

Simpson, E.L. and House, A.O. (2002) 'Involving users in the delivery and evaluation of mental health services: systematic review', *British Medical Journal*, 325 (7375): 1265–7.

Sinclair, R. and Bullock, R. (2002) *Learning from Past Experience: A Review of Serious Case Reviews*. London: DH.

Singhal, A., Kumar, R., Belgamwar, B. and Hodgson, R.E. (2008) 'Assessment of mental capacity: who can do it?' *The Psychiatrist*, 32 (1): 17–20.

Slack, K. and Webber, M. (2008) 'Do we care? Adult mental health professionals' attitudes towards supporting service users' children', *Child and Family Social Work*, 13(1): 72–9.

Slade, M. (2009) *100 Ways to Support Recovery*. London: Rethink. Available at www.rethink.org/100ways

Smith, G., Gregory, K. and Higgs, A. (2007) *An Integrated Approach to Family Work or Psychosis: A Manual for Family Workers*. London: Jessica Kingsley.

Smith, R. (1991) 'A study of Mental Health Officers' work in Scotland', in M. Ulas (ed.), *Mental Health and Social Work*. London: Jessica Kingsley.

Smith, R. (2009) 'Inter-professional learning and multi-professional practice for PQ', in P. Higham (ed.), *Post-Qualifying Social Work Practice*. London: Sage.

Social Care Institute for Excellence (SCIE) (2007) *SCIE Position Paper 6: Supporting Self-advocacy*. London: Social Care Institute for Excellence.

Social Care Institute for Excellence (SCIE) (2009) *Think Child, Think Parent, Think Family: A Guide to Parental Mental Health and Child Welfare*. London: Social Care Institute for Excellence.

Social Exclusion Unit (SEU) (2004) *Mental Health and Social Exclusion*. London: Office of the Deputy Prime Minister.

Social Services Inspectorate (2004) *Inspection of Social Work in Mental Health Services*. Belfast: Department of Health, Social Services and Public Safety.

Stanley, N. and Manthorpe, J. (2001) 'Reading mental health inquiries: messages for social work', *Journal of Social Work*, 1 (1): 77–99.

Stanley, N., Penhale, B., Riordan, D., Barbour, R.S. and Holden S. (2003) *Child Protection and Mental Health Services*. Bristol: University of Bristol Press.

Stein, L. I. and Test, M. A. (eds) (1978) *Alternatives to Mental Hospital Treatment*. New York: Plenum Press.

Stewart, D. and Thompson, K. (2005) 'The FACE YOUR FEAR club: therapeutic group work with young children as a response to community trauma in Northern Ireland', *British Journal of Social Work*, 35 (1): 105–24.

Stratton, P. (2005) *Report On The Evidence Base Of Systemic Family Therapy. Association for Family Therapy.* Available at www.aft.org.uk/docs/evidencedocsept-05creditedSS.doc (last accessed 15 December 2010).

Strier, R. (2008) 'Community anti-poverty strategies: a conceptual framework for critical discussion', *British Journal of Social Work*, 39 (6): 1063–81.

Sudbery, J. (2009) *Human Growth and Development: An Introduction for Social Workers*. London: Routledge.

Surgeon General (1999) *Mental Health: A Report of the Surgeon General*. Rockville, MD: US Department of Health and Human Services.

Szasz, T.S. (1960) 'The myth of mental illness', *American Psychologist*, 15: 113–18.

Szasz, T.S. (2008) 'Debunking antipsychiatry: Laing, Law, and Largactil', *Current Psychology*, 27 (2): 79–101.

Szmukler, G. and Appelbaum, P.S. (2008) 'Treatment pressures, leverage, coercion, and compulsion in mental health care', *Journal of Mental Health*, 17(3): 233–44

Tait, L. and Lester, H. (2005) 'Encouraging user involvement in mental health services', *Advances in Psychiatric Treatment*, 11 (3): 168–75.

Tanzman, B. (1993) 'An overview of surveys of mental health consumers' preferences for housing and support services', *Hospital and Community Psychiatry*, 44 (5): 450–5.

Taylor, P.J. and Gunn, J. (1999) 'Homicides by people with mental illness: myth and reality', *British Journal of Psychiatry*, 174 (1): 9–14.

Tblisi State University, Georgia, 1–2 July 2008. Available at www.ceimh.bham.ac.uk/documents/Ann_Georgia_presentation.pdf (last accessed 10 September 2010).

Teater, B. (2010) *An Introduction to Applying Social Work Theories and Methods*. Buckingham: Open University Press.

Test, M.A. (1999) 'Book Review' of C.A. Rapp (1998) *The Strengths Model: Case Management With People Suffering From Severe and Persistent Mental Illness*, New York City, Oxford University Press, in *Psychiatric* Services, 50 (11): 1502–3.

Tew, J. (ed.) (2005) *Social Perspectives in Mental Health*. London: Jessica Kingsley.

Tew, J. (2010) *Social Approaches to Mental Distress*. Basingstoke: Palgrave Macmillan.

Thompson, A., Shaw, M., Harrison, G., Davidson, H., Gunnell, D. and Veue, J. (2004) 'Patterns of hospital admission for adult psychiatric illness in England: analysis of hospital episode statistics data', *British Journal of Psychiatry*, 185 (4): 428–31.

Thompson, N. (2003) *Promoting Equality: Challenging Discrimination and Oppression*. Basingstoke: Palgrave Macmillan.

Thompson, N. (2005) *Understanding Social Work: Preparing for Practice*. Basingstoke: Palgrave Macmillan.

Thornicroft, G. and Tansella, M. (2004) 'Components of a modern mental health service: a pragmatic balance of community and hospital care: overview of systematic evidence', *British Journal of Psychiatry*, 185 (4): 283–90.

Thornicroft, G. and Tansella, M. (2005) 'Growing recognition of the importance of service user involvement in mental health service planning and evaluation', *Epidemiologia e Psichiatria Sociale*, 14 (1): 1–3.

Time to Change (2008) 'Stigma shout: service user and carer experiences of stigma and discrimination', London: Time to Change. Available online at hrrp://www.time-to-change.org.uk

Tomlinson, M. (2007) *The Trouble with Suicide. Mental Health, Suicide and the Northern Ireland Conflict: A Review of the Evidence.* Belfast: Department of Health, Social Services and Public Safety (NI).

Traynor, M. (2003) 'A brief history of empowerment: response to discussion with Julianne Cheek', *Primary Health Care Research and Development*, 4 (2): 129–36.

Trevithick, P. (2003) 'Effective relationship-based practice: a theoretical exploration', *Journal of Social Work Practice*, 17 (2): 163–76.

Twelvetrees, A. (1982) *Community Work*. London: Macmillan.

Twigg, J. and Atkin, K. (1994) *Carers Perceived: Policy and Practice in Informal Caring*. Buckingham: Open University Press.

Vetere, A. and Dallos, R. (2003) *Working Systemically with Families*. London: Karnac.

Von Bertalanffy, L. (1950) 'An outline of general system theory', *British Journal for the Philosophy of Science*, 1 (2): 139–64.

Warner, J., McKeown, E., Griffin, M., Johnson, K., Ramsay, A., Cort, C. and King, M. (2004) 'Rates and predictors of mental illness in gay men, lesbians and bisexual men and women: results from a survey based in England and Wales', *British Journal of Psychiatry,* 185 (6): 479–85.

Warren, F., McGauley, G., Norton, K., Dolan, B., Preedy-Fayers, K., Pickering, A. and Geddes, J.R. (2003) *Review of Treatments for Severe Personality Disorder* (Home Office Online Report 30/03). London: Home Office.

Webber, M. (2005) 'Social capital and mental health', in J. Tew (ed.), *Social Perspectives in Mental Health*. London: Jessica Kingsley.

Webber, M. (2008) *Evidence-based Policy and Practice in Mental Health Social Work*. Exeter: Learning Matters.

Weiner, N. (1948) 'Cybernetics', *Scientific American,* 179 (5): 14–18.

Weir, A. and Douglas, A. (1999) *Child Protection and Adult Mental Health: Conflict of Interest?* Edinburgh: Butterworth-Heinemann.

Weiss, E., Gal, J. and Katan, J. (2006) 'Social policy for social work: a teaching agenda', *British Journal of Social Work*, 36 (5): 798–806.

Welsh Assembly (2008) *Talk to Me: A National Action Plan to Reduce Suicide and Self Harm in Wales 2008–2013*. Cardiff: The Welsh Assembly.

Wetzel, J.W. (2000) 'Women and mental health: a global perspective', *International Social Work*, 43 (2): 205–15.

Whiffen, V.E., Thompson, J.M. and Aube, J.A. (2000) 'Mediators of the link between childhood sexual abuse and adult depressive symptoms', *Journal of Interpersonal Violence*, 15(10): 1100–20.

Whitaker, R. (2002) *Mad in America: Bad Science, Bad Medicine and the Enduring Mistreatment of the Mentally Ill*. Cambridge, MA: Basic Books.

Wilkinson, R. and Pickett, K. (2009) *The Spirit Level: Why More Equal Societies Almost Always Do Better*. London: Allen Lane.

Williams, J. (2005) 'Women's mental health: taking equality into account', in J. Tew (ed.), *Social Perspectives in Mental Health*. London: Jessica Kingsley.

Wilson, G. and Daly, M. (2007) 'Shaping the future of mental health policy and legislation in Northern Ireland: the impact of service user and professional social work discourses', *British Journal of Social Work*, 37 (3): 423–39.

Wilson, M., Williamson, L., Williams, R. and Griffiths, S. (2004) 'Black and minority mental health', in T. Ryan and J. Prichard (eds), *Good Practice in Adult Mental Health*. London: Jessica Kingsley.

Wing, J.K. and Brown, G.W. (1970) *Institutionalism and Schizophrenia*. Cambridge: Cambridge University Press.

Winness, M.G., Borg, M. and Kim, H.S. (2010) 'Service users' experiences with help and support from crisis resolution teams: a literature review', *Journal of Mental Health*, 19(1): 75–87.

Winter, K. (2011) *Building Relationships and Communicating with Young Children: A Practical Guide for Social Workers*. London: Routledge.

World Health Organisation (1992) *The ICD-10 Classification of Mental and Behavioural Disorders: Clinical Descriptions and Diagnostic Guidelines*. Geneva: World Health Organization.

World Health Organisation (2008a) *Stigma: An International Briefing Paper*. Geneva: World Health Organisation. Available at www.supportproject.eu/news/stigma/stigmatoolkit.htm

World Health Organisation (2008b) *Stigma: Guidebook for Action*. Geneva: World Health Organisation. Available at www.supportproject.eu/news/stigma/stigmatoolkit.htm

Zubin, J. and Spring, B. (1977) 'Vulnerability: "a new view on schizophrenia"', *Journal of Abnormal Psychology*, 86:103–26.

Index